TO THE READER

This book is a revised edition of the award-winning *Don't Murder Your Mystery*. It offers the same information about the craft of writing and the publication submission process. *What's different?* 130 new excerpts in addition to 100 of the original 140, for a total of 230 positive examples of effective techniques from 215 authors in many genres. Also new: expanded resources for writers, a handy guide to better usage, and five pages on interior dialogue.

MORE PRAISE for the ORIGINAL EDITION of THIS BOOK

Agatha Award; Macavity, Anthony, & ForeWord finalist: *DON'T MURDER YOUR MYSTERY*

Of all my books on writing, it's the one I would not part with.
Phil Hardwick, 7 novels in The Mississippi Mystery series

When a writer becomes serious about having an agent or editor look at your masterpiece, you must use *Don't Murder Your Mystery* to even have a shot at being read past the first page.
Steve Brown, 16 novels in 3 genres

Great book. I am recommending it to new writers.
Michael Allen Dymmoch, award winner, 7 novels

Patrons have told me the book is packed with useful, sensible hints to improve their writing. I recommend it.
Karen Kiley, Wake County NC Public Library System (6 copies circulate throughout 19 branches)

Outstanding guide to improving one's critical reading and writing skills.
Alix Dobkin, feminist singer-songwriter, forthcoming My Red Blood

I used most every technique in your book recently. I was stunned by how much better even my first draft was when I did what you suggested.
Heather Hutchins, new writer, Chicago

Indispensable tool... I've learned more from it than any of the numerous other instructional manuals I've read.
Scott Nicholson, 7 fantasy novels

Experienced writers may also find the tips helpful and inspiring if they hit a roadblock.... I rewrote an entire first page after reading *Don't Murder Your Mystery*.
PJ Parrish, NYTimes best-selling author of 9 thrillers

A terrific job...a great service to experienced writers as well as newbies.
Jeanne Dams, 14 novels, Agatha Award-winner

Immensely insightful....I've never before seen a guide that does such a great job detailing the no-no's.
Lori L. Lake, 8 standalone novels

One of the best writing tools I've ever read.
Craig Faris, Carrie McCray Literary Award for Best Short Fiction

It has circulated well. I recommend the book to patrons who have an interest in the writing process or love mysteries.
Ronald Headen, Greensboro NC Library (owns 3 copies)

Belongs in every library.
Kate Flora, past internat'l pres., Sisters in Crime

The best book on its subject out there.
Michael Mallory, co-author with Marilyn Victor, Death Roll

I believe libraries ought to add this book to their collections for patrons who are writers or who teach writing. A terrific resource.
Linda Lemery, Mary B. Blount Library, Averett Univ., Danville VA

Basic enough for beginners, thorough and deep enough for seasoned writers, and humorous enough to read just for fun—the best how-to I've read.
Betty Beamguard, recipient of over 30 writing honors and awards

This book is good.... I highly recommend this title to anyone wanting to publish any type of novel.
Jane Cohen, reviewed for the DorothyL listserv

MORE PRAISE for the ORIGINAL EDITION of THIS BOOK

Agatha Award; Macavity, Anthony, & ForeWord finalist: *DON'T MURDER YOUR MYSTERY*

A superb book. Lots of good information, even for experienced writers, presented with wit.
Cynthia Riggs,
7 Martha's Vineyard mysteries

[CLUE #21] has been more help to me than almost any editing advice I've received.   *Kathryn R. Wall,*
7 Bay Tanner novels

I'm currently using *Don't Murder Your Mystery* in my class on writing popular fiction (UNCA's Great Smokies Writing Program), and like my three previous classes, all the students say this is the most useful book for writers they've ever seen.   *Vicki Lane,*
4 Elizabeth Goodweather novels

Every thoughtful writer will find at least a half-dozen tips that directly apply...I certainly did.
Margaret Maron, winner of every
major mystery-writing award; 2005
president of Mystery Writers of America

I have shelves filled with how-to-books about writing, but *Don't Murder Your Mystery* instantly surpassed them all and became my #1 guide.
Sandra Parshall, Agatha Award for
Best First Novel, The Heat of the Moon

Your whole approach is so original.... I'll certainly keep recommending this book, beginning with a fiction workshop I'm teaching.
Nancy Means Wright, 6 Vermont novels

PRAISE for other books by Chris Roerden:

WHAT TWO CAN DO: SAM & MANDY STELLMAN'S CRUSADE FOR SOCIAL JUSTICE (2002)
Wonderful book. *Donna Shalala, HHS Cabinet Minister under Pres. Clinton*

OPEN GATE: TEACHING IN A FOREIGN COUNTRY
Handy guidebook and fascinating look into the courtesy and hospitality of the Korean people. *Milwaukee Journal, Dec. 30, 1990*
Humorous and insightful. *Midwest Book Review*

ON TO THE SECOND DECADE
Requested by the Smithsonian Institution for its Special Collection on Women, 1977

COLLECTIONS FROM CAPE ELIZABETH, MAINE
A wonderful book. *Gov. John N. Reed, 1965*
A miracle! *Mrs. Durward Holman, Head Librarian, Thomas Memorial Library,*
quoted in Portland Press Herald, Aug. 5, 1965

Also: four ghostwritten books of nonfiction, and a simulation game adopted for
the officer training program at Rickenbacker Air Force Base, Ohio

DON'T SABOTAGE YOUR SUBMISSION

SAVE YOUR MANUSCRIPT FROM TURNING UP D.O.A.

CHRIS ROERDEN

BellaRosaBooks

ROCK HILL, SC

Published by Bella Rosa Books
P. O. Box 4251 CRS, Rock Hill, SC 29732
www.bellarosabooks.com

Publisher's Cataloging-in-Publication

Roerden, Chris.
    Don't sabotage your submission : save your manuscript
from turning up D.O.A. / Chris
Roerden.
    p. cm.
    Includes bibliographical references and index.
    ISBN 978-1-933523-31-6 (1-933523-31-X)

    1. Fiction—Technique.   2. Editing.   I. Title.

PN3355.R62 2008   808.3

    18 17 16 15 14 13 12 11 10 09 08   2 3 4 5 6 7 8 9 10

DEDICATION

To the writers, already published and still submitting, who have trusted their best efforts to me and asked for assistance:

You taught me what you need.

This book is one way I can show my gratitude for your trust and pay it forward.

TABLE OF CONTENTS

"In the book publishing business, an observer can reasonably conclude that there are an infinite number of manuscripts chasing a finite number of opportunities to publish with established publishers."

John B. McHugh, publishing consultant

PRECAUTIONS

R

For long-lasting benefits, apply this remedy to drafts that have finished digesting. Attempting to revise while still writing, like exercising while eating, may shut down the body's flow of creative juices and produce verbal constipation.

Double vision and intermittent paralysis of the hands are signs of early self-editing disorder, which may be alleviated by rest and large doses of Dorothy Cannell.

Minor irritants include a pain in the neck and discomfort in the shoulder, as if an editor were looking over it. Severe cases are marked by schizophrenia, in which writers hear voices of critiquers that temporarily smother one's own voice.

Use caution when applying any writing remedy.

NOT ABOUT RULES

Despite my parody of a prescription warning, I don't call myself a book doctor. To me, the term implies that a writer's work is sick. Neither do I talk about writing as good or bad, right or wrong. That presupposes rules. This book is not about rules. It's about effectiveness.

What counts in any work of fiction—whether literary fiction or genre (a.k.a. category) fiction—is its effect on the reader. Content is important, but technique is the means by which that content creates its effect. Some techniques are more effective than others; some, less effective.

For more than forty-four years, editing has been my full-time day job. I love my job, but I am saddened by witnessing, year after year, the same ineffective writing habits continuing to sabotage one submission after another.

Though my own focus in this book is on genre fiction, my goal is to help *all* writers:

1. find and fix the clues to the ineffective use of key techniques;
2. survive the first cut of the submission process so plot and characters can get a fair reading.

Why send a manuscript off to self-destruct?

PART I: DEAD ON ARRIVAL

"Idealistic young scribes who insist their work is
for them alone will disagree, but a writer without
readers is like shouting in an empty room."
Leonard Pitts Jr., syndicated columnist [1]

JUDGE AND JURY

Remember when you first learned to identify spam in your email? Once you realized what it was, the clues seemed to fall into place: senders you didn't know and subject lines with unrealistic promises: "Lose fat while sleeping," "Your tax refund" (fat chance), and "I found your wallet." You learned to spot the clues quickly, didn't you?

Me too. In fact, anyone who knows me would know I'd never fall for anything resembling "URGENT RESPONSE NEEDED!!!" or any offer that for me is anatomically impossible.

And how about those telemarketers? Once you learned how to spot their calls, you cut them off after hearing only the start of their pitch. Now you get rid of calls and emails the moment you see the first clue.

The same quick decision-making applies to most submissions that flood literary agencies and publishing houses every day. In the same way that you developed your own shortcuts for rapidly screening spammers and telemarketers, the publishing industry developed its own shortcuts for rapidly screening manuscript submissions.

One form of flood control is the literary agency, the industry's first responder. Whether your manuscript lands in a pile at an agency or a pile at a publishing house, the screening process is essentially the same. An optimist known as the first reader, or "the reader," has the job of lowering the leaning tower of printouts as efficiently as possible—all the while hoping to rescue the rare beauty imprisoned within.

Readers work rapidly, spotting the clues that separate the manuscripts with no chance of publication from those that may deserve a second look. Gatekeepers know what to screen for. More accurately, they know what to screen *out*. We might as well call them by their function: screener-outers.

The piles of submissions are large; made larger still by multiple copies of the same manuscripts making the rounds of agents and royalty publishers all across the country. Think what's involved in simply handling those millions of manuscripts, much less attempting to actually *read* them. Some of us can barely handle a day's worth of spam.

SPEEDY EXECUTION

When busy screeners pick up your 12-point Courier, double-spaced, laser-printed, return-receipted priority-posted submission, they do what you and I do when we log on to our email or pick up a ringing phone. We become alert for the earliest clue enabling us to reject, ASAP, whatever someone else is selling that doesn't interest us.

> "Despite the statistics that we are a country suffering from functional illiteracy, we seem to be producing an extraordinary number of imaginative, interesting writers. The problem is that they can't get anyone to read what they write."
>
> Rayanna Simons, about her four years as first reader for Macmillan[2]

At this make-or-break moment in which a first impression is the only impression, appearance is everything. Submissions that merely *look* unprofessional get shoved back in the box or the bubble wrap, unread.

Because appearance involves mechanics, not writing skill, you can find information about formatting at the end of this book in Exhibit A of the POST-MORTEM.

Another rapid disqualifier of submissions is wrong category or genre. A sci-fi/fantasy house won't buy a cozy mystery, no matter how well written. A literary press won't redirect its editorial and marketing strategies to publish a vampire romance, no matter how cleverly crafted. For your novel to reach the audience most likely to buy it, your submission must aim for the publishing pros who court the same market you do.

Just as you recognize which over-the-phone and email offers don't interest you, agents and publishers recognize which genres don't interest them. It's up to you to research who is interested in what. Check the guidelines agents and publishers post on their websites and happily send to you for the courtesy of a self-addressed stamped envelope (SASE). Then:

1. Follow each agent's or publisher's guidelines, even if the variations from one to another seem minor.
2. Send your work to only those agencies or publishing houses that state an interest in your genre.
3. Identify the category or genre in your cover letter, and your subgenre if you know it.

A surprisingly large number of writers submit their work to anyone in publishing whose address they happen to come across. *My spy thriller is so good,* thinks the aspiring writer, *surely every publisher will want it.*

Nonsense. Disregarding the stated preferences of agents and royalty publishers ensures that a submission will be dead on arrival, proof that the writer is an amateur. (Because matching a manuscript to the interests of its recipient involves common sense, not writing skill, you can find information about genres among the sources listed at the back of this book. See Exhibit B of the POST-MORTEM under writing category fiction.)[3]

A GOOD FIT

If your manuscript passes the qualifying trials of mechanics and category, it becomes eligible for the opening round of the main event. That's where your submission has its first and often *only* chance of being read. That's where your writing skills are judged—rapidly, often hastily. The process is publishing's version of the survivor-based reality show.

For an agent to represent you, your submission must be a good fit for the agency. For an acquisitions editor to offer a contract, your submission must be a good fit for the publishing house.

You might scoff at the words "good fit," hearing them as weasel words. *Whatever those people want to call it,* you say, *I know rejection when I get it.*

Without discounting or denying any writer's feelings of rejection, I offer a view of the process from another perspective:

TIP: THE FITTING ROOM—A PARABLE

Let's say you need a new pair of slacks. When you walk into your favorite emporium, aren't you eliminating all the merchandise offered by every other store—at least for the time being? Is that not rejection?

Maybe it's simply prioritizing, like an agent's shifting some manuscripts to the bottom of the reading pile to look at later.

On entering the first store, you ignore half the clothing solely because it's intended for the opposite sex. You also walk past jewelry, shoes, toys, and hardware *without even looking at what they have to offer.* Is that not rejection?

When you arrive at sportswear, you brush past racks of slacks with budget-busting prices and sizes from a past life. Nothing is wrong with these armies of garments; they simply don't fit your needs—like the millions of manuscripts that don't fit the needs of every agent or publisher.

Fast-forward to the fitting room. You're about to try on six promising selections—not unlike the agent who asks to see a full manuscript based on a promising first chapter.

If none of the try-ons fits well enough to buy, you will visit another store and begin the rejection process over. But one pair of slacks happens to fit just right, so you leave the other five candidates hanging in the dressing room, pay for your purchase, and head home.

There, crammed into your mail slot, sits one of your own self-addressed stamped envelopes. Your novel has come home— again. You can feel rejected, or you can feel one step closer to finding the agency or publishing house where both of you are the right fit for each other.

You slip into your new slacks, check your email, and browse the latest postings on your favorite writers' list serve. One online subscriber is asking, "Why did they ask for my whole manuscript if they were only going to reject it?"

At that moment, thousands of underpaid department-store clerks are cleaning out fitting rooms from coast to coast, grumbling, "Why do they take so many clothes to try on if they're going to buy only one?"[4]

SUDDEN DEATH

The manuscript that's always a poor fit is one that seems unlikely to sell enough copies to push a publisher's revenues well above the break-even point. What does sell, other than a celebrity name? Enthusiasm! Book-sellers telling readers, "Here's an author you'll enjoy," and all of us readers telling our friends and librarians, "This is a terrific book! Get it!"

That's word-of-mouth. That's "buzz." It sells boocoodle books.

The promise of success begins with the enthusiasm that a manuscript generates in wary literary agents, cautious acquisitions editors, and skeptical marketing and accounting decision-makers.

Mild interest doesn't sell books. Wild interest does.

I know, I know—the industry is famously poor at predicting the success of the titles it releases. High-advance celebrity books lose tons of money, while best-selling authors admit to many early years of rejection.

In spite of cloudy crystal balls, publishing pros do foresee with some accuracy one type of failure: average writing. They call it "amateur."

As unkind as this word sounds, "amateur" is used throughout the industry to distinguish the average writer from the professional: the one in a hundred whose writing shows that she or he has studied the craft, practiced it, and appears able to make money at it.

Sadly, most submissions deserve the amateur label. That's why the industry's first readers must be efficient screener-outers. The sooner they spot a clue to average writing, the sooner they can go on to the next piece. Before you can say give my piece a chance, it goes from the slush pile to the "no" pile. Practically unread.

"No" is a rapid decision based primarily on the craft and voice heard at the start of a manuscript's pitch. You may have spent a year or more in labor to bring your 400-page bundle of joy to life, but your effort miscarries. And you don't know why. So you keep looking for the one agent or publisher who will listen to what your submission has to say.

But all are alert to the same clues.

It doesn't matter that your plot and subplots weave suspensefully from beginning to end. Few manuscripts are read far enough for the plot to reveal itself. It doesn't matter how skillfully you develop the relationship between protagonist and antagonist. Screener-outers don't hang in there long enough to see how you develop your characters.

A manuscript screener is the quicker picker-upper: a professional reader who picks up the earliest clues that separate the amateurs from the pros.

What are those clues? That's what this book is all about. If you already know how publishing decisions are made, skip ahead to CLUE #1.

A REPRIEVE

No doubt you've seen works of fiction that make you wonder how they ever made it into print. The reaction "I can do better than that" probably spawns more new writers than all the writers conferences put together.

As your own reading proves, not every piece of writing deserving of obscurity is rewarded with it. There's an exception to everything.

Luck may play a part, though few writers care to pin their hopes on being picked from fortune's fickle barrel. Most want to do everything they can to improve their manuscripts to survive that first, often *only* screen test, by a screener-outer who is the publishing police, judge, and executioner rolled into one.

Cruel? After years of rejecting manuscripts for the identical writing habits, even the kindest, most optimistic agents and acquisitions editors cannot help but feel cruelly treated by those who expect to enter a skilled profession without learning its craft.

With more self-improvement resources available today than ever before, publishing pros wonder how writers can remain oblivious to the many ways they sabotage their own submissions.

"We write all these books, how-to articles, and blogs," they groan. "We travel coast to coast giving workshops and telling writers what to do and what not to do. Are these efforts making a difference? No," they moan. "Our offices are still being flooded with the same kind of amateur submissions."

To deal with the deluge, agencies and publishers respond with brief form letters or postcards saying thanks-but-no-thanks, here's wishing you success . . . elsewhere.

If you receive one of those "elsewhere" advisories, you might feel like spending the rest of the day lying on your couch in a blue funk.

"How could they reject my story," you cry. "What do those people *want?"*

D.O.A.

PLAINTIFFS

Before we look at what publishers want, take a few moments— since you're stretched out on the couch anyway—to contemplate a want of your own. An end to those unsaintly "elsewhere" notes? That, too. What I have in mind, though, is the secret desire that lurks deep in the unconscious of the unhappily unpublished.

Like many who yearn for publication, you may be nurturing a dream in which your manuscript lands on the desk of a kindly benefactor able to look past any rough edges and recognize raw, undeveloped talent. This visionary is so taken by your *potential* that he or she shows you how to fix whatever little flaws might be getting in the way of your success.

Wouldn't it be wonderful to encounter a nurturing mentor willing to mold you into the accomplished writer you know you can become?

Like any fantasy, this secret desire is based on an unreal premise—the result, perhaps, of growing up with all those inspiring biographies in the school library that told of misunderstood geniuses who struggled and eventually made good.

Biographies are by definition inspiring. Who wants to read of the shlimazel who hasn't succeeded at *something?*

In publishing, mentors and fairy godparents exist, but they are rare. Teaching writers their craft is not the job of an agent or a publisher's in-house editor.

"[P]eople tend to think, I can take this horrible mess of a manuscript to a benevolent genius who is going to turn it into a masterpiece and teach me how to write. The function of the [in-house] editor is not to run a writing school; it is to edit and publish books."

Justin Kaplan, editor of *Bartlett's Familiar Quotations* [5]

9

CALCULATED GAMBLE

Royalty publishers are professional gamblers. They bet on an acquisition's netting a large enough profit to make their risk worthwhile—larger by far than their outlay for production, marketing, distribution, and the author's modest advance and equally modest royalty.

Agents are risk-takers, too. They gamble on an acquisition's generating a large enough advance plus royalties to produce a meaningful commission. Other than that large commission and small reimbursements for postage and photocopying, professional agents are not paid for the time they invest in seeking homes for the work they represent. Nor should they be.

Therefore, if these risk-takers believe their projected ROI (return on investment) will be modest, a reasonably well-written manuscript that generates mild but not wild enthusiasm is unlikely to attract either an agent or a publisher, *even when nothing is wrong with it.*

Moreover, if this nicely written manuscript does get published and nets only a small profit, that profit will be seen as a loss. To understand this paradox, we have to consider what's known in all business ventures as the *opportunity cost*—more accurately, the *lost* opportunity cost. That is, an investor's decision to put resources behind Book A means not investing in Book B—and Book B *might have yielded a higher profit.*

So you can see why agents and publishers must feel passionate about a new writer's chances for success before risking time and resources on an unknown. This reality applies equally to the mid-list writer who is eventually convinced by unspectacular sales to start fresh under a pseudonym.

How often do you feel passionate enough to gamble your time and money on the future of a stranger? For agents and royalty publishers, gambling is a given—unlike those whose job is to help writers learn their craft, such as the professional writing instructor, coach, or independent manuscript editor. These fee-for-service providers are paid at the time they render their professional services. Now that publishers no longer subsidize the editorial costs they once did, the burden of who pays for editing has shifted to the writer, who is expected to do whatever it takes to come up with a highly polished, profitably publishable manuscript.

Writers serious about their work are well advised to put aside their fantasies, get up from the couch, and learn as much as possible about the craft of writing *before* subjecting themselves to near-certain disappointment.

D.O.A.

DEFENDANTS

We can now look at what publishers want. Writers are always being told, write what *you* want, not what you think publishers want, unless you're a writer for hire. "The first person you should think of pleasing, in writing a book, is yourself," advised bestselling author Patricia Highsmith. She felt strongly enough about this issue to put it on page 1 of her classic *Plotting and Writing Suspense Fiction.*

However, Highsmith and others are not saying write in whatever way you want. They are saying don't try to second-guess the next trend. "Are they still buying cozies?" asks the *trendinista.* "Has the serial killer been overdone?" "Paranormal romance seems hot right now. Maybe I'll try it."

Pleasing yourself applies to selecting your genres and topics. It does not apply to writing well, which never goes out of style.[6]

Comments that occasionally accompany a returned manuscript sometimes tell what a specific agent or publisher is looking for.[7]

> "What's sought is a fresh voice, a magical individuality that is both unique and indefinable. . . ."

Magical? Indefinable? Maybe the next rejection letter is more helpful:

> "We are always looking for the writer with that extra pizzazz."

Is this any clearer? Stay tuned—we place our order for pizzazz later.

BACK TO BASICS

To review, publishing is a profit-driven business based on a gamble in which the odds favor no one. Most new titles have short, unprofitable shelf lives of twelve to thirteen weeks. Most lose money, their losses offset by the earnings of the few titles that do exceptionally well.

How many other industries turn out between 65,000 and 100,000 different products every year? Only a small number of these titles bring in extra income by being reissued in film, paperback, and foreign reprints. Note that book revenue comes from *new* units sold. Not a penny from the huge market in used books goes to the producers: authors, agents, or publishers. (Raise your hand if you buy only brand new books. I thought so.)

Because the goal is to get through the pile, literary agent Noah Lukeman says that agents and editors read solely with an eye to dismiss a manuscript.[8]

In contrast, Hollywood produces a little over 300 films a year for theatrical release,[9] which earn residuals whenever they are licensed for TV, video, and DVD *whether or not the original did well at the box office.* Furthermore, film has no competition from sales of used movie tickets.

These realities force the publishing industry's risk-takers to select manuscripts likely to spill less red ink than previous gambles. That's why the odds-pickers attempt to maximize the sales potential of their already-established high earners, and to:

A. cut further losses by dropping existing authors whose sales are less than stellar;
B. minimize risks by taking on a small number of new writers who look like sure winners; and
C. ignore the rest, especially those whose writing skills are average.

Everything else that can be said about publishing is based on these ABCs. The industry cannot afford to gamble on writers who are still developing their potential, show little evidence of having studied the craft of the profession they aspire to, or don't follow the submission guidelines that publishers and agents make available. At times, guidelines serve as a screening device to identify writers who don't or won't follow instructions.

TIPSHEETS

Submission guidelines are also known as tipsheets. These specify each recipient's genres handled, preferences for querying and submitting, policy on multiple submissions, interest in a synopsis, number of pages to send, and many other dos and don'ts.

Advice and opinions on the pros and cons of what to send and how to write that all-important query letter are available in dozens of excellent books, magazines, and blogs for writers. Because that information is plentiful, and because the writing skills needed to produce nonfiction marketing materials are not the same as the skills needed to create a work of fiction, I do not cover marketing. Instead, you can find pre-publication and post-publication resources listed among the recommended nonfiction titles and popular Internet sites at the back of this book (in Exhibits B and C of the POST-MORTEM).

Often, submission guidelines mention the need for fresh characters, plausible plots, and lively dialogue. They do not tell you how to correct implausible plots, avoid stale characters, and eliminate other signs of average writing. That's not the job of a tipsheet. It's the writer's job.

The responsibility is also yours for delivering the indefinable magic and pizzazz.

Your most valuable resource for learning the craft of writing is the work of other authors. Steep yourself in fiction and nonfiction of all kinds. Read and reread the authors you feel an affinity for and study their techniques. Analyze the way they set a scene, construct dialogue, develop characters, and build suspense.

Jason Epstein, publisher of Anchor Books and a founder of the *New York Review of Books*, writes that when he got his start in publishing at Doubleday, for several weeks he was given no further assignment than to read unsolicited manuscripts, which he soon learned could be "disposed of on the evidence of a paragraph or two."[10]

The advantage of reading a novel or a short story for the second or third time is that you avoid getting caught up in questions of what happens next, thereby freeing yourself to concentrate on the how-to of creating the effects you admire.

Effective techniques, when added to your own natural ability to spin a great story, prepare you to give publishers what they are really looking for: good writing.

BEYOND TIPSHEETS

1. Join organizations of writers, attend their meetings and conferences, and participate in their online discussions. (For popular Internet sites for writers, see Exhibit C of the POST-MORTEM.)

2. Take courses on technique at local colleges and online. To learn which courses are worthwhile, ask your online discussion buddies.

3. Join a local support group for writers or an online critique group—or start one. Some writers find such groups extremely helpful; others find them taking time and energy that could better be used for writing. (There's a reason that Milwaukee's Redbird Studios has a waiting list for its "Shut Up and Write" program.)

4. If possible, work with a professional writing coach or personal editor to build your writing strengths, identify your weaknesses, and produce a manuscript with promise.

5. Read books about the craft of writing—and not merely one or two, because no book, including this one, has all the answers. Advice ranges from how to write and market your book to how to edit it, and from "My way is the only way" to "See all the options you have."

6. Read novels in your genre and other genres, and soak up the sound of good writing.

7. Keep returning to the quick FIND & FIX checklists throughout this book. And don't hesitate to write in the margins, highlight, put sticky-notes wherever you want to, and add your own listings to the index of topics you want to return to again.

D.O.A.

CORRECTION FACILITIES

Now that we've considered a few fundamentals that drive the publishing business, we can look at what you have some control over. Whether you love revising or hate it, revision is where a writer's craft shows itself—where the real writing takes place. Step 1 is to put your completed first draft aside for a week or a month to gain a fresh perspective on it. The longer its forced exile, the fresher your vision.

In Step 2, some writers read only for plot on their first pass through, taking notes but making no corrections. On their next pass, they focus only on characters. They recommend reading for specific elements on each subsequent pass. Why work over the phrasing of a sentence when the whole scene might be dumped?

Other writers revise each scene before writing the next one, reviewing where they've been so they know where they're heading. Only when the first draft is finished and brought out of exile do they begin at page 1 and make several complete revision passes through the whole, as needed.

Both approaches have merit, as do other methods. What works for you depends on your own experience with writing a full-length novel. First-timers can benefit from trying several methods, because I strongly advocate revising, revising, revising.

Between revisions put your manuscript out of sight and read a good novel. Let the voices of skilled writers refresh your hearing and expand your sensibilities. The moment you feel inspired to let your own voice resound, stop reading and start revising again.

Author of *The Sterile Cuckoo*, John Nichols, talks of writing his first draft very quickly, then rewriting and rewriting—loving the process. For him, "really writing" is that final stage in which he dwells on lines and words.[11]

15

Without these mind-cleansing interludes, a too-frequent self-edit of your draft can counteract the fresh approach gained by its temporary exile.

If you reach revision overload, try an about-face. Work your way from the last scene to the first. A change in sequence breaks the continuity of the plot and keeps you from missing the same weaknesses again. This altered perspective can reveal scenes that go nowhere, plus action, dialogue, and characters who contribute nothing. Whatever works for you, go for it.

NO "RIGHT WAY"

When the subject of revision comes up at writing conferences, some workshop leaders who are also successful authors put forth their way as "The Right Way." This makes me uncomfortable, because the audience is filled with writers eager to believe that all advice from an author who glitters is gospel. When aspiring writers, already insecure, realize they aren't doing things the way they think a *real* author is supposed to, they have one more reason to feel inadequate.

The truth is, no one way is the right way. Revising, like writing, is a creative process, too complex to reduce to a formula. As convinced of this truth as I am, I was nonetheless gratified to come across support for it from the award-winning novelist Jan Burke. Her essay "Revision" appears in *Writing Mysteries,* the Mystery Writers of America handbook edited by Sue Grafton:

> "Revision is one more process through which each writer must
> find his or her own way, and while it may take some time and
> experimentation to learn what method works best for you,
> mastering this part of the craft of writing will be well worth it."
>
> [p. 182]

Revise as much as you can before submitting your manuscript. Do the same even when the only one looking at your draft is your personal editor, critique partner, or writing coach.

Wait a minute—if you hire your own editor can't you expect that person to find and fix all those little details? Yes, and many editors do just that, but most are able to see the forest *and* the trees more clearly if you first hack away at the underbrush and dead stumps. It's a fact: certain issues become evident only as smaller obstructions are removed. To get the most from any editor, provide the cleanest manuscript you can.

The more problems you can keep from murdering your manuscript, the more attention a writing coach or editor can pay to these two necessities:

- helping you overcome the weaknesses invisible to a critique group and to you, the only *self*-editor, and
- reinforcing your writing strengths.

The professional editor takes no pleasure in fixing what you can be taught to find and fix yourself. By mastering the dozens of techniques in this book, you save your manuscript from instant rejection, improve its chances of being *read,* and enable those who edit your work to focus on the subtler challenges that help you grow as a writer. Professional editors get a kick out of witnessing the development of new talent. I know I do.

THE BIG STUFF

Chances are you've been concentrating on developing your characters, weaving your plot and subplots, and refining other large-scale, whole-book concepts. These big-picture elements comprise your manuscript's content— what your novel is *about.* Slight one and you have no story.

Those large-scale concepts are not what I deal with in this book. One reason is that many other resources do precisely that (see Exhibit B of the POST-MORTEM).

> "Most cuts are made in the first three pages. The 'yes' pile is cut two more times."
>
> Barbara Gislason, literary agent [12]

Another reason is that handling large-scale issues in a book involves talking about general principles, but general principles are not easy to apply to one's own writing.

Third, many writers expect the agents and editors who read their work to view plot and character as the key to publication. That may be true for submissions that reach the higher levels of decision-making, but for the majority of manuscripts, the first reader rejects the quality of the writing long before reading far enough to evaluate the development of your plot or characters.

This reality is my main reason for not dealing with a novel's whole-book concepts. As you now realize, the most efficient way for the readers at agencies and publishing houses to process mountains of submissions is to stop reading at the earliest clues to average writing.

THE SMALL STUFF

Unlike large-scale, whole-book elements, the small stuff in writing deals with formatting and what I call PUGS: punctuation, usage, grammar, and spelling. I don't cover mechanics in this book, either, though such details are critical to getting read. Making errors in grammar or spelling, or failing to mirror formatting preferences, gives busy screener-outers the first clue and often the only reason to be able to say, "Whew! Another four-pounder I don't have to read."

Why offer your first reader an invitation to quickly reject your work?

Most editors-for-hire do a decent job of cleaning up PUGS for you. Scores of books and magazines advise you about format and other mechanics (e.g., p. 284), as do the free tipsheets from publishers and agents.

All tipsheets are similar but not identical, so customize your every submission to meet the requirements of each recipient. Evidence of a writer's ignoring a specification could annoy the screener, disqualify a submission immediately, or peg the writer as careless or a prima donna. No publishing pro wants a long-term relationship with a high-maintenance author.

IN THE MIDDLE

Between the large-scale elements of plot and character, and the small-scale PUGS and mechanics, a large middle ground exists. That's my focus in this book, because my goal is to give you a fair chance at getting your manuscript past its hasty initial screening to actually being *read*.

Picture a pyramid. Its base represents the major whole-book concepts that call for macro-editing. This is the province of acquisitions and developmental editors. The top of the pyramid represents the small stuff that demands the finicky, narrowly focused approach of micro-editing. This is the province of copy editors and proofreaders.

In that broad middle ground between the pyramid's base and its apex lies the wide-ranging province of the line editor. Line editing encompasses large areas of

> "Never start a sentence with a comma." That's the only rule in publishing, said Bill Brohaugh, former editorial director for Writer's Digest Books, speaking at a Mid-America Publishers Association conference. "Everything after that is up for discussion."[13]

both developmental editing and copy editing, but it is especially attuned to helping writers shape their techniques and sharpen their writing skills.

WHY THESE CLUES

You and I know that creating a publishable manuscript goes well beyond the ability to master several dozen writing techniques. Though some aspects of craft are more important than others, any technique used ineffectively is a dead giveaway to the kind of writing that is merely average.

Ineffective, average techniques share these characteristics:

1. Their use—or rather, misuse—is pervasive throughout a manuscript as well as throughout the typical stack of submissions. The resulting voice makes ninety percent of all manuscripts sound as if they were written by the same person. That's why I call it average writing. It may have been good enough to earn A and B-plus in high school and college, but it's not professional enough for commercial publication.

2. Clues to ineffective techniques remain invisible to most writers until pointed out. Pointing them out is exactly what I am about to do.

3. The same clues are equally invisible to one's writing buddies, who usually address the big stuff, and to the English major in everyone's life, who tends to tinker with the small stuff. (Take no offense, please; I'm a former English major and a life member of Tinkerers Anonymous.)

4. Screener-outers learn to spot the clues to average writing immediately.

And now for the good news...

5. Clues to the problem techniques I analyze are relatively easy to learn, and to find and fix. So easy that you'll forget where you read them.

ABOUT THE EXAMPLES

What follows are 230 excerpts from more than 215 writers working in a dozen different genres. Together, you and I shall analyze how those writers successfully dealt with the techniques that challenge every writer.

As often as possible, I present excerpts from first novels and stories because I believe a developing writer might identify more readily with others at the beginning of *their* publishing careers.

Every passage bearing an author's name is offered as a positive example of a specific technique. The few negative, nameless ones I wrote, using the identical phrasing that I encounter repeatedly in manuscripts. Only the identifying details are changed, because I have no wish to embarrass anyone. Writing is difficult enough, and the professional skills a writer must demonstrate to be taken seriously in a highly competitive marketplace require a long and challenging process to develop—much longer and more difficult than the new writer imagines.

All the excerpts I quote make up my show and tell. The rest is opinion, mostly mine, based on a lifetime of editing, coaching, teaching, reading.

I do not expect you to agree with every one of my opinions or admire every example I review. In fact, the wording of some excerpts could be improved. However, I chose each because it is a good example of a particular technique that I'd like every writer to be aware of.

Some caveats:

- I don't claim to know what effect an author intended—only the effect on me and what my years in publishing have shown me is the effect on others.

- By offering specific examples that I find particularly effective, I am not necessarily endorsing the books from which they come or all the techniques within their pages.

- Each selection I review is meant to stimulate your imagination and inspire your experimentation, not imitation.

- In no way am I laying down *rules*. In fiction, there are no absolutes. There are, however, guidelines.

What's more, in all things editorial:

- No solution is right for every situation. Evaluate my suggestions in relation to what is most appropriate for your own work.

- There's an exception to everything—a caveat that bears repeating.

- The choices are always yours, no matter what I or any editor recommends at any stage of your manuscript's development.

PART II: EVIDENCE COLLECTION

"It's interesting that the word 'plot' can mean a place for the dead, an evil intrigue, or a story line."

Sandra T. Wales, author of the Warrior Queen series[14]

TERMS OF THE WILL

Writers inherit a legacy of terminology from past generations. They add to it, modify it, and pass it along. Terms used in unique ways in a profession are usually stuck in a glossary at the back of a book, where readers discover the meaning of those terms long after they have made assumptions about them.

So here, up front, is a brief overview of some terms I use in this book.

Of the narrative forms available for presenting a story, the easiest to recognize, but the most difficult to write well, is **dialogue**. The least understood is **action**, which is not anything that moves; it is behavior that reveals character, advances the plot, and provokes reactions and conflict. At the opposite end of the action continuum are **gestures** and **body language**—little behaviors that reveal a character's attitude and feelings.

Description is another narrative form, as is **thought**—also called **self-talk, monologue,** and **interior dialogue.** Everything else is **exposition**, sometimes called by the general term **narrative**. Exposition is efficient for condensing, explaining, and summarizing. Action and dialogue are less efficient but more compelling, presenting behavior that lets readers interpret meaning for themselves.

The main character is the **protagonist**, who often is also the **viewpoint character**, whether the story is presented from a first-person or third-person **POV** (**point of view**). The romance genre uses the terms **hero** and **heroine**, with the protagonist usually the woman.

Today's audiences expect a **developing character**—one who experiences an internal change in the course of overcoming external opposition.

The **antagonist** in the crime genre is always a person. Other forces may also thwart the main character, like social mores, personal beliefs, or nature's elements—common obstacles in literary fiction. In fiction with **paranormal** content or "**woo-woo**," such as **fantasy**, **horror**, and some **romance** and **science fiction**, antagonists are often supernatural.

What characters want produces their **motivation** for action. Conflicting wants create the **story problem**, the **situation**, or the **predicament**.

Plot is carried out through **scenes**. Each is made up of at least one character, a **setting** in time and place, and action propelled by a **goal** and an **obstacle** to that goal, which produces **tension** and **conflict**. The scene's **resolution** advances the plot by creating a new problem, often a **setback** or **redirection**. A **red herring** is a false lead that takes the protagonist further from the goal.

A **beat** is a statement that takes the place of a *he said/she said* **dialogue tag**. It can dramatize **body language** or a **gesture** that identifies the speaker and **grounds** or **anchors** the character in time and place.

Story time is real time for the characters. It is usually presented in past tense, although fiction can be written in present tense. **Backstory** tells of events that occurred before story time. **Background** is information that was or continues to be true.

The opening lines that grab attention and get readers involved in the story situation are called, appropriately, the **hook**. The plot's forward movement toward its conclusion is known as **progression**. The rate of progression is controlled by **pacing**. A story's pace, action, and tension reach their height in the **climax**. This penultimate scene is followed by the **dénouement**, a brief scene to tie up any loose ends and explain the **solution**, solidify the **payoff**, and provide reader satisfaction.

Density refers to using the same story element for more than one purpose. Density is a highly valued quality in fiction, especially in the more condensed genres such as mystery, romance, and sci-fi.

WITH PURPOSE AFORETHOUGHT

Every element in a work of fiction—every character, scene, setting, action, image, description, detail, and word—should serve a purpose. Elements that serve more than one purpose at a time or fill more than one function enrich the writing by multiplying its density.

Evaluate the density of your writing by seeing how many of the following purposes are served by each of your novel's elements:

advancing plot
dramatizing action
evoking mood
introducing sexual tension
escalating conflict
sketching a description
revealing a buried agenda
thwarting a goal
raising the stakes
supplying information
establishing a sense of place
embedding a first reference
making a second reference
expanding a character's insight
identifying a speaker
furnishing visual interest
appealing to the other senses:
    sound, smell, taste, touch
offering another perspective
grounding or anchoring characters
regrounding or re-anchoring
setting up a surprise
introducing irony
contributing humor
arousing emotion

portraying character
hooking interest
increasing motivation
adding to sexual tension
intensifying suspense
expressing an attitude
provoking a reaction
triggering a counter-reaction
differentiating characters
changing tempo or pace
transitioning in time, place
suggesting elapsed time
misdirecting
showing a relationship
planting a clue
providing texture
comparing or contrasting
    with similes or metaphors
extending a metaphor
symbolizing meaning
creating counterpoint
constructing parallel actions
developing theme
delaying resolution
enriching the writing style

A SUCCESS STORY

Joe Konrath is the author of six (so far) mystery novels
and a horror novel under the name Jack Kilborn.
His short stories have appeared in more than sixty
magazines and collections, and his work has been
translated into ten languages.
Winner of the Derringer Award, he's been nominated for
the Anthony, Macavity, Gumshoe, and Barry.

It wasn't luck. It was researching, analyzing the writing
of others, and determined self-editing.

"After a million written words and over four hundred rejections,
I decided to take a different approach. Instead of writing
something, sending it out, and adding the subsequent
bong letter to my Rejection Book, I dedicated myself to
figuring out what I was doing wrong.

"I write genre fiction: mystery, suspense, horror.
For comparison, I selected some current, best-selling
examples of each of these forms and read them back to back.
Then I reread my early novels with the same critical eye.

"The conclusion was startling; my first novels weren't very
good. They were riddled with typos, poor grammar, and
creative spelling. They were also remarkably self-indulgent,
showcasing a writer who was in love with his own voice
rather than the one who made every word count.

"The plots weren't bad, but they could have been streamlined.
The pace was messy, sometimes grinding to a halt with
long sections of clunky exposition. The characters were pretty
good but spent a lot of time doing things that had nothing
to do with furthering the plot. Plus, I'm ashamed to admit,
I had a modifier problem. No verb or noun went without
several helpers. It was really extraordinarily amazingly
hugely very unfortunately bad." [15]

D.O.A.

PART III: FIRST OFFENDERS

Elizabeth Daniels Squire, author of the Peaches Dann mystery
series, shared what a publisher told her a manuscript had to do to
get his attention. He suggested watching readers in a bookstore
deciding which book to buy. They look first at the jacket,
which is largely out of the author's control, and the first page.
Writers have the first page at most to sell the reader.
"So you have even less space than that to sell me." [16]

CLUE #1: HOBBLED HOOK

Every submission needs a hook—something sharp to catch the attention of a busy screener. A celebrity byline is a great hook, but if you don't own that particular bait, you have to lure the reader into your story the way the rest of us do, with an interesting, intriguing opening line. As in fishing, an effective hook not only arouses curiosity but also holds on to it, not letting it get away, not even letting it . . . uh, flounder.

The typical submission begins effectively enough with a line or two of dialogue or action about a character in some kind of predicament. But this soon drifts into description and backstory, which tells of the protagonist's past instead of continuing to show that character in action in the present.

By the time the writer gets around to picking up the opening action where it left off, the screener-outer is picking up the next submission.

25

When you edit your opening, determine whether it fulfills its primary function of making readers want to read the next line, the one after that, and the line after that.

Sustaining interest is primary, because the busy screener is looking for the earliest excuse to stop reading.

To heighten the effect of your action opening, omit description and background altogether, or severely limit them to a word or two that you work in with the main action. Don't upstage either dialogue or action, the two narrative forms that bring readers into direct contact with your main character. If possible, add just a suggestion of the setting:

> "He was murdered upstairs, in that front bedroom where you sleep, Ashley dear," Binkie said.

This is the first line of the first Magnolia mystery novel by Ellen Elizabeth Hunter, *Murder on the Candlelight Tour.* Dialogue introduces the main character (Ashley), briefly sets the scene (in the house where she sleeps), and makes the powerful statement that someone was murdered in her bedroom.

Opening with the word "He" indicates that Binkie and Ashley are in the midst of discussing the murdered man, creating the sense that we've dropped into a scene *in medias res*—in the middle of things. This opening technique immerses readers in the story situation right away.

FAST START OR SLOW

To increase the feeling of a fast start, use short sentences and paragraphs and open with action or with quick, punchy dialogue. Begin more slowly if you are establishing a mood foreshadowing danger and intrigue, as Marcia Muller does in her opening to *The Cheshire Cat's Eye:*

> The row of Victorian houses loomed dark in the early June fog. I put my hand on the cold iron railing and started up the stairway from the street. As I pushed through the overgrown front yard, blackberry vines reached out to tear at my clothing.

Fast start or slow, verify that your main character appears as soon as possible and is faced with an immediate situation that leads the reader to want to know who, what, where, when, how, and why. Foster-Harris, in

The Basic Formulas of Fiction, defines the hook as "the first brief, potent statement of what is the matter with the central character, what his problem is, what difficulty he is facing."[17]

> As far as Brian Donnelly was concerned, a vindictive woman had invented the tie to choke the life out of man so that he would then be so weak she could just grab the tail of it and lead him wherever she wanted him to go.
>
> Nora Roberts, *Irish Rebel* (romance)

> It's never a good thing when the flight attendant is crying.
>
> Hank Phillippi Ryan, *Air Time* (mystery)

> "For the crime of causing irreparable sexual mischief through magic, I hereby banish the defendants, Dorcas and Ambrose Lowell, to Big Knob, Indiana, until such time as they straighten out the dragon living there. So mote it be."
>
> Vicki Lewis Thompson, *Over Hexed* (paranormal romance)

> My eyes weren't fixed on the direction I was driving, but on the words "Nigger Landlord" slashed in bright neon paint across the ribs of the oak tree that stood in front of my new home.   Gammy L. Singer, *A Landlord's Tale* (first mystery)

Examine your opening line to verify that it hooks readers into your protagonist's situation from the get-go.

DOING IT ALL

If these recommendations seem too numerous for any one hook to support, here's an opening that covers them all in a single sentence. It's from *Dead Over Heels,* an Aurora Teagarden mystery by Charlaine Harris:

> My bodyguard was mowing the yard wearing her pink bikini when the man fell from the sky.

Despite some playful details, we know a murder has been committed, because no self-respecting reader would believe that a body falls from the sky by accident. The author's multi-pronged opening line raises all the important questions: whose body is falling, whodunit, how, and why. A minimum of description raises enough additional questions to pique our curiosity and prompt us to read further. Why is a bodyguard performing yard duty? Why is she doing so in a bikini—a pink one, no less—and how come she's a she? Who *is* this narrator that needs a bodyguard?

Now that you've seen how many questions can emanate from a tightly worded opening line, compare Harris's opening sentence with one I'm making up to show the kind of writing I see all the time:

> I was lazily watching my tall, tanned bodyguard mowing the lush green lawn in her bright pink bikini when I heard the loud, insistent buzz of a small private airplane flying overhead. When I looked up I saw the very scary sight of a man's limp body falling from the cloudless blue sky.

What's wrong with this picture? It's awkward and wordy. Actions are buried in redundancies: *airplane flying overhead . . . When I looked up I saw.* Every noun suffers from an overload of adjectives: *tall, tanned; lush green; bright pink; loud, insistent; small private; very scary; man's limp; cloudless blue.* The relentless pattern of modifiers creates a rhythm you could polka to—if you haven't been laid low by infectious adjectivitis.

Wordiness destroys a hook's impact. How many readers would be motivated to endure such unimaginative prose for the length of a novel—other than Mom?

Cramming multiple actions into a single sentence can make even a well-written hook sink of its own weight. Exception (there's always an exception): where the weight of repetition creates a deliberate effect:

> Claire Jenson was out back in her favorite part of the garden, the section where she'd tossed seeds here and there this past spring, nothing structured, nothing formal, just scattered here and there the way her grandmother had taught her, when the call came from Chicago telling her that her youngest daughter had been murdered.
>
> Beth Anderson, *Murder Online* (first mystery)

This novel, a Frankfurt Award nominee, opens with a leisurely pace and a homey setting. Anderson makes us feel at ease, laid back, off guard. We picture a favorite place and a familiar routine performed with a casualness learned from grandma, a figure associated with love, old-fashioned comfort, and safety. The mood is one of security, calm, and normalcy, when . . . WHAM! We're slammed into the worst scenario any parent could imagine, made more powerful by the contrast.

CONTRADICTION

Anderson's opening sentence illustrates a concept that underlies much genre fiction: nothing is as it seems. A contradiction or paradox adds intrigue. Look for the contradiction in this opening line:

> The perfect windless day kept the tear gas hovering near the ground. Susan P. Mucha, *Deadly Deception* (first mystery)

Can a day be perfect if tear gas is hovering? Analyze the incongruities or potential reversals you sense in the following openings:

> Men did not dump Lena Caprell. She dumped them. That was how it went. That was how it *always* went.
> Lynn Viehl, *Dark Need* (vampire romance)

> From the waist down, he was promising.
> Barbara Delinsky, *The Carpenter's Lady* (romance)

> I was admiring the view from my second story window when the screaming started. Betty Webb, *Desert Noir* (mystery)

> It was a dark and dirty alley and a very expensive dress.
> Evonne Wareham, *Out of Sight, Out of Mind*
> (paranormal romance-in-progress)

> I wondered if anyone would be there to meet me. I hoped not.
> Gene Hull, *Hooked on a Horn* (memoir)

> He was the man every woman dreams about—in her worst nightmares. Edna Buchanan, *Miami, It's Murder* (mystery)

> There was a dead man in my freezer.
> Wendy Howell Mills, *Callie & the Dealer*
> *& a Dog Named Jake* (first mystery)

> At night, Mr Phillips lies beside his wife and dreams about other women. John Lanchester, *Mr Phillips* (mainstream)

TONE

Decide the tone of voice or attitude you want your opening to project—amused, cynical, snide, or something else. Tone helps readers get in the mood for the type of story to come. Though a humorous opening signals a lighthearted story, the same opening for a dark drama mixes the message.

Tone also reflects the protagonist's attitude toward his situation, putting readers in a frame of mind to accept his response to that situation.

The tone of Charlaine Harris's fell-from-the-sky opening is whimsical; that of Beth Anderson's in-the-garden hook is soothing—at first. What's similar about the next two openings, and what's different?

> At the very beginning, she had seen his face and knew he
> would not let her live.   Allison Brennan, *Speak No Evil* (mystery)

> The day I died started out bad and got worse in a hurry.
> Mary Janice Davidson, *Undead and Unwed* (vampire romance)

Each line refers to the character's death, but the tone is different. One sounds sinister, ominous; the other, light, almost humorous. Readers can decide what they're in the mood for. How about the tone of this opening:

> Call me Snake.
> Michael Mallory and Marilyn Victor, *Death Roll* (first mystery)

A spare three words. Matter-of-fact. Suggests the straightforward tone of its protagonist, a zoo keeper. Also a fast pace. Snappy dialogue.

Some openings name the protagonist while indicating the situation and the tone of the work as a whole. Listen for tone of voice in these openings:

> On the day she was chosen for death, Dana Enfield rose early
> and made coffee for her husband in the hushed November dawn.
> Francine Mathews, *Blown* (suspense)

> Kate McKenna's Wonderbra saved her life.
> Julie Garwood, *Slow Burn* (romantic suspense)

> "When we chose this book to read, I had no idea it would be
> so . . . explicit," murmured Carolyn Turner, Viscountess Wingate.
> Jacquie D'Alessandro, *Confessions at Midnight* (romance)

> When Briana Devon surfaced, her boat was gone.
> Karen Harper, *Below the Surface* (romantic suspense)

Some openings get their edge from a single word or phrase:

> The first one was a mercy killing.
> > Julie Garwood, *Mercy* (romantic suspense)

> That Thursday morning had been going so well until I found
> the local handyman dead on my workroom floor.
> > Cricket McRae, *Lye in Wait* (mystery)

> I felt *almost* wonderful.
> > Phyllis A. Whitney, *Woman Without a Past* (mystery)

Notice which of the above words suggest additional contradictions between what *is* and what came before or lies ahead: "The first one" (is there a second one?), "until" (what's next?), "almost" (why not all wonderful?).

Review the hooks presented so far. Put content aside for a moment and choose which of those hooks arouse an emotion in you that's similar to the emotion you want to create in your reader. Which come close to the tone of voice you want your own work to express?

If the mood of any of my selections feels wrong for your story, try to identify why without falling back on a simplistic *I like / dislike* response. Tone becomes easier to identify when you analyze how other authors achieve their effects. Granted, I offer here only a few of the many interesting, effective openings that authors craft to hook their readers. To expand your awareness of them, scout your library, prowl the bookstores.

SUSTAINABILITY

There's a reason "angling" is synonymous with fishing. Angling is defined as attempting to get something by *artful means.* In the creative arts, technique is the means. It involves selecting and manipulating content (the subject, the details) and mood (through tone and foreshadowing) until the desired effect is achieved.

To continue the angler's analogy, a novel's first line should be a high-tensile line. *Tensile: capable of being stretched or drawn out.* An effective hook stretches our curiosity beyond the first sentence. It raises a question that teases us into seeking the answer in the next sentence. There, we learn just enough to want to learn more.

The high-tensile line is sustainable. It keeps stretching, stringing us along, drawing us from one sentence to the next—preferably nonstop.

Many a manuscript comes close to hooking readers with an interesting line or two, but it doesn't sustain interest. Faltering curiosity is reason enough for a busy screener to move on to the next manuscript, and from that one to the next—also preferably nonstop.

To discover how far a high-tensile line can take you, look at the opening to *Midnight Hour,* the first mystery novel by Mary Saums:

> The phone hit the far corner of my bedroom like a blast out
> of a shotgun.

This sentence is all action, no background. It raises questions we want answered: what, who, when, how, and why. "Where" is already established: "my bedroom." The only description is "far corner."

Is this violence really occurring in a bedroom? And to a telephone? To find out, we're obliged to read on:

> Its plastic parts slid down the wall and fell in a heap.

Yep, it's a phone all right, and there's the wall it hit. So much for the *what,* which makes us want to find out *why.* Let's read another sentence before deciding how far to let this hook take us:

> After a few seconds of quiet it sputtered a final electronic cough,
> then flat-lined like a dead man's monitor.

From the first line's *shotgun* simile to the *dead man's,* the images are sinister, the tone is not. Who could quit now? Okay, one more sentence:

> "You deserved a slower death, you demon tool of iniquity!" I
> yelled. I tugged the straps of my push-up bra, part of a fancy set
> I'd bought specifically for the evening—a truly joyous occasion.
> It was my fortieth birthday.

Oops! We meant to read one sentence, and three whizzed by. How'd that happen? What does Saums do to keep our eyes pasted to the page?

- ☙ Her structure continually provokes new questions because the hook keeps stretching, adding more interest, not letting go. To see where it leads, we have to read more, don't we?
- ☙ Her character is quirky—a desirable trait in any protagonist.

Saums has her character do to her phone what most of us only dream of doing to ours. We like this person already. In addition, the author has her character reveal intimate details about herself, strong personal feelings, and a hair-trigger mood—which anyone over twenty who turns a divisible-by-ten birthday can identify with.

Whaddya know, our emotions are engaged. We're starting to care about this Ma Bellicose mangler and want to know what happens next.

> The dial tone was driving me crazy. I stomped across the room and slammed the receiver onto what was left of its cradle. Sitting down at my dressing table, I rubbed my face and tried to calm down. *To hell with that jerk,* I thought. I shook my new bottle of age-denying makeup and slathered it on.

What jerk? Something else to find out? Oh, all right, one more line:

> Much to my surprise the debris-that-once-was-my-phone rang.

Do you think it's the jerk calling? If so, we have yet another reason to stay tuned—we want to hear him reamed out by this spitfire. Her name, Willi Taft, we learn *after* she picks up the phone. Saums skillfully works these details and bits of background and description in with the action.

You might ask how much of all this activity is the hook itself, since we keep being strung along from one sentence to the next, one passage to the next. It doesn't stop.

Precisely! The function of an effective hook is *not* to stop; it's to draw readers into the character's situation to a point of no return. The goal is to keep readers *reading*—especially the first reader. The plan is to build staying power. Tensile strength.

Here's an opening that similarly sustains curiosity. It's from a novel-in-progress by Heidi Anna Johnson titled *Flash Memory:*

> I shot the first deputy just after ten. It wasn't easy; he kept squirming around and cracking jokes. I was planning to shoot the second deputy at eleven and I hoped he would behave himself.
>
> "One down, one to go," I said to my assistant as I slid the check for $150 into the deposit bag. Not bad for an hour's work. There was still the editing and the printing to be done. . . .

By the third paragraph, Johnson's protagonist tells us she is the sole proprietor of a photography studio in Lost Hat, Texas. And we thought "shot the first deputy" meant . . . oh, you know. It's a great set-up.

Jerrilyn Farmer's *Perfect Sax,* one of eight (so far) Madeline Bean culinary mysteries, also opens with a double meaning to provoke interest:

> "I love big balls."
> Wesley Westcott took his eyes off the road for a moment to glance over at the tall, thin blonde sitting beside him.
> "Oh, stop!" Holly caught his look and laughed. "You know what I mean," she said, flushing. "Big *fund-raising* balls. Banquets. *Parties.* "

TURN OF THE SCREW

Many authors open more sedately and sharpen their hooks gradually, letting a slightly later sentence be the one to turn the screw:

> Hannah Dain parked her Subaru behind a stand of sun-faded palo verde. She didn't know much about breaking and entering, but figured that hiding the getaway car was probably a good idea.   Twist Phelan, *Spurred Ambition* (mystery)

> No one understands my world except the man in the garden who lives in a suitcase. I gave him permission to live there last month. The next door neighbor complains constantly about it. Calls it a disgraceful state of affairs.
> I ignore her and visit him often.
>   Anne Segard Godden, "The Garden Lodger" (fantasy)

> If my grandson, Little Donny, hadn't taken so long getting out of bed this morning, I would have been at Chester's hunting blind in time to see them haul Chester out. I've never seen a bullet hole smack in the middle of someone's head before.
>   Deb Baker, *Murder Passes the Buck* (mystery)

> "We don't get much snow, and we hardly ever murder one another. Suicide is more our style. . . ."
>   Michael Malone, *Uncivil Seasons* (mystery)

Here's another provocative opening that keeps stretching, then turns the screw:

> Someone was watching her.
> Hope Farrier's nerves pinged as her mount skittered across the riding ring. The prickle of awareness that slid across the back of her neck wasn't going away.
> She glanced over at the dense hardwood forest that bordered her farm. Nothing unusual there.
> The thin chestnut snorted and tossed his head up, tugging the reins from her hands. "Easy, Jocko," she crooned. "It's all right."
> Someone was out there. She was sure of it. After another lap around the ring she had Jocko at a slow trot and risked another glance at the perimeter. No one by the woods, but a tall man in a dark business suit stood by the barn.
> A business suit. Old fears resurfaced. Men in suits came from foster care. From funeral homes. From foreclosing banks. Men in business suits were bad news.
>
> Maggie Toussaint, *No Second Chance* (romantic suspense)

Identify the openings shown so far that make you want to keep reading. Analyze how each of those authors captures your interest. Contradiction? Tone? Double meaning? Which techniques might work for your opening?

Christopher Park used his blog to solicit feedback on the "log line" or pitch he was developing for submitting his manuscript to an agent. Over the course of many months he received about thirty comments from readers, and his pitch went through nine iterations. Eventually he realized the result made a better hook for his manuscript than the hook he'd written. I agree. His opening line became:

> Nine years had passed since the Dead ended civilization.
>
> Christopher M. Park, *Longer the Night* (science fiction)

WEATHERING OPINION

Opinion is split on opening with the weather. One objection is the tendency toward clichés—not as rusty, perhaps, as "It was a dark and stormy night,"[18] but close. Another is that the weather seldom plays a relevant role in the story. Most opening weather reports seem stuck on, like gum.

Leann Sweeney reminds us that readers are interested in people, so for the weather to work in fiction, someone has to *experience* the weather's effect. The opening to *Pick Your Poison,* the first of her Yellow Rose mysteries, shows how Abby Rose experiences Houston's climate:

> The sun could have melted diamonds that day, and I spent the afternoon poolside, wasting away in Liptonville for the thirtieth time in a month.

Weather continues playing a role in Sweeney's plot, as it does in *Act of Betrayal,* a thriller by Morgan Avery. It opens:

> It was hot in the apartment, but Cut was used to the heat. His lean body sweated freely and the undershirt he wore was soaked under the arms and down his back. The last week of July in St. Louis was bad enough when a person could lie in the deep shade of a tree and let the breeze take away the sweat. . . . Compared to an afternoon under a shade tree, the apartment was a little slice of hell.
> It would have been nice to open the window.

Cut won't open it, because the plot is intricately connected with the heat—and because he "always associated the summer heat with the day that his boy died."

Nature and the environment are especially effective for creating an atmosphere of foreboding, as in the following first lines:

> Legend says that overcast skies are nature's way of hiding evil, protecting the gods from seeing sinister deeds.
>> S. D. Tooley, *When the Dead Speak* (first paranormal)

> The late morning blazed with blue skies and the colors of fall, but none of it was for me.
> > Patricia Cornwell, *Black Notice* (mystery)

> I had forgotten the smell.
> > Sara Paretsky, *Blood Shot* (mystery)

> The drought had lasted now for ten million years, and the reign of the terrible lizards had long since ended.
> > Arthur C. Clarke, *2001: A Space Odyssey* (science fiction)

These lines paint no leisurely panorama of the sky, water, or landscape for their own sake. Rather, the environment is called upon to create an effect that's quick and sharp: nature with a twist.

If you open with the environment, check your follow-through. Is the opening relevant to your plot? To the actions of your main character? Or is it background only? Do readers sense what the character is feeling, both physically through selected sensory data and emotionally through mood, tone, and anticipation of what lies ahead? If not, take a hint from the developers of real estate and don't let your grand opening depend on the weather.

CLICHÉD OPENINGS

One of the most clichéd openings is the protagonist's being jolted awake by a ringing telephone, especially after a hard night. That situation was sharp in the early days of the hardboiled detective story. Today, hooks that start off the day demand originality—which the following offer:

> I had become so used to hysterical dawn phone calls that I only muttered one halfhearted oath before answering.
> "Peacocks," a voice said.
>> Donna Andrews, *Murder with Peacocks* (mystery)

> I sat on my living room sofa at five o'clock in the morning with a copy of the mock-up of the front page of the day's *New York Post* in my hand, looking at my own obituary.
>> Linda Fairstein, *Final Jeopardy* (mystery)

Rapidly becoming a cliché is the hokey hook, one contrived for quick shock value but without staying power. After delivering its initial punch it drifts off to pursue other thoughts, and meanders for another chapter or two before returning to the opening incident. To warn you against this type of hobbled hook, here's my parody of a best-selling author's opening:

> The morning the severed finger arrived in the mail, I was still thinking about Hawaii. The blinding sun, the fragrance of yellow hibiscus, and Lola's sleek body riding the waves.
> We'd arrived on a balmy Tuesday evening after a long, sleepless flight listening to some moron in the seat behind us trying to impress the blonde traveling alone. A pretty woman, she wore. . . .

If you are a new writer, don't try to get away with this bestselling author's empty shock hook and his meandering irrelevancies. The busy screener recognizes the technique for its hokey pokiness and might look for the story line to reappear by skipping ahead a few pages. Or not.

So don't hobble your hook with backstory, description dumps, odd fits and starts, clichés, pile-ups of adjectives and adverbs, or the hokiness of a gratuitous severed body part. Those techniques deserve the finger.

Choose an opening action you are prepared to build from and sustain. A hook does its job by continuing to engage our attention until we are firmly caught and cannot get away. Nothing should divert our attention or cause reader interest to . . . um, you know . . . flounder.

Caring about the main character is the ultimate hook.

FIND & FIX CLUE #1: HOBBLED HOOK

- See how many of the following characteristics are true for your hook:
  - arouses curiosity about who, what, where, when, how, and why;
  - introduces the main character as soon as possible and leaves no doubt about who is the lead;
  - begins with the problem, predicament, conflict, threat, or change;
  - plunges into the middle of the situation;
  - creates a mood through tone, not with adjectives and adverbs;
  - stirs emotions that keep readers identifying with the central character's feelings;
  - sets a tone consistent with the main character's attitude;
  - avoids being clichéd, boring, or hokey—not contrived solely for shock value;
  - sustains curiosity well past the first chapter;
  - keeps action going without submerging it in backstory or description;
  - suggests a contradiction or incongruity of some kind.

D.O.A.

CLUE #2:   PERILOUS PROLOGUE

New writers may be surprised to learn that a novel is not obliged to open with a prologue. Avoid this device whenever you can, because readers tend to skip anything they view as a barrier to the story—along with all the other body parts known collectively as front matter: the legal notice, acknowledgments, dedication, author's note, and so on. In addition, nonfiction conditions readers to skip the preface, introduction, and much-despised "How to Use This Book."

Front matter gives a whole new meaning to the term "page-turner."

Whenever I encounter the prologue to a novel, I envision the public speaker who approaches the microphone, looks at the audience, and announces, "Before I begin. . . ." News flash: You just began.

Although walking out on a speaker's drawn-out warm-up would look rude in an auditorium, prologue-skipping is common in a bookstore. Why should readers browse front matter when thousands of other crisp new spines stand at attention waiting to be selected for active duty?

Meanwhile, back at the prologue, the author's carefully wrought hook lies undiscovered among all the other superfluous body parts.

REASONS OR EXCUSES?

Why do some novels open before Chapter 1? Here are the reasons I'm given when I ask writers who use prologues:

- *My first chapter is not that exciting.*
  My reply: Let's work on your first chapter.
- *My editor made me do it.*
  Probably for the above reason. See above reply.
- *Writing the prologue was the easiest way to get started.*
  True, but even jumper cables are temporary.

➽ *I introduce my protagonist after the prologue because I have the rest of the book to build interest in her.*
Who told you that? The rest of the book is for *developing* the character. Interest must begin on page 1.

If you need help getting started, consider this tip from Denise Dietz, creator of the Ellie Bernstein series and the Ingrid Beaumont series:

> "Most of the time I write a prologue, then delete it later. For me, it's a way to get my act together (since I don't outline). For *Footprints in the Butter,* my prologue became my second chapter."

Another reason some writers give me for opening with a prologue is:

➽ *I'm writing a* [fill in the genre]. *I thought a prologue was required.*

If your reason is equally lame but you are set on using this controversial device anyway, my next question is, are you willing to buck the bias?

BIAS?

What bias?

Agents and editors know all about the page-skipping that goes on in the aisles of the book nook and the privacy of the bedroom. Even *writers* admit to not reading other writers' prologues.[19] At least one acquisitions editor has not made a secret of his shifting front-loaded manuscripts to the bottom of his pile. *And those were agent-referred.*

As someone who reads front matter even when I'm not paid to, I agree that the majority of prologues are unjustified, unconnected, and unnecessary. So the rest of this CLUE presents a number of basic types of prologue together with their pros and cons. Mostly cons.

Literary agent Jessica Faust finds that material put in a prologue seldom belongs there. It often gives away crucial plot elements too early and ties in to the main story too late.

"If you must use the device," Faust advises, "tie its content in with the main story almost immediately. For example, if the prologue introduces a time when the characters are children, at least one of them has to be introduced right away in Chapter 1."[20]

Let's see how your prologue, if you use one, measures up.

TYPE 1: CHRONOLOGICAL CONNECTION

The most immediate connection between a prologue and its main story—therefore the most justifiable form of the device—occurs with the chronological or backstory prologue. The gap in time can be a few hours, as in Dan Brown's *The DaVinci Code,* or twenty-three years, as in Meg Chittenden's *More Than You Know.*

The latter opens with thirteen-year-old Nick Ciacia attending his father's funeral. He's given a tip that his father's killer might be a white-haired man known only as the Snowman. Nick tells this to the police captain, who ridicules the tip. The boy vows to find the mystery man himself.

The prologue's tie-in to Chapter 1 is immediate. Nick, now an FBI agent, learns the Snowman's real name and begins tracking him. Same objective, same narrative POV, same central character. The only change is time.

Not all writers who open with a backstory prologue dramatize it. Some present history in the form of news clippings or correspondence, often in italics. If you must italicize, keep the text as brief as possible, preferably under four lines. One hardcover I saw from a major publisher opened with fourteen pages set entirely in italics, despite the type style being notoriously unappealing to read at length. See what I mean?

An effective alternative to opening with backstory is to select essential bits of it and weave them into the main story a little at a time (discussed in CLUE #3). Or simply name the prologue Scene 1 of Chapter 1.

A top candidate for renaming is *The DaVinci Code,* because its prologue's structure is no different from that of other chapters in the book:

- ◆ The time interval from the opening event to the main story is only a few hours, an interval that occurs between many other chapters.
- ◆ The post-prologue switch to a different viewpoint character and a different setting also occurs between other chapters.
- ◆ The narrative uses a third-person POV throughout.

Renaming Brown's prologue Scene 1 of Chapter 1 would involve only the renumbering of chapters—no change in content. If your prologue could as easily become part or all of your first chapter, why not renumber? Although sales of Dan Brown's best seller have not been hurt by its prologue one iota, if your novel is not even a first-time seller are you willing to put it at risk by opening with a device widely considered unpopular?

TYPE 2: FUTURE CONNECTION

Alas, a frequently used type of prologue is the least chronologically connected, and is therefore the hardest to justify. It's the flash-forward or peek-ahead prologue in which a high-anxiety event from later in the story is mounted on the front end, like a hood ornament.

Its purpose is supposedly to let readers know certain facts without letting the protagonist learn them until later in the plot. To that end, the prologue's POV is often that of a victim, villain, or objective third person. One problem: by the time the plot catches up to the events of a flash-forward prologue, readers have forgotten the particulars. Should we plow on, hoping those details are unimportant? In fiction—especially mystery, suspense, science fiction, and fantasy—details are always important.

Or should we stop reading, turn to the beginning, and read the opening again? Hah! Another reason to skip a prologue the first time around.

Advocates of the peek-ahead form defend it as the only way to keep the narrator's first-person voice consistent once the main story begins. Here lies the second problem: the case has yet to be made for narrating in first-person. Often, the protagonist's POV can be put forth just as effectively in third-person, and with fewer restrictions. (More on POV in CLUE #11.)

> "I find that prologues are vastly overused in mysteries and almost always a mistake. They get in the way of a good story, rather than enhance it."
>
> Jim Huang, publisher, Crum Creek Press[21]

First-person benefits include intimacy, immediacy, and—if a crime is involved—a fair shot at solving it alongside the narrator. We enjoy the illusion of sharing a close, personal relationship with this character, privy to his thoughts, feelings, and information.

Moreover, we expect to stay in step with the narrator while he stays one step behind the antagonist—until the climax, that is. At that breakthrough moment, readers accept (sort of) being shut out of the protagonist's thinking as he puts the last piece of the puzzle in place, triumphs over his adversary, and wows us with his superior deductive abilities.

Which brings us to problem number three for the flash-forward prologue. From the outset, possessing information the protagonist does not have puts readers in a superior position to the one character who is expected to be the story's most resourceful, admirable individual.

When readers start out with the advantage of knowing something the main character doesn't, the benefits of intimacy and fair play diminish. If it's a mystery, for example, it slides partly into the category of thriller. Blending those elements is yet another challenge for new writers who might not be that familiar with the industry's expectations for every genre.[22]

A more consistent way of keeping information from a main character—when that's essential to the plot—is to merge the prologue with the first chapter and use third-person throughout.

There are no simple answers to questions about which point of view to use. Writers demonstrate their skill by the choices they make—presumably *after* they experiment with alternatives. Successful writers have boxes filled with such experiments. These are known in the business as first drafts.

CHEAP THRILL

Let's be honest. The reason for most peek-ahead prologues is to heat up a lukewarm opening. Does it matter if this quick fix for a slow start gives away too much too soon, or is unrelated to the chapter that follows? Yes, it does. Imagine you and I are reading a story that plunges into action on page 1, without our noticing the small type that says "Prologue." Heading, shmedding—form shouldn't call attention to itself anyway.

Just as we become interested in the high-anxiety threat to the character we believe is the protagonist, she suffers a gruesome, gory, graphic end. This evil deed barely pushes our emotional buttons, though, because so far we've had little opportunity to care about this victim. You and I may feel sympathy for her but not empathy. Not good.

We turn the page and "Chapter 1" shouts the start of the main story in 48-point type. Now we cannot help but become aware of form. Worse, we seem to be reading a different novel: actions are unrelated to those of the prologue, time and place are ambiguous, and every character is a stranger. Our link between the prologue and the main story just disconnected. *Click.*

What happened to the need to identify early with the main character? Our first relationship ended when she turned into the victim and got bumped off on page 2, 4, 6, or 8. *Now* who do we appreciate? Someone new is emerging as the possible protagonist, but we're slow to invest in this newcomer because the prologue's cheap thrill trifled with our emotions. What if this relationship turns into yet another brief fling? Will the real protagonist please stand up?

A bigger problem with the peek-ahead prologue is that after it raises the goose bumps, what follows has nowhere to go but down. Invariably, the content morphs into backstory and action downshifts to description. Although a change of pace is usually welcome after a high-tension scene, we just got here. We are not yet fully hooked. We're not even sure who the main character is. Chapter 1 is too early for a meltdown.

But here we are, mired in the same slow-moving chapter that the thriller prologue was mounted in front of in an attempt to keep the story from opening with originally. We've been had by a blatant appeal to sensationalism. The nightly news exploits the same principle: if it bleeds, it leads.

> "The well-told story, with characters who interest us, does quite well, no matter when the murder takes place."
>
> Pat Browning, author of *Full Circle*

I like an exciting opening as well as anyone. What is not desirable is the tension drop that occurs when a prologue disconnects from the main story. *Click click.*

Those who review submissions—screeners, agents, editors—tend to see such disconnects as spoiling a novel's structural unity. The reading public finds Chapter 1 just as dull with or without a prologue, which they skip anyway. And the writers who use the device continue believing it's okay for a strong opening to be followed by a first chapter that suffers from chronic post-prologue, low-tension, backstory ache.

TYPE 3: BODY ON PAGE 1

A variant of the cheap thrill is the "body on page 1." In the mystery subgenre known as police procedural, a dead body does kick off the investigation. Think *Law and Order.* For other genres, the "body on page 1" is shorthand for whatever shock occurs in the opening scene. Some writers believe an actual body in Scene 1 is a rule. It is not a rule. It is a precipitating event. Make it a good one, whatever your hook's emotion-grabber.

Turn a prologue into Scene 1 of Chapter 1 if there's no disconnect between it and the main story, which is usually the case when professional crime-fighters begin their investigation upon discovery of the corpse.

That unfortunate fellow is not, however, under contract to pop up at the start of every suspense novel.

In fiction that features a nonprofessional or "accidental sleuth," the investigative role seldom begins immediately. The writer has to first justify why an ordinary citizen would become involved in tracking an evildoer. It takes time to dramatize the circumstances that would make such an extreme risk appear credible. Often, the writer has to first portray:

1. the character's customary behavior under normal circumstances— like her quirkiness and propensity for getting into trouble;
2. events that increase her motivation to take such a risk (more on motivation in CLUE #15, BURIED AGENDA);
3. her initial resistance to being drawn into the situation;
4. her failed attempts to get others to believe her suspicions.

While these scenarios unfold, the high-tension action of the typical prologue too often skids to a halt at the threshold to Chapter 1, where it causes a noticeable disconnect. *Click click click.*

If this result resembles your own opening, have your hook kick off the story at a more modest anxiety level so the drop in tension is less severe. Build up from there.

Avoid divorcing your audience's emotional investment in your central character so early.

Though a mystery, for example, does not have to open with a murder, you might want to commit the wicked deed before page 100. Again, this is not a rule; it *is* an expectation. Today, genre fiction is in trouble if *something* doesn't cause tension from page 1.

> "Give them no reason to reject your work."
>
> Harry Arnston,
> quoted by Peter Abresch

It's in bigger trouble if its *only* tension comes from a body on page 1.

Consider *Dead Ringer* by *New York Times* bestselling author Lisa Scottoline. The murder occurs as late as page 195. What could possibly hold the reader's attention until then?

Answer: Constant action and conflict.

There's a trial that protagonist-lawyer Bennie Rosato wins—but she is devastated by not getting paid. Then there's her struggle with too-tight pantyhose, fear of not making the payroll and losing her law practice, shock over an associate's dyeing her hair hot pink (a shtick that turns into a running gag), stress over the arrival of a charming new client with a big commission, conflict over whether she should take this lucrative case, and worry over the loss of her wallet. All this before the end of Chapter 2.

In later chapters, the Italian community takes over Bennie's office with a food orgy, her house is ransacked, her dog is nearly killed, and on and on, from one scary event to the next humorous upset. I could tell you more, but then, as they say, I'd have to kill you. My point is, Scottoline invents more uproar to keep her pace barreling along, bouncing from one emotional high to the next, than most writers put into an entire novel. Do you?

THE HE-HE-HE VILLAIN

When a prologue dramatizes a crime, it tends to conceal the bad guy's identity until the climax—a technique that lets him play a dual role in the story: a Mr. Hyde in private and an ordinary Dr. Jekyll in public.

Some writers try so hard to conceal the identity of their Mr. Hyde that they refer to him only as "he," "the man," "him," "the dark figure," "he," "he," and "he." Soon, the profusion of indefinite pronouns becomes tedious and grammatically ungainly.

Sol Stein, author and editor, points out that ideally the protagonist should play an important role in the first scene so there's no mistaking another character for that primary role.

He says that one mark of amateur writing is a "lack of early clarity as to whose story we, as readers, should be following."[23]

Jan Burke has the right idea in *Flight,* her eighth mystery featuring Irene Kelly and Detective Frank Harriman. Burke gives her unidentified murderer a specific nickname: the "Looking Glass Man." Using a consistent third-person POV throughout, she periodically cuts to scenes that focus on this villain, starting with Chapter 2. Before we meet him, Burke dramatizes his brutal assault on a father and two teenagers. A less-skilled writer would have framed that opening attack as a prologue.

Wisely, Burke uses no such device. She opens with a fully developed Chapter 1 that gives us the opportunity to care about the teenagers before they are attacked—especially one of them.

CONTINUITY

Tell No One, Harlan Coben's tenth novel, offers a variation of the body on page 1. The story opens with David Beck hearing his wife being assaulted. With her screams still ringing in his ears, he, too, is attacked.

No heading identifies that opening scene as a prologue and no dateline appears. This sly evasion of truth-in-labeling lets us approach the story with no expectation of a disconnect—except for David's warning to us on page 1: "There was my life before the tragedy. There is my life now. The two have painfully little in common."

Given the shocking events following that warning, we might not recall David's observation about *before* and *now*. I didn't. So I was unprepared for the next scene's arrival, on page 9, introduced with these headings: Chapter 1, and Eight Years Later.

Aha! That opening scene *is* a prologue after all. Yet Coben quickly establishes continuity between it and his first chapter. Here's how:

1. He limits change to one factor: time. Although the eight-year gap comes as a surprise (I can't be the only one), the dateline keeps us from having to puzzle over the "when"—unlike other novels that disconnect the prologue from the main story.
2. Coben continues the same POV, as with a true backstory-type prologue. (Three chapters later, the first-person viewpoint shifts to third-person, but that's a different issue.)
3. The first words of the main story are: "Another girl was about to break my heart." This opening acknowledges the events of the prologue and connects the two scenes.
4. A few pages into the main story, Coben has David refer directly to his efforts over the years to find some trace of his missing wife. This tightens the connection and unifies the story's structure.

Supposing you, as a non-bestselling author, were to develop the same four unifying features for your opening scenes. Would I then say, "Aw shucks, go ahead and use a prologue"? Not a chance. What I *would* say is: "Think. If your prologue is so well-connected to the main story that it could *be* Chapter 1, have you any reason for risking the potential sabotage of your submission by not making it Chapter 1?"

TYPE 4: SUMMARY PROLOGUE

Another prologue to become aware of is the summary, in which the narrator looks back on the experience about to be told and hints at the lessons learned. Often, in those lessons, lies the story's theme.

A summary is not a scene, however, and philosophical reflection is not action. Moreover, summary prologues are usually so generalized that if page 1 fell to the floor of the book bindery it would never be missed.

Reflecting on lessons learned is a type of foretelling. Whereas *foreboding* is a mood-setting technique, and *foreshadowing* legitimizes future events by hinting about them early, *foretelling* is too similar to the aptly named had-I-but-known gimmick. Observe:

> Had I but known I'd be dangling from a ledge a hundred meters above the Pacific Ocean, I'd never have opened the lilac-scented envelope.

How suspenseful can a cliffhanger-dangler be if it reminds us that the narrator survived to tell of it? This once-fashionable foretelling device is today's object of ridicule.

In truth, slight foretelling is tolerated but not encouraged. Did you notice it in the sentences from *Tell No One* quoted two pages ago? Here is Coben's opening to the prologue preceding the attack. It starts with foreboding to establish a mood, slides into foreshadowing, hints at the theme about violence altering everything, and ends with foretelling:

> There should have been a dark whisper in the wind. Or maybe a deep chill in the bone. Something. An ethereal song only Elizabeth or I could hear. A tightness in the air. Some textbook premonition. There are misfortunes we almost expect in life— what happened to my parents, for example—and then there are other dark moments, moments of sudden violence, that alter everything. There was my life before the tragedy. There is my life now. The two have painfully little in common.

Coben's opening blends three types of prologue: the chronologically connected, the dramatized "body on page 1," and the summary.

BREVITY COUNTS

Once in a while I come across a prologue that enhances the story it precedes but isn't a scene and might—or might not—work as part of the first chapter. But it has a good chance of being read solely because of its brevity and the inviting white space on the page. One of these is from Alexandra Sokoloff's first novel, *The Harrowing,* a supernatural thriller.

The memorial was buried deep in an oak grove in the heart of campus. A graceful circle of trees, and the curved marble bench.

On this late November day, the grove was dark and hushed, just a whisper of rain that dripped from the thick canopy of branches, leaked down onto the aged marble, streaking the stone with black, like tears.

Vines and brambles had crept over the path, cutting off access to the quiet circle, leaving the bench all but forgotten now, like the students whose names it bore.

Above the layer of rotting leaves covering the seat, they were cut into the marble like names on a tombstone. Five names, a date, and a simple epitaph:

IN MEMORIAM

Five students dead, so long ago.

What could it matter now?

These 131 words establish the environment and the mood for the shocking events to come. The memorial to five students hints at the backstory that's revealed—as backstory should be—a little at a time throughout the novel.

The question, "What could it matter now?" is one the reader answers as the story unfolds. An epilogue echoes this memorial. All these elements serve to unify Sokoloff's first novel.

Another prologue that works effectively introduces *A Woman's Place*, the fourth Catherine Sayler mystery by Linda Grant. It's a brief looking-back summary, with an important difference: specific images replace generalizations.

> The hardest part of revising, author Raymond Obstfeld observes, is not the cutting of bad stuff, but the cutting of "good stuff that . . . diminishes the story as a whole."
>
> *Fiction First Aid*, p. 154

Grant uses only fifty-one words to evoke a mood, arouse our curiosity, and express the protagonist's fears—without giving away their source:

I don't dwell on the past. No point in that.

But I still can't stay in the same room with a man wearing

Paco cologne. And there are times when a ringing phone makes my heart race. I read the newspapers, but I skip certain stories. The nightmares come less often.

This is the entire prologue. I like to think that the line about not dwelling on the past is a playful slap at novels overloaded with backstory. That's the next CLUE.

FIND & FIX CLUE #2: PERILOUS PROLOGUE

- If you use a prologue, be sure it serves a useful, well-integrated purpose essential to the story.
- Double-check that any prologue:
  - does not inhibit bonding with the protagonist;
  - does tie into the main story right away;
  - exists for a reason other than a cheap thrill;
  - avoids giving away important developments from the middle of the book;
  - is not a disguise for a first chapter that sags with backstory and description.
- See if your prologue could more properly become Scene 1 of Chapter 1.
- Confirm that the character directly affected by your opening situation is someone readers will care about. Don't answer until you work through the issues raised in CLUES #1 and #3.

D.O.A.

CLUE #3: BLOODY BACKSTORY

When you meet a stranger at a party, do you want to stand there while your host launches into a lengthy introduction about the stranger's past, keeping you from discovering whether that individual interests you in the present? Yet writers often dump a large amount of information about the past that gets in the way of the character's making his or her own first impression on the reader. The past is history. In fiction it's called backstory. It's a technique. Unless you are writing memoir, the technique of backstory is a means to an end, not an end in itself.

Readers do need to know something about the events that affect the current story and its characters. But techniques are available for revealing the past more effectively than by playing the intrusive host—such as dramatizing one event that would make us care about the protagonist *now.*

Writers who tell of the past usually tell too much of it too soon. This is the wretched technique that makes backstory so maligned, so bloody unpopular.

One thriller I edited bumped off five victims, and chilled any thrill by stopping after each killing to tell about the victim from childhood to adulthood. Five victims, four pages of backstory apiece: twenty tiresome pages.

SATISFYING CURIOSITY

A novel is in trouble if what already happened gets more attention than what's currently happening. Backstory may advance our store of data, but data does not necessarily advance a story or build a desire to learn more. Much of what I see in manuscripts is not essential or even relevant. Rarely is it needed soon after a scene opens or a character appears.

If events from the past are important to your plot, remember that long before plot reveals enough of itself to be appreciated, the busy screener finds other reasons to stop reading. Too much backstory too soon is a great reason. Before you risk killing a screener's interest in your story, do this:

- ➡ Edit your first two chapters to sustain the tensile quality of your hook.
- ➡ Force yourself to stop telling what has already happened and show what is happening in present story time.

Once readers are hooked by a character's immediate problem, insinuate one or two *sentences* of backstory. Don't try to satisfy reader curiosity; you want to increase it. By Chapter 3, after readers care about what's happening to the protagonist *now,* they are more accepting of a few paragraphs of what happened *then.* Be selective. Free yourself from explaining your characters and concentrate on the real work of character portrayal.

WHERE TO BEGIN

Begin too early and you bury your story in history. Begin too late and you have all that backstory on your hands. Where *is* the beginning, anyway? It's where the first sign of trouble appears for the protagonist, the pivotal moment of change when someone's actions upset the status quo.

Author and literary agent Jack Bickham says, "Nothing is more threatening than change. . . . Identify the moment of change, and you know when your story must open."[24]

Memory Can Be Murder, the third Peaches Dann mystery by Elizabeth Daniels Squire, opens with these three sentences:

> "I'm scared." The voice on the telephone wavered. "Maybe I'm losing my mind."

The story does not open with the telephone ringing and the too-conventional "Hello, who is this?" Neither does the action stop to unload explanation. Readers learn what led up to the caller's situation in the same way Peaches does: from the action and dialogue that occur when she goes to meet the woman who phoned. The narrative moves forward, not backward.

This forward movement is known as *progression.* In popular fiction, whether character driven or plot driven, progression builds a sense of inevitability—the conviction that once events are set in motion, all that follows moves toward resolution. The

"Only that part of *then* that is important to, that has a bearing on, *now* is worth being told."

Robie Macauley and
George Lanning,
Technique in Fiction[25]

behavior of characters affects the plot's *direction* as it moves forward, but trips into the past stop the action, reverse direction, and kill momentum.

To analyze the backstory in your first three chapters, use a highlighter to identify all references to past events. Chances are you'll come across statements of background as well as backstory. Whereas backstory tells what took place before a story opens, background supplies information that was or still is true, such as references to a character's occupation, age, status. Highlight background too, but in a different color.

Next, examine the evidence to see where and how your backstory occurs. Do you work the past into the present with dialogue and action? Or do you unload it in a *backstory dump*—a paragraph of exposition occurring shortly after each new character appears?

If you're a dumper, clean up the wreckage with some clever slicing, dicing, and splicing:

1. Evaluate how much of your (highlighted) backstory is not vital to the story or to the reader's understanding of the scene where it now appears. Cut or *slice it* and put it in a new file for possible later use.

2. Take the backstory that *is* essential and *dice it*—chop it into separate bits and pieces.

3. Determine where in the story readers need which bits of essential information to understand what's happening *at that time.* Find the latest relevant location in your plot where each essential bit can be placed, and *splice it*—integrate it into the action and dialogue.

Adopt a less-and-later approach. Unless you are disguising a fact by slipping it in where you hope readers will overlook it, give them only what they need to know when they need to know it.

HANDLING BACKGROUND

Evaluate the background you highlighted and splice bits of it into your text, too. Be sure that background doesn't dominate the foreground. Subordinate the bits to whatever action, dialogue, or description is taking place.

Sara Hoskinson Frommer does this in *The Vanishing Violinist,* fourth in the Joan Spencer mystery series. The story opens with the man on Joan's sofa nibbling her ear and showing impatience over a delay in their wedding date.

"Only don't rush me, Fred," she said.

"Rush you!" Detective Lieutenant Fred Lundquist pulled away and patted her hand the way she occasionally patted the hands of the old ladies at the Oliver Senior Citizens' Center she directed. "I wouldn't dream of it. Now that you mention it, we'd probably better wait a few more years. You'll need grandchildren first, to throw rose petals."

"You!" She punched him lightly on the shoulder. At the moment, she was feeling anything but grandmotherly.   [p. 7]

Frommer slips in the fact that Joan directs the senior center by subordinating it to the more visual, character-revealing action of Fred's hand-patting. She does not use a technique common among average writers:

"As you know, Fred, I'm the director of. . . ."

Dialogue that informs characters of what they already know is *phony dialogue,* a corny device invented by the unimaginative for the convenience of the desperate. Frommer does not state background directly, either:

Joan Spencer directed the Oliver Senior Citizens' Center.

A line as brief as this would not seriously impede the flow of the scene, but as a direct statement of fact it's flat. It simply lies there, like road kill.

Instead, Frommer reduces Joan's job to a comparison: *the way she occasionally patted the hands . . . at the Center she directed.* This roundabout method subordinates background to dramatization. It puts us front and center to witness Joan's feelings and her interactions with Fred.

By minimizing background, Frommer makes her opening more multifaceted than it first appears. The scene has *density.* Do your scenes?

BACKGROUND EXPLANATION

If your story opens at the perfect moment, can it go back to fill in the blanks? You do have to show what shaped the antagonist's psyche, no?

No. That's the short answer. The long answer agrees that all characters have a past and their life experiences form an integral part of who they are. You have to know all of it. But readers don't. Although events occurring before the story opens may cause the problems that affect your characters *now,* readers can often get the picture from a single sentence, like this one:

"The neighbor told me of hearing the old man beating on the kid almost every night."

A brief reference like this is sufficient to account for the way this kid turned out, with no need for his life's story. Be sure to dramatize his grown-up actions in story time so readers can observe his current behavior—good and bad—and interpret it for themselves.

Another technique that's more effective than a backstory dump is to have a character drop hints about himself, never quite telling all until later.

Sometimes I receive an e-mail that says, in effect, "I took out as much backstory as I could, like you said to, but I had to keep a lot of it because if I cut any more, I'd have no story."

This is true, unfortunately, because some writers start their novels with the unexamined assumption that backstory *is* the story. If you believe a considerable amount of information from the past must be included in your story, take a hard look at what you want to be writing. Maybe your story is history, biography, or memoir, not genre fiction. Are you sure you are working in the right genre?

> Phyllis Taylor Pianka advises starting with the protagonist actively confronting the story's issue, then filtering in background through dialogue. Getting to know and care about the main character is accomplished in part "by seeing how she reacts to the problem with which she must come to terms."
>
> *How to Write Romances*, p. 86

Long ago, when I first got hooked on books, long passages of explanatory background were common. Today's aspiring writers need to meet today's market expectations.

The character profiles or bios you create are for your own guidance. Not every fact and personality trait in a profile can or should show up in your manuscript, any more than every job you've ever held should show up on your résumé.

BE SELECTIVE

The most important skill for any writer, I'm convinced, is the ability to *select*. The best time for a vigorous application of this skill is during self-editing. The key to being selective is the delete key. Use it to make your writing not merely shorter but *sharper.*

Begin your revision process by presuming that all backstory is unnecessary. Not all of it is, of course, but if you're not used to making major cuts in your own writing, this presumption makes the process easier.

The genre known as YA—young adult—offers many examples of clean, uncluttered writing. Observe these opening lines from *Mrdr Mystri* by Teresa Fannin. Tommie is eighth-grader Thomasa, a detective-in-training.

> The sirens stopped, finally. The halogen headlights and the bouncing flashlights converged on Temels' backyard, and a black body bag was placed on the snow beside the playhouse. There was the glimpse of a leg or maybe it was an arm. Then it was gone.
>
> "Don't move." Mom appeared briefly on the lowest limb of the pine tree.
>
> "Mom!" Tommie looked up. "They've found a body next door. A real live dead body."
>
> "I said, don't move. I'm coming down."

What's Mom doing in a tree? Gosh, no backstory! A few lines later we learn that Tommie was hoping Mom would fly around the pine trees:

> Unfortunately, Mom didn't fly but she could jump, she could jump really, really high.

Still no backstory! But we're hooked by our curiosity. Not until the end of the seventh paragraph does Fannin give us the first bit of backstory:

> Even before last Thursday's accident Mom was fast. But since she was doused with those strange chemicals in that freak accident on the Pike, well, since then. . . .

Notice the lack of elaboration, the scarce details. Notice how those details are doled out a little at a time. The technique teases our desire to learn more and increases our questions, all the while keeping us interested in the unfolding of a unique story with action in the present. Less is more.

MULTIPLE PURPOSES

The writer who develops a series knows that some readers forget background from earlier titles, some read out of sequence, and some read only one book in a series. Each has to stand alone as well as preserve continuity from one to the next. How much background should repeat in a series? As little as possible, preferably not until the story has hooked the reader.

Refer to an occurrence from the past as it affects the current story, but minimize flat statements of fact. If the protagonist solves crimes, briefly reestablish his or her credentials. Show relationships through action and dialogue, and avoid the phoniness of informing readers of information by having your characters tell each other what they already know.

In *Snipe Hunt* by Sarah Shaber, the second title in her Professor Simon Shaw mystery series, Simon's background is relevant to the story. It is revealed by Simon's friend, Morgan, to the owners of a general store where the friends are vacationing.

In an interesting twist, Simon is present while his reputation is being aired. One of the shopkeepers asks:

> ". . . Aren't you the history professor who figured out who killed that woman in Raleigh? The one that disappeared so many years ago?"
>
> Damn, Simon thought.
>
> "Yeah, that's him," Morgan said. "You probably saw the big article the *News and Observer* did. They called him a 'forensic historian.' A couple of national papers picked the story up off the wires and ran it, too."
>
> "It was a slow news day," Simon said.
>
> Morgan selected a twelve-pack of Miller draft and a jumbo bag of potato chips and took them to the cash register, chuckling.
>
> "Next thing you know, *Newsweek*'s got a whole page on him and *People* wanted to do a profile—"
>
> "That's enough," Simon said. He handed Morgan the Coke and a box of Goody's headache powders. "If you're going to embarrass me, you can pay."   [pp. 21–22]

This dialogue does more than "out" Simon's credentials; it works his background into a scene that establishes how and when the mom-and-pop shopkeepers learn that the visitor to their town is a forensic historian. It dramatizes the relationship between the two friends, whose give and take of protest and persistence adds a wry humor and lighthearted conflict to what might otherwise seem too mundane to dramatize: a trip to the store for a headache remedy.

Shaber keeps the history brief and the facts few. Her focus stays on the interactions among her characters while she slips in just enough background to establish Simon's credentials. That, in turn, leads a family to later request his help in an investigation—and the plot takes off.

This scene is deceptively simple, but it works overtime to function on multiple levels. That's density.

FIND & FIX CLUE #3: BLOODY BACKSTORY

- Determine the moment of change and begin your story there.
- Approach self-editing with the presumption that backstory is unnecessary.
- Highlight all passages of backstory and background in your first three chapters; then be selective and slice what's non-essential.
- Dice what's left into small, manageable bits.
- Splice those bits in with the dialogue, action, exposition, and description only where needed for readers to understand what is happening at the time.
- See if background can serve more than one purpose.
- Replace the too-much-too-soon approach with a less-and-later restraint.
- Break the habit of inserting a background dump immediately after each new character is introduced.
- Identify phony dialogue using your word processor to search your manuscript for the words "As you know" and "Remember."
- Verify that your story keeps moving forward with the least amount of stopping, side-stepping, or reversing.

PART IV: KILLING TIME

"The number of authors who are irritated by copy editors, brush off their queries, and can't be bothered to work with them only demonstrates to publishers that many authors are in fact amateurs. [The editor's] only aim is to make the writer look as good as possible."

Clarkson Potter, *Who Does What and Why in Publishing*

CLUE #4: FATAL FLASHBACKS

A flashback is backstory dramatized. The power of this technique is tempting to harness, but publishing professionals strongly recommend that new writers not try to mount this particular charger. Even experienced writers have problems with it. Here's why:

1. Shifts in time challenge every writer; they're an invitation to crazy time.
2. Flashbacks don't merely apply the brakes to a story's forward drive, as backstory does; they shift it into reverse. When the gears don't mesh, the collision can be fatal.
3. Information is too often included that adds no value to the story.
4. Readers need less history than some writers believe. That small amount can almost always be presented less intrusively.
5. The longer the flashback, the greater the risk of destroying the story's momentum.
6. Any scene that occurs within another scene is difficult to get into and out of gracefully.

7. The hint that a flashback is beginning can prompt readers to skip ahead.

8. The device is often an indulgence used for the writer's convenience, not for its primary purpose—which, as editor and author Sol Stein says, is to *illuminate the present story in a significant way.*[26]

SMOOTH SEGUE

An excellent example of significant illumination is found in *Delayed Diagnosis* by Gwen Hunter, first in her series of medical thrillers featuring Rhea Lynch, M.D.

The scene is a hospital emergency room. Rhea silences a drunken bully and misogynist so she can tend to the injuries of the son he obviously abused. Action changes to thought as she realizes she'd rather be looking into the medical records of her lifelong friend, Marisa, who lies badly beaten and comatose in another part of the hospital. But:

> Instead of paperwork, I pulled together layers of muscle
> and flesh and stitched up the laceration. And thought about the
> moaning child under my hands. He was so innocent and so at
> risk of being warped. Just as I had been at one time.   [p. 81]

Parallels between the little boy of the present and Rhea as a little girl in the past establish a theme of vulnerability. Hunter uses a single paragraph to start a gradual process of moving us from the present into Rhea's past and to the day her friendship with Marisa began:

> Risa and I were seven the year we met, and to this day it was
> the best year of my life. Better even than my senior year of med
> school, when John noticed me for the first time and began
> pursuing me as if I fit into his parents' upper-class lifestyle.
> Better even than the year I graduated medical school and was
> accepted into my first choice of residency programs. Better even
> than that perfect summer when John and I became engaged.
> Better because there were no butterflies, no uncertainties, no
> hormonal confusion, no stress, no self-doubt. No grown-up
> angst. Just childhood perfection.
> We had met. . . .   [pp. 81–82]

Before we enter the flashback itself, I want to point out the richness of Hunter's technique. The repetition of "Better even than" creates a framework for backstory. With each major event in Rhea's life reduced to a small, specific chunk of background, the passage becomes a model of compression. The compare-contrast structure further increases its density.

The next line sets the scene for that long-ago time and place in which "We had met . . . where Mama had rented a house":

> Though fairly stable at the time of the move, Mama had been drunk since, and the groceries had run out. Her next trust-fund check wasn't due to arrive for a week. And it wasn't as though I could ask my daddy for money, as he had died before I was born. Even when Mama was sober, I was alone. . . .   [p. 82]

An alcoholic parent creates yet another parallel between the physically hurt little boy of the present and the emotionally hurt little girl of the past.

> Hungry, angry at the world, I had carried every rock, branch and construction remnant I could find to the creek and hurled them in. I had built a fine dam. Water had begun to swell and rise over the low banks, flooding the low-lying empty lot near the rental house where Mama snored in a pool of vomit on the bathroom floor. . . .
>
> And so I built a really fine dam with junk and angry frustration. Just as I dumped in an armful of wallboard scraps, I heard a voice.   [pp. 82–83]

Notice the switch from the past perfect tense (*"had built"* and water *"had begun* to swell") to the simple past tense ("Mama *snored,"* "I *dumped,"* and "I *heard* a voice"). Backstory glides effortlessly into flashback, and we find ourselves in the past, seeing the world through seven-year-old eyes and experiencing the powerful emotions of a neglected child. We glimpse a personality taking shape in Rhea's proactive response to frustration and unmet expectation—ideal characteristics for a main character who won't take "no" for an answer from anyone.

Hunter's flashback portrays the start of a lifelong friendship between Rhea and Marisa, and for the next two pages we see how unlike they are in upbringing and lifestyle, yet how alike in their defiance of authority.

Because Marisa, the adult, lies in a coma, we cannot observe the interaction between these friends in current story time. The only way to experience the strength of their relationship is through the device of a flashback.

By dramatizing this friendship and showing how important it is to Rhea —not telling about it—Hunter establishes the necessary motivation that drives the doctor to disobey orders from Marisa's husband and investigate her friend's mysterious injuries.

RETURN TO PRESENT

The first three words of the author's next paragraph, "To this day," prepare us for the return to current story time. The actual return occurs four sentences later, effective in its swiftness:

> . . . To this day I can remember the crunch of that apple and the taste of the peanut butter and jelly. It was peach jam. I had never eaten peach jam, and it was wonderful.
>
> After lunch, Risa took off her sandals and waded in with me. Together we tore down my dam. I never built another.
>
> Carefully, I tied off the last stitch.   [p. 84]

In one smooth motion Hunter brings us back to the emergency room, where the doctor is continuing the same action as before the flashback.

Let's summarize a few of the author's techniques:

- Thematically, images of the boy's physical injuries parallel Rhea's psychic injuries.

- Structurally, the departure in time fuses with the main story, engaging our interest before we realize that a flashback is upon us.

- Transitions are seamless; the same action at the point of departure —stitching a wound—picks up at the return to present story time.

- There's no overt setup for the shift in time, no clichéd "It stirred a memory of" or "My mind went back to that special day when. . . ."

- The flashback is all characterization, presented mostly through dialogue and action with a minimum of description.

- Most importantly, it serves the function widely recognized as the only justification for a flashback: to illuminate the main story in a significant way.

Flashbacks work as effectively in third-person narration as in first-person, except where writers make wordy, awkward shifts in time, such as "his memory took him" or "her mind floated back." Often, a subtle change in tense is all that's needed to complete the transition.

ALTERNATING WITH PRESENT

The Dark Side of Heaven by Tamar Myers dramatizes the banishment of a young Amish woman for refusing to submit to her community's expectations and renounce her talent for painting pictures. Her bishop says:

> "But you compare yourself to God—"
> I look at the Bishop. "I did *not* compare myself to God." Even a year ago, I would not have dared to interrupt the bishop. "What I meant to say, Bishop, is that by using my talent for painting, I am honoring God."
> "Yah, a good quilt—"
> "My talent is not for quilting. It is for painting!"
> "Then paint barns, Anna Hostetler."   [p. 5]

The novel follows Anna's adventures chronologically, using present tense to show her efforts to adjust to living on her own in Pittsburgh among "the English," as the Amish refer to outsiders. Anna makes friends with unusual characters, whose words and behaviors she comically misinterprets in her naïveté.

At the end of Chapter 8 her new gay friend tells her, "Watch your back." The next line opens Chapter 9 and takes us into the past with the words:

> I watched Mamm's back in the garden . . . .   [p. 75]

We are now in Anna's childhood, and for the first time the verbs change from present tense to past. Later scenes move randomly back and forth in time, clued subtly by verb tense, more overtly by the names of the characters associated with each of the two periods of time in Anna's life. Each flashback immerses us in one of the two worlds that shape her character, and that only her unique perspective can do justice to.

> "Anyone who is satisfied with first-draft writing is either extraordinarily talented or has low standards."
>
> Arnold Melnick, D. O.[27]

If you are using one or more flashbacks in your work-in-progress, let their story value be equal in significance to the portrayal by Tamar Myers of two different worlds as seen through the eyes of an innocent—or to the dramatization by Gwen Hunter of Dr. Rhea's interaction with her childhood friend, whose coma prevents showing via any other technique.

That is, be certain the event is essential to the story and cannot be imparted except by dramatizing it. When in doubt about using a flashback, treat its content like any backstory, by slicing, dicing, and splicing its essentials into the main action (described in CLUE #3).

This method maintains your story's all-important forward momentum.

MINI-FLASH

Here's an effective alternative to the flashback. It's the *recollection* or *flash memory,* a mini-flashback that evokes the feeling of a blast from the past without your having to construct a fully realized scene.

Mini-flashes are introduced at those moments when an incident in current story time would naturally trigger the character's recall of a past event.

Alice Orr, in *No More Rejections* [p. 102], emphasizes the need for a positive attitude toward revision. She writes that revision is where "the richness of a story comes to life." It's where authors can take the time to discover previously unrevealed story layers and elements.

The device may offer readers new information or repeat old information in a new context—either of which creates new meaning.

A memory flash needs no transition or fanfare, no *he thought* or *she remembered.* Because each recollection is brief, it may be set off by italics to distinguish it from what's taking place in current story time.

Observe how this technique is used in *The Alibi* by Sandra Brown, author of more than sixty romance and suspense novels. Later circumstances cause Hammond Cross to mentally replay lines of dialogue spoken earlier. Because we saw those early scenes dramatized, we believed we knew all we needed to of those events. We were wrong. Hammond's mini-flashes of words we were not privy to makes him (and us) realize his initial encounter with an attractive woman was not what he thought it was at the time. See how Brown integrates Hammond's flashes of recall into the later scene:

. . . They had been together at the fair for at least an hour before he even thought to ask her name. They'd laughed because it had taken them that long to get around to what was usually the first order of business when two people meet and must make their own introductions.

"Names aren't really that important, are they? Not when the meeting is this amiable."

He agreed. "Yeah, what's in a name?" He proceeded to quote what he could remember of the passage from Romeo and Juliet.

"That's good! Have you ever thought of writing it down?"

"In fact I have, but it would never sell."

From there it had become a running joke—his asking her name, her declining to tell him.   [pp. 166–67]

Had these lines of dialogue, recalled later, been included in the original dramatization, our suspicions would have run ahead of Hammond's. That would put readers in a superior position to the protagonist.

Instead, Sandra Brown's use of the mini-flash dupes both the reader and the protagonist, who—unlike the reader—possesses knowledge that he *failed to recognize the significance of at the time.*

By integrating the flashed memory seamlessly into current action, Brown raises our awareness simultaneously with Hammond's, which adds to our surprise.

If mini-flashes work for your story, you may find the technique easier to carry out than a fully developed flashback. Used effectively, the technique avoids the time warp that sabotages the momentum of many novels.

Bob Mayer tells of writers getting upset when told that a technique they're using, after seeing it used by another writer, doesn't work. They don't realize that the technique may be part of the overall structure of the other author's novel. "You can't take the type of beginning of one bestseller, tie it in with the flashback style from another, and have a similar flashy ending as another and expect [your] novel to automatically work."

The Fiction Writer's Toolkit,
2001 edition, p. 48

PAST RELATIONSHIPS

In a romance, a scene is worthy of a flashback if it features the hero or the heroine in a remembered scene that's important to the plot, or both major characters if they shared an earlier romantic relationship. Romance editor Leslie J. Wainger explains that because the past relationship colors everything that happens between the hero and heroine in the present—which is the substance of the story—telling us they used to be involved doesn't carry the emotional impact that showing a flashback does.

Whether it works is all in the execution.

> It's not what you do, it's how you do it that counts. Even though a flashback might be brief, it won't work for Leslie Wainger if "the scene itself is unnecessary or the placement is jarring."
>
> *Writing a Romance Novel for Dummies*, p. 202

FIND & FIX CLUE #4: FATAL FLASHBACKS

- If you must use a flashback, determine how *little* of the material is essential, not how *much* can be stretched to fill a scene.
- Confirm that your flashback illuminates the main story in a significant way and stirs emotions that could not be evoked through other, less time-stopping techniques.
- Verify that the scene you are choosing to show as a flashback represents a time of high drama.
- Keep the same action going before and after any flashback that you place in the middle of a scene, and edit the transitions so they are clear, seamless, unobtrusive—not clichéd.
- Instead of writing a flashback scene for your protagonist, experiment with quick flashes of memory—provided each flash is meaningful and relevant.
- Avoid transporting readers into the past if you're able to incorporate brief, selected highlights from the past into current action.

CLUE #5: TOXIC TRANSCRIPT

Y ou are sitting in a comfortable chair reading of a jealous woman who attends a party at her rival's home and sneaks upstairs to look for evidence of her boyfriend's infidelity. She approaches a roll-top desk in the study and quietly raises the top. The old wood creaks and she freezes. So do you. When her nerves calm down she resumes her snooping and discovers a small diary tucked into a cubbyhole. She opens it, sits in the desk chair, and begins reading. And reading. And so do you.

You keep reading the diary along with the character because its text is reproduced verbatim within the pages of the novel resting in your own lap.

Maybe the author is intentionally slowing the pace to set up a surprise, such as the rival's walking in on the snoop. But that doesn't happen. Nor does the pace merely slow—it stops, and it remains stopped until the author resumes some action in current story time.

No plot development can justify bringing a scene to a standstill while a character sits and reads. If a diary is so compelling, show the character's reaction to it. Interrupt occasionally for her to listen for a sound or wonder what time it is. Maybe she could scratch an itch. Stifle a sneeze. *Anything?*

Regrettably, this author is guilty of a backstory dump in the form of that clumsy device, the story-within-a-story. The busy screener is quickly bored, pages ahead to see where the narrative method changes, then realizes the passage is suspiciously like . . . ho-hum, the toxic transcript rides again.

SUSPENSION OF TIME

I'm not railing against a few lines of a letter interwoven with a story's action or dialogue. I *am* sounding the alarm for those multi-page transcripts dropped whole into a scene, from a series of letters found in a hope chest to typed pages retrieved from a wastebasket; from a collection of old newspaper clippings that fall out of a book to days of email downloaded from a computer. Sometimes the quoted material is presented as a written report, a lecture the protagonist listens to on tape, a speech she sits through, or a folk legend told around a campfire. Lengthy. Uninterrupted.

At best, a story-within-a-story creates an effect similar to that of a flash-back—but offers less to visualize. At worst, the effect is unrealistic, especially when the letter or journal starts sounding as if P. D. James wrote it, fully dramatized with characters, action, setting, and dialogue.

No matter how lively or intriguing the content of these stories-within-a-story, the form of delivery strains our credulity and our ability as readers to maintain the illusion of a sedentary figure as the transmitter of all this second-hand action.

Whereas a verbatim transcript might describe a conflict, the character's reading about it does not engage her *in* conflict.

If you wish to insert a transcript, break it up. Periodically interrupt it to show the character's reactions to its content and to her surroundings, especially if she's skulking. Occasionally re-anchor her in the scene to keep our imaginations skulking in her shadow. If she's oblivious to the possibility of being discovered where she doesn't belong, she comes across as stupid—not a desirable trait for a main character.

TIME AND SPACE

Don't lose sight of the character's presence in her own time and space, lest we, as readers of both the story and the story-within-a-story, become aware of our own time and space. Give us something to visualize other than a figure sitting and reading—which is what *we* are doing. Being reminded of what we are doing in real time takes us out of the story.

That's jarring, like catching your reflection in a trio of mirrors and having that glimpse of infinity pull you away from where you'd been heading.

Not to get too existential about it, this dual awareness reminds us that we exist in real time and space, separate from the fictional characters whose hold on our imaginations is so tenuous. Any time the momentum of a story stops and lets our attention falter, the characters we identify with cease to exist. They fade into the illusions they are, flimsier than the printed page.

FUNCTION DETERMINES FORM

Recall Scheherazade and *A Thousand and One Nights,* or Chaucer's *The Canterbury Tales.* In the days before Gutenberg and Oprah, when villagers sat at the feet of oral storytellers, the literary form later known as the frame story kept audiences entertained day after day. The frame offered a structure (or an excuse) for stringing together many unrelated tales, as if the storyteller was on a pilgrimage, or forestalling punishment.

The modern novel is the structural antithesis of the frame story. Today's publishers want stories that feature one central character and one central plot, with every minor character and every thread of subplot an indispensable part of the total fabric. Cut into that fabric and the illusion unravels.

Does this mean you can never include other material? No, not if the material is relevant, entertaining, and blended smoothly with the larger action. It does mean knowing how to make the technique work *for* your story, not against it.

CONTROLLING TIME

As you analyze the next few examples, bear in mind that I am not recommending the story-within-a-story device. My purpose here is to show how one author makes the transition to a transcript and manages a challenge that all writers of fiction grapple with in one way or another: the need to control time and space, and direct the reader's perception of it.

George Orwell manipulates our sense of time and space in the novel *Nineteen Eighty-four.* Published in 1949, this prescient work is a suspenseful political satire about a totalitarian society. In this grim future, Big Brother watches everyone through a telescreen that cannot be turned off. No written history has survived to contradict the government's propaganda—except for one banned book, which an old bookseller makes available to Winston, the protagonist.

We're as curious as Winston is to learn how so many personal liberties could have been lost. But our interest in the *content* of this secret history book cannot compensate for a *form* of presentation that involves a lengthy verbatim transcript. This form requires us to sit and read about a character who—you guessed it—is sitting and reading.

Orwell manages the problem by artfully slowing the pace, and by setting and resetting the scene to keep it grounded. Here's how he initially establishes our image of Winston in time and space:

> With a sort of voluptuous creaking in his joints he climbed
> the stair above Mr. Charrington's shop. He was tired, but not
> sleepy any longer. He opened the window, lit the dirty little

> oilstove, and put on a pan of water for coffee. Julia would arrive
> presently; meanwhile there was the book. He sat down in the
> sluttish armchair and undid the straps of the brief case.   [p. 151]

Orwell next shifts our attention from Winston to the book and to its
worn pages and amateurish printing and binding, which:

> . . . fell apart easily, as though the book had passed through many
> hands. The inscription on the title page ran:
>
>
>
> THE THEORY AND PRACTICE OF
> OLIGARCHICAL COLLECTIVISM
> by
> EMMANUAL GOLDSTEIN
>
>
>
> *[Winston began reading.]*

The bracketed, italicized phrase "Winston began reading" is not my
comment but the author's. It serves as a form of stage direction to keep the
reading of the transcript grounded in story time. An overt stage direction is
unlikely to appear in novels today, but some form of re-anchoring or grounding is appropriate, especially early in the reading of any transcript. It functions like a *he said / she said* tag inserted in a line of dialogue at the first
take-a-breath location.

Orwell's bracketed anchor seems to ask readers, "Are you with me?" It
recognizes that we still have one foot in current story time and need a little
easing into the longer transcript before we can jump into it with both feet.

After this stage direction, Orwell quotes no more than one paragraph
from the forbidden history before breaking away, mid-sentence, to drop
anchor once again. Notice the concrete details that follow, which reinforce
the scene's third grounding:

> Winston stopped reading, chiefly in order to appreciate the
> fact that he *was* reading, in comfort and safety. He was alone:
> no telescreen, no ear at the keyhole, no nervous impulse to
> glance over his shoulder or cover the page with his hand. The
> sweet summer air played against his cheek. From somewhere
> far away there floated the faint shouts of children; in the room
> itself there was no sound except the insect voice of the clock.

He settled deeper into the armchair and put his feet up on the fender. It was bliss, it was eternity. [p. 152]

With time and place under control, Orwell continues the transcript, letting it run for twelve pages before setting time and place once more. The transcript begins again but later than where it left off. No point in suffocating readers with so much exposition. Instead, Winston, knowing he "will ultimately read and reread every word" of the book, "opened it at a different place and found himself at the third chapter." Clever, yes?

By making Winston a page-turner, Orwell moves directly to the history book's secret truth: that ongoing wars and a climate of fear created the emotional basis that allowed the government to usurp its citizens' privacy.

GROUNDING IN TIME

Please remember that I'm not in favor of any transcript in fiction if it breaks the flow of the story, which is true in *Nineteen Eighty-four.* Yet Orwell's technique of grounding is worth examining because his setting and resetting of the scene does prepare us for the longer transcript to come.

To review, the initial scene-setting is followed only by the title and author of the forbidden book before Orwell reestablishes that "Winston began reading." Next, only one full paragraph is quoted from the history before the author once again grounds Winston in the scene.

This start-and-stop pattern is similar to the reinforcement used in progressive relaxation or self-hypnosis, in which the subject is deliberately brought out of an early, light trance for the purpose of being sent into a longer, deeper trance. Orwell's twice calling attention to the fact that the protagonist is reading gets us ready for what lies ahead. He does not submerge us in a full-length transcript all at once.

Next, let's examine how Orwell sets the scene for his story-within-a-story. He increases the distance between the room at the top of the stairs and the world outside by going beyond the visual, capturing the feel of the summer air and the sounds of distance: the shouts of children far away and faint; the clock with its insect voice.

Time may continue to pass in the outside world, but inside the room, everything is slowing down. These techniques give our inner clocks permission to wind down. Winston's settling deeper into his armchair helps us settle in and be read to.

PARAPHRASING TRANSCRIPTS

Be selective: quote only a few lines of a transcript at a time, not whole passages. Paraphrase some of it, and splice that paraphrase in with the character's actions to keep the scene grounded.

Nancy Pickard paraphrases all of a lengthy newspaper article in the third mystery of her Jenny Cain series, *No Body.* Jenny has asked a reporter, Lew Riss, to retrieve a story from the paper's archives about funeral scams, which she's investigating.

> When he returned, he held up the front page for me to see. "Which story?"
>
> I scanned it, looking for news about the funeral industry.
>
> "This one," I said, and handed it back to him. "Here. Why don't you read it aloud, so we'll both know?"
>
> "Sure." He folded the paper back. "And after that, boys and girls, Uncle Lewis will read to you all about Brer Rabbit and the Three Blind Mice, since Uncle Lewis doesn't have anything better to do on a Sunday afternoon, right? Draw up a rug, kiddies, here goes. . . ." [pp. 216–17]

This trailing off is the author's. Without interruption, Pickard switches from dialogue to paraphrase, *not* to a verbatim transcript:

> He read to me the *Journal*'s report that prearrangement salespeople in Texas had been caught skimming off their client's contracts. When customers paid in cash, the salesperson simply falsified the contract and pocketed a little money off the top. . . .

I'm stopping here to call your attention to three references in the paragraph coming up: the *Journal,* the paper, and the story. Each reminds us that we are hearing a paraphrase of a newspaper article:

> They were easy scams, the *Journal* pointed out, and possible not just in the funeral industry, but in any business that depends to a great extent on the inherent honesty of its salespeople. The paper went to some pains to point out that the "vast majority" of prearrangement companies dealt honestly with their customers. But if the story had an editorial slant, it was "buyer beware." [p. 217]

If the article were read aloud verbatim, it would run considerably longer than this concise paraphrase. It would also pull us out of the scene and into that suspended twilight zone of a story-within-a-story. Instead, Pickard frames her paraphrase so that "Uncle" Lewis is pretending to read to a child. Humor lightens a grim topic and adds to Lew's characterization, getting additional mileage from the scene.

MORE OPTIONS

Maybe you don't want to use a paraphrase, thinking the shortened version might call too much attention to a clue that you'd prefer to keep buried among the larger number of words of the transcript. One technique for preventing this situation is to interweave pieces of the transcript in with other action. That breaks up the material and postpones our discovery of key parts of it. By building anticipation of what is yet to be revealed, writers can intensify suspense and keep attention focused on the story—not on the reality of our sitting and reading.

Postponing information is not the same as withholding it. If you play fair with your readers and plant clues throughout, however obscure, you withhold only the correct *interpretation* of that information.

During revision, see where you might:

1. let readers learn only partial information;
2. make them anticipate the rest of it; and
3. delay its fulfillment to increase dramatic tension.

These techniques are effective whether or not you use a transcript.

TANGIBLE SETTINGS

My final example prepares us to read a transcript, but we experience a boy's recollection instead. Judith Geary's well-researched historical novel, *Getorix: The Eagle and the Bull,* is set in Rome in 101 B.C.E. The Roman victory over the Celts has stripped Getorix, almost fifteen, of his honor and thrust him into the unfamiliar role of slave. Notice Geary's appeal to the senses in showing him with the book his owner's son gives him:

> Getorix's heart beat faster. He smelled the oiled leather of the case, the papyrus, the ink, the hands that had held the spindles.
> Silence settled in like a mist. . . . Reverently, as if it were a

living thing, he eased the roll from its leather case. It had been put away without being re-rolled. . . .

The book ended with Odysseus feasting with his son . . . and plotting his revenge. Getorix rolled the scroll carefully back to the beginning. There were sticky spots—honey, his nose and the tip of his tongue told him—usually on the pages where the people were eating. It seemed they ate a lot. He hadn't noticed that when he himself had enough.

Dogs barked in the street outside, but the house was silent. Everyone had gone to watch the parade to the Circus. . . .

Instead of having Getorix read the scroll through the device of a transcript, Geary brings us closer to his feelings through rich sensory details:

He drew the blanket around his shoulders even though the afternoon was warm enough, leaned against the rough stone wall and gave himself up to memory.   [pp. 143-45]

Instead of Homer, we read of the boy's images of his people's final battle—until the roar of the circus crowd reminds him to stop remembering before he begins to feel, once again, the disgrace of the Celts in defeat.

FIND & FIX CLUE #5: TOXIC TRANSCRIPT

- See that any transcript is kept as brief as possible.
- Break it up with paraphrase, action, description, setting, dialogue, or thought in story time (not in transcript time)—techniques to keep readers from losing touch with the character.
- Gradually slow the pace that leads into a transcript, or begin a new scene with the desired pace.
- Set and reset the scene to keep it grounded in story time and space.
- Consider revealing quoted lines from a transcript over several scenes, knowing that postponement builds suspense.

D.O.A.

CLUE #6: DECEPTIVE DREAM

A sinister figure steps from the shadows and begins to chase the main character. She tries to run but her legs turn to stone. She feels the presence getting closer. It's right behind her. Now it's reaching for her! She opens her mouth to cry out but there's no sound. Suddenly, she hears a terrifying scream. It's so loud it wakens her, and she realizes she's the one screaming.

Surprise! It's only a bad dream.

Fooled you, right? Not even a little? Good. You recognize the scenario—it's been done often enough to have become its own cliché. This is the deceptive dream, typically placed at the start of a chapter to make readers think the villain is about to inflict actual harm on the character we've come to care about. But today's sophisticated readers wake up to the illusion well before the character does.

A dream that arouses emotion for its own sake is a gimmick—which the busy screener recognizes. Gimmicks can turn an already challenging submission process into a nightmare.

KEEP IT BRIEF

If you intend to mislead, keep the dream brief. Readers who catch on by the second or third line quickly tire of the charade and want to move on to the real story. Screeners want to move on to the next manuscript.

Often, writers use dreams for the purpose of dumping backstory. You already know how backstory can stop a story cold. Many readers say they skip past dreams or skim them, just as they do with prologues, transcripts, and long italicized passages. In their experience, such devices get in the way of the story. In most cases they are right.

Dreams are also hard to present effectively. If you must use one or more, I suggest not dramatizing them. To reverse the show-don't-tell mantra, describing a dream is often more effective than dramatizing it.

To demonstrate this upended principle, here's a passage from Jan Burke's first mystery novel, *Goodnight, Irene,* an Agatha and an Anthony nominee. The dream scene takes place after the brutal murders of several people known to the series character, investigative reporter Irene Kelly. Irene's sleeping companion, as you might not guess from his name, is a cat.

> As I crawled into bed later that night, I thought about how I
> had made it through two days in a row in a fairly peaceful
> fashion. Cody jumped in with me and I snuggled close to him.
> I felt good all over. I don't know how I could go from feeling so
> good to the nightmare, but that night I dreamed that someone
> was trying to cut off my hands and feet.   [p. 287]

Dramatizing a dream lengthens it. Burke's paraphrase condenses it— even as it incorporates Irene's comments, which give the dream its power. Brevity adds its own power, too. The quick ending contrasts sharply with the relaxed pace and feel-good mood leading up to it. A violent image ends the chapter, an ideal place to shake readers awake so they cannot put the book down and nod off on dreams of their own.

HIDDEN EMOTIONS

When dramatized effectively, a dream becomes a vehicle for taking us places we could not otherwise go. If steered competently, that vehicle can:

- take the story to a deeper level by probing a situation or a character in ways that could not be achieved by other means;
- suggest parallels and symbolize relationships by juxtaposing two or more of the story's themes;
- reveal contradictions and bring out emotions that the character may be hiding from others or from himself; and
- expand characterization.

All four purposes are served by the dream scene in *Playing God,* the first police procedural in the second series by Kate Flora, an Edgar-nominated author. Sergeant Joe Burgess is investigating the murder of the doctor who misdiagnosed the cancer that led to his mother's death. Burgess is a conflicted man, unable to mourn, unable to put the preventable loss behind him after two years. He considers mourning as wallowing:

He hated wallowing. Self-pity was such a useless emotion.
[pp. 19-20]

When he is injured on the job, he views his pain as penance for having let himself be ambushed. Once the pain pills kick in, he sleeps and dreams:

He sat beside his mother, holding her swollen, unresponsive hand, watching the electronic read-outs of hope and hopelessness, as she failed in full-screen living color. Doing the death watch, there for her as she'd always been for him. His sisters came and cried and left and came to do it all again, making him the rock for everyone. He'd never cried.

In his dream, he cried with a dream's surrealism. Tears flowed in silver columns down his face, tracing silver stripes down his clothes, pooling at his feet like mercury. In the hospital he'd sat silent. In his dream, he spoke of those magical nights by the window when she taught him to see, of his anger toward his father, his sorrow that her life had given her so little of what she deserved. Said all the things she'd died without hearing.   [pp. 161-62]

The author's third-person point of view makes possible a literal description of the tormented man's memories, as well as a symbolic representation of his grief in tears that flow like a heavy, toxic mineral. His dream continues, juxtaposed with another event that similarly evokes a heavy burden of suppressed emotion:

The dream took him, floating like a man on a magic carpet, to the place he always went, awake or asleep. The darkest spot on his soul. He hovered there in the crystalline blue light of a morning just past dawn, looking down on the sprawled white body of little Kristin Marks. Thrown away on a landfill like an empty can, worn shoe, or yesterday's news.

Every cop had them, the cases that wouldn't let go. Kristin was his. . . .

He groped his way out of bed, staggered into the bathroom, and threw up. Kristin lived inside him like a chronic disease, occasionally flaring up. . . .   [pp. 162-63]

ADDING MEANING

Skillfully managed, dreams can add meaning to memories about the past and foreshadow the future. Note that I am not suggesting *foretelling* the future, except perhaps in some stories featuring the paranormal. *Foreshadowing* is about creating the mood in which later events occur. Dreams can reveal a character's fears or anxiety, conscious or not. A sequence of dreams can be used to build suspense and raise tension.

In deciding to use this device in your fiction—like the decision to use the device of a flashback, which a dream is, in many ways—consider whether it meets Sol Stein's criterion of illuminating the story in a significant way. Does your story benefit in ways that could not otherwise be achieved?

Grave Secrets, a romantic suspense by Dixie Land, tells the story of a woman who discovers, after the deaths of her adored parents, that she had been sold to them. What follows is the first nightmare in the novel's dream sequence:

> Susan Slade woke chilled, shaking and sobbing. It had happened again . . . that awful dream. It came frequently in her early childhood. Then for years it remained dormant, buried within her.
>
> In the month since her mother died, it had resurfaced. In it, she was bitterly cold . . . an ice child, enclosed in something dark, utterly alone, weeping mournfully. When she'd been a small child, her mother always heard her cries and hurried to her room. She slipped into bed next to Susan and held her until her tears subsided, until she felt warm and safe again.
>
> But Ella Slade was no longer there to comfort her.   [p. 1]

Susan's efforts to learn the truth are continually thwarted. Each time she feels she may be getting closer to her secret past, the dream recurs. Ultimately, it's part of her discovery of her scandalous lineage.

PURPOSEFUL DREAMING

Know what purpose you want a dream to serve. If its purpose is to foreshadow an upcoming event, be sure your protagonist has a reason to feel anxious, suspicious, or fearful before having the nightmare.

For the short story "The Dream Delicious," author Susan Malone begins with a dream that lets us know how much her protagonist has been dreading the next day's events:

> She dreamed that night of descending into a watery grave—literally—complete with rectangular gray headstone at the bottom of a rancid sea, hammerhead sharks nibbling on her lengths of blond curls before death took her into dark night. So when the alarm of Dylan's lamenting a hard rain raised her from the dead dream, she sighed with relief.
>
> Short lived, of course. She'd almost rather fend off the fishes than go to this audition.
>
> Okay, so the nocturnal vision wasn't in the least original, and Freud needn't be in the building to decipher it. Even Dr. Phil could've nailed that one.

Without trying to trick the reader, Malone acknowledges at the start that we're entering a dream. And before she shows us why the protagonist, an unemployed actress who needs the work, doesn't want to attend an audition, the author also acknowledges that this nocturnal vision is neither original nor difficult to interpret. By opening the short story as she does, Malone is able to place another dream at the end of the story—brief and "delicious"—and thereby achieve a purpose valued in all artistic endeavors: unity.

In examining your purpose for including a dream, distinguish foreshadowing (a legitimate literary device) from foretelling (legitimate in genres with a paranormal element). However, in traditional mystery or romantic suspense, avoid using a dream to reveal a missing piece of the puzzle that your main character does not already possess. Your protagonist should be smart, not psychic.

> Many people hear voices when no one is there. Some of them are called mad and are shut up in rooms where they stare at the walls all day. Others are called writers and they do pretty much the same thing.
>
> Anonymous

More effective, as well as less controversial, is the clue revealed in a dream about something the protagonist *already knows but doesn't know she knows*. If, for example, the trauma of witnessing a horrible event has blocked a character's conscious memory of someone's identity, let his face gradually become more distinct over the course of several dreams. Although this scenario has been done before, when carried out with thought and purpose it becomes fully synthesized with the plot, an organic element in the story.

Despite my cautions about dreams in fiction, in the right hands the device can be effective. After all, one of the most famous works of literature—a novel that writers themselves often cite as the most well-constructed precursor to the modern mystery—opens with the following line:

> Last night I dreamt I went to Manderley again.
>
> Daphne du Maurier, *Rebecca*

FIND & FIX CLUE #6: DECEPTIVE DREAM

- ➤ If your manuscript includes a dream scene, be sure the purpose it serves is worthwhile to the story.
- ➤ Determine whether that purpose could be achieved as effectively by paraphrasing the dream instead of dramatizing it.
- ➤ Establish a reason for the character's feeling the anxiety that leads to dreaming.
- ➤ Select details that add meaning and value to your story and to the character's thoughts and emotions.
- ➤ Keep a dramatized dream brief; briefer still if you are attempting to deceive.

D.O.A.

CLUE #7: TIME BOMB

The need to handle time effectively is not limited to dreams, transcripts, flashbacks, backstory, and prologues. It affects everything in a typical day in the life of the lead character. I've read mystery manuscripts packed with so much running around from one end of Chicago to the other, I thought the mayor had decreed the thirty-six-hour workday after I'd moved south.

Even Superhero cannot travel faster than a speeding bullet on the Eisenhower Expressway.

Writers occasionally get so caught up in the plotting of their stories that they lose track of time—story time, that is. (Losing track of mealtime and bedtime is nothing I'm qualified to discuss.) Their scenes open with profuse descriptions of the morning sky and the weather—but if the plot doesn't require a change in the weather, no further mention is made of the environment or of time's passage. The protagonist takes off and keeps going like the Energizer bunny on NoDoz (generic name: caffeine).

That's why readers get a jolt when Superhero, having driven across town to check out a suspect's reported hideout, conceals his approach by turning off his headlights a block away. Headlights? Nothing about the drive through the city even hinted at the sun's setting or the streetlights coming on. In fact, we realize that nowhere has the writer intimated what month or season it is, or prepared us for either an early or a late sunset.

This is crazy time. It sabotages the story like a time bomb.

Writers who disorient readers by suspending the lead character's clock quickly diminish the busy screener's willingness to suspend disbelief.

TRACKING TIME

As a writer, you control how time passes. That's the nice thing about fiction. Three hours in the life of your lead character might take only five minutes of real time to read, unlike literary fiction, in which five minutes in the life of the lead could take three hours to read. But that's another story.

When revising, review how you help readers account for the passage of time in the lives of your characters. One option is to state the day and precise hour as titles for your chapters. These examples are from Elizabeth Daniels Squire's first mystery, *Who Killed What's-Her-Name?*

> *Chap. 1:* Friday Morning, May 24
> *Chap. 2:* A Few Minutes Later
> *Chap. 3:* That Afternoon
> *Chap. 8:* Monday Afternoon, After the Funeral

Or you could state how much time remains until an anticipated threat is carried out—a tension-building countdown known in suspense fiction as a ticking time bomb.

Perhaps your story lends itself to a technique found in the mystery subgenre known as police procedural, in which the plot follows an investigation step by step, chronologically. Eleanor Taylor Bland, creator of the first black woman homicide detective, Marti MacAlister, keeps her readers oriented by suggesting—in the opening lines of each chapter—time of day, day of week, and location. In *Done Wrong,* for example:

> *Chap. 4:* It was after nine o'clock Thursday night when Marti parked at a beach in Evanston near the Northwestern University campus.
> *Chap. 5:* After court on Friday, Marti and Vik went to the Barrister, a pub not far from the precinct.
> *Chap. 6:* DaVon was whistling as he parked the van alongside a U-shaped apartment building Saturday morning.
> *Chap. 7:* On Saturday afternoon, Marti met. . . .
> *Chap. 33:* It was still dark when Diablo walked. . . .

The author's method is obvious here because I deliberately stack one example on top of another. In practice, the technique is subtle. Notice how Bland controls the grammatical structure of her opening lines to subordinate all time references to the action. In other words, subject and verb carry the action, dependent clauses keep the time references in their place.

Time is a structural element in Nancy Pickard's standalone suspense, *The Virgin of Small Plains,* winner of the Agatha and Macavity awards and an Edgar nominee. The story is set in two time periods: 1987, when the body of a young woman is found in a small community in Kansas, and seventeen years later, when the main characters learn the truth.

For each chapter that unfolds in a different year, Pickard opens with an unobtrusive dateline:

> *Chap. 1:* .... January 23, 2004
> *Chap. 2:* .... January 23, 1987
> *Chap. 3–6:* .... (no dateline—meaning no change)
> *Chap. 7:* .... January 23, 2004
> *Chap. 8:* .... (no dateline, meaning no change)

With or without a dateline, most chapters open with orientation, such as: *By the time Mitch got home that night from Abby's house. . . .* (readers already know which night is meant), and *On the Memorial Day after Nadine Newquist died. . . .* After a while, most of the action occurs in 2004, and almost no assist is needed, because we can tell which year we are experiencing solely from its opening situation.

A third-person POV lets chapters be seen through the eyes of different main characters, but unlike the flashbacks found in most novels, no 1987 chapter is presented as a 2004 memory; rather, the setting *is* 1987.

Pickard's techniques are effective, and the result, powerful, comparable in impact to the techniques of Tamar Myers in *The Dark Side of Heaven,* which move in and out of the present and the past (discussed in CLUE #4).

PASSING TIME

A fourth method of time orientation can be seen in *Naked Once More* by Elizabeth Peters, Agatha winner for best mystery novel. I'd like you to observe both the frequency and the variety of clues that keep readers time-oriented. The following lines represent five consecutive scenes spanning twenty-seven pages:

> *Chap. 10, Sc. 1:* Monday morning. Seven glorious empty days ahead. . . . There was also the delightful possibility of catching some of them still asleep, blissfully unaware of the fact that it was Monday morning.

Chap. 10, Sc. 2: As she drove back . . . she felt like bursting into
    song. . . . "Oh what a beautiful morning. . . ."
  It was afternoon, not morning, but she could not think of a
    song celebrating that time of day. . . .
  On her way through town she stopped at the supermarket to
    pick up a few supplies. School would be out shortly. . . .
  As she approached Gondal, the mutter of an engine greeted her
    and she saw a riding mower lumbering across the lawn. . . .
  When she reached the door the child was standing outside. She
    must have come directly to the cottage after getting off the
    school bus. . . .
Chap. 11, Sc. 1: The sound of the mower had stopped. Sunlight
    turned the stubbled grass to gold. . . .
  A chilly finger touched her foot and she looked up to see that
    the shadows of the surrounding pines were creeping upon her.
Chap. 11, Sc. 2: Twilight had fallen by the time she got home,
    and as she lugged the half-filled carton of books along the
    shadow-enshrouded path, she found herself moving a little
    faster than she had intended . . . dusk was not as pleasant a
    time of day as she had once thought it. Fumbling for the light
    switch in the dark house. . . .
Chap. 11, Sc. 3: Jacqueline was at her desk at nine the following
    morning. . . .
  For the next few days. . . .
  On the morning of the third day. . . .
  After leaving the cottage she stood breathing deeply of the
    winy autumn air. . . .
  A stroll down the sunny street restored her. . . and [she] paused
    to say good morning.
  ". . . and I thought, why not drop in and see if she'll join me
    for lunch?"   [pp. 147–73]

Elizabeth Peters offers clues to time's passage ranging from the specific *it was afternoon* to the metaphorical *chilly finger* of creeping shadows. Her less obvious hints are unrelated to light. Twice she mentions
school letting out. Especially effective is the reference in one chapter to
the mutter of the lawn mower, and in the next, to its sound having stopped.

SENSING TIME

In manuscripts that lack time techniques or environmental clues to echo real-world rhythms, characters seem stuck in a time warp. Readers experience a disorienting sameness, like that described by private investigator Bill Smith in *Winter and Night,* from award-winning author S. J. Rozan:

> The sun never showed that morning, so I had no real sense of the passing of time. In diffuse gray light that was always the same. . . .   [p. 138]

This passage's diffuse gray light is more than setting. It is also a metaphor to emphasize the sameness of the investigators' results:

> The light was the same and the guarded faces of the kids were the same and the answer was always the same.   [pp. 138–39]

Look for opportunities to drop brief, subtle clues about changes in the environment during the course of a day. Perhaps your protagonist looks for her sunglasses or adjusts the angle of her car's sun visor. After a long day of activity, she might notice the lengthening shadows or the coming on of lamps at dusk. Perhaps she has difficulty at night making out street names or unlit house numbers, as real people do. As I do.

Add sounds and smells to make the season vivid: squeals of children under a sprinkler, the scent of new-mown grass. Unless the environment plays a significant role in your story, keep such references brief, subordinate to the action. One or two brushstrokes can be more vivid than a brilliantly rendered dawnscape or detailed landscape. Readers of genre fiction pay less mind than readers of literary fiction to elaborate descriptions of settings. They focus on what the characters are up to—just what you want.

All the techniques I describe involving time are unobtrusive enough for your readers to skip. As a writer, you may prefer more detail or less. As an editor, I value these remedies for crazy time, and I can tell you that more manuscripts would benefit from similar techniques.

NATURE CALLS

It's hard to relate to a character who puts in an eighteen-hour day of constant activity without a break or something more substantial than a cup of coffee. Yet I've heard some interesting defenses from writers for not mentioning anything so natural as a lunch stop or a bathroom break. Supposedly, bathrooms are too "delicate" an issue to acknowledge. They could offend genteel readers.

Baloney. Who says the mere mention of a break requires indelicate details? What could be less offensive than these lines from *P is for Peril* by Sue Grafton? Kinsey Milhone is about to question a hospital employee:

> I . . . was given directions to the office of the Director of
> Nursing Services. I passed a ladies' restroom and made a brief
> detour before I continued my quest.   [p. 125]

A brief detour. No fuss, no muss. In a later scene after Kinsey waits hours for a sign of the killer, she tells the first person who joins her:

> "I missed dinner. I'm about to eat my arm."   [p. 217]

Kinsey's dinner alternative may be indelicate, but not the normal bodily function that prompts it. Don't mention every break, of course, and only suggest a few, such as: *After a quick TV dinner I drove to. . . .*

ILLOGICAL SEQUENCE

Frequently I come across manuscripts with another kind of unnatural time, the result of actions presented out of sequence:

> "Let's go, Henry." The two of them turned and left the room.
> Peg reached behind him to switch off the lights on her way out.

Their having *left the room* takes me outside the doorway into the hall. For the next action to occur *on her way out* makes the movie in my head run in reverse—the way my Uncle Sol used to show home movies. I see Peg stepping back into the room, then going forward into the hall again.

Put actions in sequence and watch certain repetitions resolve themselves.

> Laci decided to leave the stupid party and go home. She could
> feel Don's warm embrace enveloping her tired body, kissing
> away all distractions. After an hour of small talk and large
> drinks, she slipped away and began the long drive home.

In my made-up example, we buy into Laci's decision to leave, intensified by the writer's getting us to feel the warm embrace waiting for her. At first, the sensory data seems to transport Laci to her destination, and our imaginations along with her, when—whoops! Fast rewind. For the next hour she's still at the stupid party. Though she hasn't yet gotten behind the wheel, we're already experiencing whiplash.

Can you fix the sequence of events? Avoid suggesting that the character's goal has been realized before it has. Here's one possibility:

> Laci decided she'd tolerate the stupid party for no more than
> an hour of small talk and large drinks, all the while aching for
> Don's warm embrace to envelop her tired body. As soon as
> she could, she left for the long drive home.

A small change, but the new sequence keeps our imaginations at the party together with the long-suffering Laci, not leaping ahead of her.

Another cause of illogical sequencing comes from delaying a character's reactions to her environment. Visualize someone arriving at a house and taking the time to notice the expensive-looking Queen Anne chairs, tall reading lamps, gold-framed paintings on the wall, and luxurious beige broadloom, *then* mentioning the distinguished-looking host walking toward her with his hand outstretched.

> Jane Austen managed to put fruit trees in bloom in a scene where her characters are picking strawberries. She had to endure much ribbing from her brothers.
>
> Kim Wilson, author of
> *Tea with Jane Austen*

She hadn't noticed this guy among all those tall lamps?

Or the character treats us to a similarly detailed *House Beautiful* spread, *then* tells us of the dead body sprawled in the middle of that bonnie beige broadloom. Gimme a break.

Examine your manuscript for instances that defy the logical sequence in which a supposedly keen observer would notice obvious things first—unless you have an equally logical reason for defying that sequence. (Like, if your protagonist is a complete ditz.) If your reason is to shock readers with a corpse by slowly leading up to it, let the slowed pace precede the entry into the room where the body lies. Avoid crazy timing; it's a time bomb set to sabotage your submission.

CALENDAR

As many authors do, make a calendar of the events taking place in your novel so that all times of day and days of the week make internal sense. Also note the location of each of your characters at key times. When you revise your manuscript, double-check that every entry on your calendar has an actual counterpart in the story, and vice versa. Without such a guide, your use of time can make readers crazy.

When I edit a manuscript I construct my own timeline as I follow the unfolding plot, and I let the writer know of any discrepancies I find. According to the calendar I produced for one author, the protagonist rose "early the next morning to beat the rush-hour traffic heading downtown."

On a Sunday?

FIND & FIX CLUE #7: TIME BOMB

- ➥ See if your narrative goes beyond the initial scene-setting to suggest time's passage throughout your manuscript.
- ➥ Keep readers subtly oriented as to time of day, day of the week, and location, especially at the opening of a scene when a little time has passed or the location has shifted.
- ➥ Use sensory details that reflect changes in time, thereby lending authenticity and depth to your story.
- ➥ Be alert for the ways your readers might mistake the order of events in a sequence.
- ➥ Don't avoid referring to a washroom break or other physical need if its absence would create an unrealistic passage of time over a long day's events.
- ➥ Use an actual calendar to note every event in your story, together with the whereabouts of each character, and double-check your manuscript as you self-edit to confirm the chronological accuracy of the days and weeks of your plot.

D.O.A.

PART V: THE LINEUP

Lawrence Block said he learned more about writing
while he worked for a literary agency reviewing bad
books, learning things not to do, than he ever learned
from reading the masters.[29]

CLUE #8: DASTARDLY DESCRIPTION

Pretend you're telling a friend about your newest coworker. Would you be more likely to mention his height and weight or to tell how he spreads his papers out on the conference table and takes up enough space for three people? Are you more likely to say his eyes are brown or his eyes never seem to meet yours?

Because you choose to describe your coworkers in terms of their behaviors, surely you describe your fictional characters through their behaviors, too. Many writers do not.

Behavioral quirks and habits are not only more interesting than direct physical description but also reveal more of a character's personality and attitude. Behaviors create stronger, more memorable impressions, engender feelings in readers, and help set characters apart from each other.

Regrettably, the majority of submissions confront the busy screener with passages indistinguishable from this one:

> Jack was six-feet-two, 325 pounds, with blue eyes and gray hair combed straight back. He wore dark blue pants, a brown jacket, wire-rimmed glasses, and a thick salt-and-pepper beard.

89

This is a description dump. It shows no sign of the writer's having selected one or two unique details to make an unforgettable impression on the reader. Instead, the dumper unloads a Hefty bag of unremarkable features from two typical sources: the driver's license and the clothes closet.

Such choices lack purpose, as if a child reached into Barbie and Ken's trunk and pulled out whatever items were not already assigned to others.

SELECTING BEHAVIORS

Include a physical detail or an article of clothing if it expands the reader's understanding of a character, but know that the sharpest impressions come from behavior: what characters say, what they want, what they do.

See how Vicki Lane captures all three types of behavior in this description from *Old Wounds,* third in the Elizabeth Goodweather series:

> A heavy, pasty-faced woman in green sweatpants and an
> ample Hawaiian shirt stubbed out her cigarette on the arm of
> her chair, tossed the butt into the scrawny evergreens that did
> service as foundation planting, and hailed Phillip and Elizabeth
> as they approached the steps.
> "You folks in the market for good help?" she rasped. "I work
> cheap. Cook, clean, take care of kids? Hell, I'm a goddam
> Mary Poppins."   [p. 110]

With a minimum of physical description, Vicki Lane depicts what the woman says, what she wants, what she does.

In *The Violet-Crowned Corpse,* Judy Bartlett Creekmore introduces us to a character by means of two physical features, her taste in cars, and her behavior behind the wheel. We also learn a little about the main character, Tilda, from her actions and choice of vehicle:

> Tilda Sundown stopped her silver Camry at the sign on the
> corner of Cane and Camphor and watched as the Powder Pink
> 1968 T-bird coming from the opposite direction screeched to a
> halt. They were the only two cars in sight, so she motioned for
> Clyda Stern to go ahead. Clyda, a raven-haired grandmother
> with high, Lucille Ball-style eyebrows, nodded energetically in
> response to Tilda's wave and revved the engine twice before
> peeling through the intersection.   [p. 1]

The image of Lucille Ball is strong; her look-alike's laying rubber with a '68 pastel-colored T-bird is stronger still. Compare Creekmore's and Lane's descriptive techniques with the following line from a story in a published anthology. I changed the details to shield the guilty:

> Jake led the tall, slender, pretty reporter with straight black hair into the squad room.

Lazy choices—a sure sign of average writing. Examine your own descriptions and know why you select certain details over others. Whim? Impulse? Or to serve a purpose relevant to something in your story—something to expand character, perhaps, or create emotion in your readers.

Whenever I encounter the usual assemblage of features—this color eyes, that color clothes, or anything else that could be changed *without affecting the story in any way*—I am reminded of the days of youthful innocence when my world of creativity was defined by a box of sixty-four Crayolas.

Carla Damron says, "Don't describe a character so much that a movie star couldn't play the role."[30]

Piling on more colors, features, and details makes a character's appearance harder to visualize, not easier. Tall or short, blond or bald—it's all a Crayola-and-Barbie-doll grab bag. These ho-hum choices are precisely what fills the majority of submissions.

A careless choice can lead readers to false expectations. One first-time writer whose novel I edited included one brunette and five blondes. *Five?* Hmmm, the little grey cells believed this was significant. I kept watching for blondness to become relevant to the story. Nothing did. Nada. Bupkiss. So I queried the writer. He said he'd been unaware of the repetition; he simply liked blondes.

Hair color may be relevant if, say, a spy disguises himself with a dye job, a stalker has a thing for redheads, or a blonde is seen speeding away from the scene of a hit-and-run. In a romance, hair plays a sensual role. (More on this in CLUE #10.) Hair*style,* if unique, might expand characterization by indicating its wearer's lifestyle. But if one's thatch or lack thereof has no connection with anything in the story and no bearing on our perception of the character, why mention it?

I agree that readers need to visualize your characters. However, stats from a driver's license and garments from a clothes closet rarely create lasting, distinct impressions. Besides, readers take for granted that each character is dressed, unless you say otherwise. A fashion report is justified when its details add characterization and clarity—not clutter.

The idea is to include only those specifics that matter, that set cast members apart from each other. Thus, facial features rarely merit attention, because readers correctly assume every character has a face—though if you write sci-fi or horror, I can't be sure about *your* characters.

MAKE AN IMPRESSION

Here's a face worth describing. It's from *Rescuing Maria,* a novel-in-progress by Betty Beamguard, an author who's received more than thirty honors and awards for her writing:

> A bedraggled redheaded woman wearing a faded housedress shuffled in holding a burning cigarette at her side. Her thin face looked like the dried-apple dolls in the shops in Gatlinburg, the ones where they peel an apple and let it turn brown and shrivel before sticking in tiny black beads for eyes.

Beamguard's selection of details raises her description to the level of an impression. Impressions are sharper than the average description and longer-lasting in the minds of readers. Others that I find especially memorable include this one by screenwriter Daryl Wood Gerber from her novel-in-progress, *Cut! Cut! Print!* It features a sassy independent filmmaker:

> Hank was walking the site with a man who reminded me of a #2 lead pencil, skinny and jaundiced with a flattop crew cut.

Reed Farrel Coleman, winner of the Shamus and Anthony and twice an Edgar finalist, writes this in his fourth Moe Prager mystery, *Soul Patch:*

> Tall, broad-shouldered, thin-waisted, Larry wore his clothes the way a smooth plaster wall wears wet paint.   [p. 3]

DESCRIPTION AS METAPHOR

When an impression is based on a concrete image, such as a #2 lead pencil or a freshly painted plaster wall, a single word can instantly evoke the desired effect. In the next description, the one word is "grape." It's from *Push Comes to Death* by Nancy Gotter Gates, the second mystery in her series featuring sixty-four-year-old Emma Daniels:

> [A] short roly-poly woman apparently in her sixties appeared at
> the door. She was dressed in a bright purple dress with match-
> ing purple shoes that gave her the appearance of a large grape.
> Her dark hair was skinned back tightly into a knot at the base of
> her neck, adding to the effect. I hoped that the grin I couldn't
> stifle would be taken as a friendly greeting rather than my real
> amusement at the spectacle of Miss Truesdale, the human
> grape.   [p. 83]

Metaphors have the clever ability of extending. That is, the key word
can be mentioned again later to call up the desired image, no explanation
needed. Nancy Bartholomew uses the technique with the race track photographer in *Drag Strip,* the second mystery of her first series:

> . . . a short oval of a man, with a belt line that hit him just
> below the armpits, white socks, black sneakers, and a bald
> head. He looked like a brown shiny egg, and the closer he
> came, the more I realized that he smelled much worse than a
> rotten egg.   [p. 18]

Bartholomew takes baldness and body shape, two features that establish
their own literal image, and likens them to an egg. The payoff is a metaphor
strong enough to serve yet another function: as an epithet or stand-in for
the photographer when he is mentioned again three pages later:

> I could've told her I'd seen it all before, but I was busy having
> my picture taken by a smelly egg.   [p. 21]

To visualize an egg taking a picture makes for a sharper image than
(duh) a photographer doing so. By extending the original metaphor, the
author enriches the reading experience, letting us enjoy the "aha" that comes
from recognizing an allusion to something mentioned pages earlier. The
technique gives readers a sense of being part of an inside joke.

DESCRIPTION AS SYMBOL

Symbols offer both a literal meaning and a deeper significance. In description, symbols can suggest a character's personality and feelings. From
the following details, see what you interpret about the character of Percey
in *The Coffin Dancer* by Jeffrey Deaver:

> . . . The pug face. Black hair in tight, stubborn curls. (In her
> tormented adolescence, during a moment of despair, she'd
> given herself a crew cut. That'll show 'em. Though naturally
> all this act of defiance did was to give the chahmin' girls of the
> Lee School in Richmond even more ammunition against her.)
> Percey had a slight figure and marbles of black eyes that her
> mother repeatedly said were her finest quality. Meaning her
> only quality. And a quality that men, of course, didn't give a
> shit about.   [p. 24]

Deaver could have written *black hair* and *black eyes*. Instead, his choices show us *tight, stubborn* curls and eyes like *marbles*. Together with bits of backstory that recall Percey's adolescent acts of defiance, even a crew cut, this description prepares us to more readily accept her reckless behavior as an adult and her uncompromising determination and motivation. These personality traits are significant, not only because they add to our understanding of a major character but also because her risk-taking drives the series of events that propel the plot of *The Coffin Dancer.*

DESCRIPTION AS MOVEMENT

When presenting a description, combine it with other information about the characters, as in this passage from *A Well-Manicured Murder,* first in the forthcoming LitChix series by Georgia Adams:

> Andrea was looking especially good. Her black and white
> designer jumpsuit revealed a figure maintained by hours of
> working out with a personal trainer. Her blond hair fell in
> waves, nearly covering the Hermes panther print scarf knotted
> around her neck. She stood on impossibly high Manolo
> Blahnik zebra print stilettos.   [ms. p. 8]

With hours of workouts forming the context for Andrea's clothes and figure, and the stilettos presented as the object of the verb *stood*—which grounds Andrea in the scene—we realize what this well-to-do Atlanta socialite puts herself through to maintain her image. This is more than description; it's characterization. (Actually, it's torture, but that's just me.)

Unlike the unimaginative descriptions I come across in which hair is a feature someone *has,* the verb introducing Andrea's hair is *fell*—and it nearly obscures something that will be found later at the murder scene. In this way, Adams's description does double duty.

Look to your verbs to overcome the static condition of the typical description, in which a feature *has* a property or *was worn.* Instead, show it in use or in motion. Observe how Nancy Glass West animates a single feature for the office receptionist in this line from *Nine Days to Evil:*

> When [they] peered in, Gloria looked up expectantly and set
> her brown pageboy in motion.   [p. 63]

West's choice of words is more effective than if she wrote: Gloria *wore* or *had* a brown pageboy. Also note the verbs in the next description from Connie Shelton's *Memories Can Be Murder,* fifth in her Charlie Parker mystery series. Shelton mentions only those features that are part of the building manager's behavior as he tries to hastily repair his appearance:

> The manager snatched open the door, expecting to snarl at a
> tenant with a stupid complaint, and looked totally surprised to
> find me standing there. He made a quick attempt to smooth the
> few threads of hair that covered his shiny head and to tuck in
> the T-shirt that boasted a large dollop of salsa at the point where
> his round belly jutted out.   [pp. 82-83]

Examine Shelton's style closely for the way she subordinates all physical details to the man's actions. She also avoids the overused *He ran his fingers through his* [x-color] *hair.* Too many mussy heads already populate fiction solely to facilitate a writer's ploy for establishing hair color.

DESCRIPTION AS REACTION

Here's how J.T. Ellison describes an assistant district attorney in *All the Pretty Girls,* first in a new mystery series set in Nashville:

> . . . she looked more like a Pomeranian fluffed out for
> Westminster than the cutthroat attorney that she was. Her light
> brown curls framed her face, making her seem innocent and
> pure, a tactic that had snowed many a criminal. They got on the
> stand and saw her sweet blue eyes and cupid-bow lips and just
> knew that this sweet young thing was no threat. How wrong
> they were.   [p. 140]

Similar to Connie Shelton's showing the building manager's reaction to being visited by a non-tenant, J.T. Ellison describes her ADA's features in terms of how they affect the criminals she prosecutes.

Ellen Elizabeth Hunter also uses a reaction, this time by her series protagonist, Ashley Wilkes, to the physical endowments of another character. The passage occurs in Hunter's fifth book in her Magnolia Mysteries, *Murder on the ICW.* (For readers unfamiliar with the coastline of the Southeast states, ICW stands for Intracoastal Waterway.)

> Mrs. Crystal Lynne Boleyn was at his side, a Dolly Parton look-alike with flowing platinum blond hair and implants so big they cleared a path for her. Melanie had clued me in about the breast implants. I need clues about such matters because the truth is I don't have a clue. I just thought Mother Nature had been generous to Crystal Lynne.   [p. 69]

Hunter mentions only hair and implants but strengthens the impression they give by effectively utilizing two literary techniques: hyperbole *(cleared a path)* and allusion *(a Dolly Parton look-alike).* Adding Ashley's reaction expands her characterization. We learn she is clueless about such matters—and willing to admit it.

MEMORABLE DETAILS

Collect your own favorite examples from the authors you read to remind yourself of the infinite possibilities for creating your own fresh descriptions. Analyze the techniques you admire to sharpen your ability to spot the dastardly descriptions in your own writing before a busy screener does. Record how others use impressions to go beyond description to enhance characterization and create multi-layered effects.

See what Denise Swanson accomplishes by focusing on a single feature in this example from *Murder of a Sweet Old Lady.* It's second in her series of ten (so far) mysteries featuring school psychologist Skye Denison:

> Scumble River High School Principal Homer Knapik was seated to her right, and every time she glanced his way, her attention was drawn to the hair growing out of his ears. The long wiry strands quivered like the curb feelers on a car's wheels.   [p. 1]

Quivering like curb feelers—what an original simile. And it's presented in the context of Skye's reaction. Trim your own descriptions to the sharpest, most memorable impressions. Focus. Go for quality, not quantity.

In Pat Browning's first novel, *Full Circle,* which combines romance and mystery, reporter Penny Mackenzie says of her fellow reporter:

> Maxie was built for stakeouts—short, wiry, collapsible. [p. 1]

Less is more—as the above minimalist description demonstrates.

Consider the following line from James Lee Burke's *A Morning for Flamingos,* the tenth novel of the more than twenty-eight he's written:

> I took out another girl, a carhop from up north who wore hair rollers in public and always seemed to have sweat rings under her arms.   [p. 78]

Because we hold some opinion of people who similarly disregard their appearance in public, details such as Burke chooses do more than paint a striking picture. They stir an attitude, an emotional response in his readers. They do double duty. That's density.

In choosing your own details from unlimited opportunities, go for those that create an emotion, attitude, or opinion in your readers.

Note the precise details in this scene from Jeri Westerson's short story, "The Tin Box." As you read it, determine who feels the emotions it stirs:

> "Pick the right essential details to show readers how to complete the non-essential details in their minds that you don't need to tell."
>
> Bruce Holland Rogers, reviewed by Roxanne Aehl[31]

> *"Yes, Father?" Father. How many boys his age called their father "Father"? No other dad insisted on it. . . .*
> *"You left the rubbish bin. You didn't take it out. There'll be maggots by morning."*
> *"I forgot."*
> *"But you remembered to ride your bicycle to Hurly's Drug Store with your chums."*
> *"I'm sorry."*
> *Griffith brought out a little notebook from his coat pocket. He pulled the pencil free from the rubber band wound round it and*

dabbed the lead point on his outstretched tongue. He opened the cover, turned several pages, and scribbled with the tiny pencil.

"That's another mark off your allowance, boy. That's so many that soon you'll be owing me." He almost smiled.

Westerson's details are powerful. No further description is needed to make this scene more vivid. Would you agree that her writing creates emotion, and that its origin lies within our own childhood experiences?

The excerpts I present throughout this CLUE demonstrate that memorable descriptions of characters are not diminished by abandoning the driver's license approach or coming out of the clothes closet.

Create impressions. Stir feelings for your reader.

To further emphasize the low value of an unremarkable, undistinguished physical description (if I still have to), here's a quick test. At the start of this CLUE when I introduced Jack, did I say he wore a dark blue jacket and brown pants, or a brown jacket and dark blue pants?

Does it matter? Not in the least—not unless a jacket is found at the scene of a crime.

FIND & FIX CLUE #8: DASTARDLY DESCRIPTION

- ❧ Double-check that you select the fewest descriptive details for creating memorable impressions, and use those impressions to serve some purpose in your story. (Please review WITH PURPOSE AFORETHOUGHT in PART II.)

- ❧ Verify that the features and other details you introduce to describe your characters are incorporated into their behaviors instead of presented as an inventory.

- ❧ Evaluate the impressions you create for their ability to stir an emotional response in your readers.

- ❧ Be alert for verbs such as *have* and *had* that indicate static properties of a feature, and replace them where possible with active verbs that show a character's behavior.

- ❧ Experiment with ways to make your descriptions do double duty.

D.O.A.

CLUE #9: POISONOUS PREDICTABILITY

You now realize the *type* of description that occurs with predictability in the average submission. Next I want to show you how predictable its *placement* is. In a great many manuscripts, the moment a member of the cast steps on stage for the first time, dialogue and action stop and physical description begins. Never mind that it's too early in the character's dramatic career for anyone but the writer to know whether the new arrival is someone we should care about. Ready or not, here comes a dose of dastardly description administered with poisonous predictability.

Remember Jack of the unmemorable description? See where that description typically occurs in a manuscript: on page 1.

> Long after midnight, the bell at the back door broke the silence, followed by loud, insistent pounding. Jill jumped and peered at the figure through the rain-spattered glass. Quickly she unbolted the door.
>
> Jack rushed in, breathless. He was six-feet-two, 325 pounds, with blue eyes and gray hair combed straight back. He wore dark blue pants, a brown jacket, wire-rimmed glasses, and a thick salt-and-pepper beard.

"Wait," shouts the reader, "get on with the story!"

Stopping the action to describe Jack's appearance sends the message that the situation couldn't be as serious as this middle-of-the-night door-pounding would have us believe. Putting action on hold contradicts its urgency, shatters the mood, and undermines the writer's credibility. Description is supposed to *support* the action that develops characterization, not overthrow it and establish its own regime.

Busy screeners, like jaded readers, have learned to skip description dumps and scan ahead for the next sign of life: dialogue and action.

Elmore Leonard says, "Try to leave out the parts that readers tend to skip."[32] The writer who has not yet learned the value of Leonard's advice might write this reaction to Jack's out-of-breath arrival at Jill's back door:

> "At last! I thought you'd never get here," cried Jill. She was petite and wore her straight blond hair in a braid. Her sweater was blue and matched her eyes, and her slacks were black. . . .

Whenever I read Jack's stop-action description aloud in a workshop, followed by Jill's, the writers roar with laughter. The pattern of poisonous predictability has exposed itself with all the absurdity of the flasher in socks and shoes and nothing under the raincoat.

> "Any time you stop to describe something, you have *stopped.*"
>
> Novelist and educator Jack M. Bickham[33]

By the third or fourth time that the same pattern occurs in a novel, what seems laughable at first becomes irritating. Predictability is desirable in a weather forecast. In fiction it's fatal; in novels of suspense it's murder.

Delivering a description dump the moment a new character comes along suspends the action's momentum and forces readers to meet all characters in the same way. We really have to stop meeting like this. The busy manuscript screener stopped long ago.

As the following extracts show, a more effective way to handle description is to slice, dice, and splice a few details in with the continuing action and dialogue. Both description and action benefit when they work together.

ECONOMY OF STYLE

Look at Karen McCullough's description of Ray in *A Question of Fire,* her sixth mystery novel. Ray is the newspaper editor who sent reporter Cathy Bennett to cover an event that turned into murder:

> . . . Ray clomped into the room an hour later, in the midst of her second detailed recounting of the events of the evening.
>
> He plopped into a chair in a corner, nodded to her, shut his eyes, and gave a good imitation of falling asleep. Cathy wasn't fooled. Ray might look like a large, sloppy puppy, but the mind behind the unruly brown hair and rounded features was sharp and alert. More than could be said of her at that point.   [p. 4]

McCullough works Ray's description in with the clomping and plopping actions that ground him in the scene. We form a picture of Ray from his actions before we come to the simile comparing him to a large, sloppy puppy, before the first mention of his hair and features.

The author shows even these physical details indirectly, subordinate to the point about Ray's mind, not as direct description—not he *had* unruly brown hair and his mind *was* sharp and alert. Subtle. Effective.

UNINTENDED MISCONCEPTIONS

If you furnish no visual evidence about a character, readers fill the vacuum with their own mental images. There's nothing wrong with that, and in many cases it's desirable—except where later events are likely to contradict a reader's initial visualization. Here are some guidelines:

- Include, at first, the fewest attributes that distinguish a character on the basis of gender, age, and maybe skin color—demographic information that's part of most character introductions anyway. For example: "The young white guy shifted from one foot to the other."

- Bring characters to life through their actions and dialogue. Keep their descriptions subordinate to the action.

- Show characters interacting with their environment and with others, opening doors, spilling drinks, plopping into chairs, and doing a thousand other things to affect their surroundings and be affected by them.

- Anticipate any physical abilities or inabilities that may become significant later. Plant the first reference to that ability early, before readers make faulty assumptions and form contrary images.

A friend wrote to tell me her enjoyment of a book was spoiled by the author's placing the character's description too late. It seems the protagonist was introduced shuffling around the house, leading my friend to visualize an old woman. When the story eventually made clear that the character was not old but suffering from a bad cold, my friend said the contradiction took her "completely out of the book," and she had trouble revising her image.

Would a full physical description be appropriate from the start? No. Should the writer anticipate and head off the unintended contradiction? That would be nice. Yet the responsibility for avoiding a false image falls on the book's editor, who could suggest the earlier inclusion of some indirect clarification along the lines of "every bone in her forty-year-old body ached," or "the flu was making her feel twice her thirty-five years."

I recommend postponing or eliminating most descriptions unless new information contradicts the initial image readers are likely to form. What if a strangler turns out to be a mousy salesclerk who is much stronger than she looks? To avoid a reader's calling "Foul!" when the strangler's identity is later revealed, treat her strength as you would any other clue: plant it early and minimize it by surrounding it with other details.

If you intend to mislead, do so with a deliberate plot twist, not with contradictions that yank readers out of your story. Writers are seldom aware of such contradictions, because their mental images of their own characters are strong and clear. Familiarity with one's own story gets in the way of predicting how different readers might interpret it.

I fault the line editor for such contradictions. It's our job to anticipate the variety of audience interpretations and recommend revisions. (Of course, authors can and do ignore editorial recommendations. Worse, not all authors seek the professional editing that publishers no longer provide.)

INTENDED MISCONCEPTIONS

Describing a character at first sight may be desirable if, for instance, two characters originally meet by phone, letter, or e-mail, and form impressions of each other that prove false when they eventually come face to face. Perhaps a wrong impression can get a point across about these characters that would be difficult to express in some other way.

In *An Eye for Murder,* Libby Fischer Hellmann's first mystery novel, Ellie Foreman visualizes a woman based only on her voice over the phone:

> "Hello?" The voice was somewhere between a bleat and a
> foghorn. I pictured a woman with too much makeup, dyed hair,
> and lots of jewelry.   [p. 13]

Three pages later Ellie arrives at the woman's house:

> Ruth Fleishman's face was thick with powder, and her arms
> jangled with bracelets, but her hair wasn't dyed. A brown
> bouffant wig in a young Jackie Kennedy style covered a
> seventy-year-old head. She was either a cancer survivor or an

> Orthodox Jew who still wore a *sheitel*. Most likely an Orthodox
> Jew. This part of Rogers Park has replaced Lawndale as the
> center of *frum* life in Chicago, and she looked too vigorous to
> have suffered a round of chemo.   [p. 16]

Here, the pace slows enough for the author to address the discrepancy
between what Ellie imagined and what she later observes, thereby adding
a bit of background about Chicago neighborhoods and an Orthodox Jew-
ish tradition. This regional and ethnic detail adds what is known as *texture*.

TIMED RELEASE

Instead of launching into an immediate description of your characters,
try this alternative:

1. Select one key attribute, physical or not, and slip it in while
   dramatizing the character's first action.
2. Work other details in with the rest of the action a little at a time,
   keeping the description subordinated to the dominant action.

A timed release is easier to apply than you might think. Anne Underwood
Grant uses it to describe Fred in the first of her Sydney Teague mysteries,
Multiple Listing. Our initial impression of Fred comes well before we see
him, when Sydney remarks that her secretary, Sally, has a self-centered
jerk for a brother. Not until Scene 2 of Chapter 2 do we meet Fred in
person. He is being held by the police on suspicion of murdering his soon-
to-be ex-wife.

> Sally and Fred sat huddled at the far end of a long metal
> conference table. They looked like both sides of a bipolar per-
> sonality, she depressed and he manic.
> Fred's voice was strained, a loud, raspy whisper. "I will not
> stay here any longer. How dare they suggest. . . . "   [p. 18]

So far, we have an impression of Fred, not a description. Grant offers
the sound of his voice, the words he speaks, the attitude his words reveal,
and a clever simile to show he is acting manic. Four more paragraphs of
action and dialogue occur before Grant gets to the first of his features.

Nothing about the postponement of Fred's physical description is predictable. Delaying it neither risks our forming an earlier, contradictory

image of the man nor robs him of substance. When he is shown to us he is sitting in a specific place in a specific way, looking—don't you love it?—like the manic side of a bipolar personality.

DIALOGUE IS PARAMOUNT

More minimalist still are the details Richard Helms selects for introducing Hotshot in *Voodoo That You Do,* his second Pat Gallegher mystery:

> Hotshot leaned back in his seat, rubbed his ample belly, and
> belched once for effect and punctuation.   [p. 1]

That Hotshot's belly is ample is made known in the context of an action: he rubbed it. This first detail of the man's appearance occurs after an opening paragraph of 121 words, most of it a monologue expressing Hotshot's opinions. His words and forms of expression create a stronger, more immediate portrait of the man than any description could:

> "Man, it ain't so easy being a gangster anymore," Hotshot
> Spano told me as he refilled his wine glass with the valpolicella
> he'd ordered to go with his veal piccata. "When I got into the
> game up in the Bronx, it was a breeze. Some guy got in your
> face, you took his off for him. Bodda bing, he's toast. You just
> push the ol' double deuce up behind his ear, pump in a couple
> of shells, and wait for the lights to go out behind his eyes. Now,
> it's like you gotta get a fuckin' act of Congress to do a decent
> whack.

And so on. Despite delaying our first glimpse of the man's appearance, Helms runs no risk of his readers' forming an inaccurate image of Hotshot, because those 121 words do introduce the character—in action. The book's opening line (the hook) is dialogue (a form of action), followed by a line that identifies only the name of the speaker. Actions show his taste in wine and food, and actions anchor him in the scene, a technique that gives substance to dialogue. Next, via further dialogue, we learn more of the man's background, values, and feelings.

All this before we see one physical attribute—presented through action: *leaning, rubbing, belching.* Nothing predictable in placement. Note, too, that the opening sentence offers an ideal start for a novel: a change in the status quo, which Hotshot experiences as a threat to his well-being.

RICHER PORTRAYALS

If you have any remaining doubts about breaking the description-first habit, let Margaret Maron's writing inspire you to renounce the practice for all time. Maron furnishes almost no physical description, yet she captures personalities so effectively that we scarcely realize the vivid images we "see" are supplied by our own imaginations.

Southern Discomfort is the second of her award-winning Deborah Knott series. Deborah's brother and his only daughter play pivotal roles, and Maron portrays them through their actions, their dialogue, the dialogue of others, some exposition—but scarcely any description. We experience their relationship as if Maron knew each of our own families.

When she introduces this parent-teen relationship, she limits backstory to one specific example of a recent clash between them:

> . . . I was glad to see that Annie Sue and Herman seemed to be speaking to each other today. A lot of days, they didn't.
>
> From infancy, Annie Sue had tested the limits of paternal authority; but she'd turned sixteen this spring and now that she had her driver's license, she wanted more freedom and less accountability than ever. According to Minnie, they'd had a monumental clash last weekend. I didn't get all the details; but I gather it involved a broken curfew and confiscation of car keys. Nothing new there except that both my brother and my niece had lost their tempers and Herman had warned Annie Sue—and in front of her friends, which made it twice as humiliating—that she wasn't too big to get a switching if she didn't apologize at once.
>
> "In the same breath as she apologized, she swore she'd never speak to Herman again as long as she lived," Minnie had reported with a shake of her head. "Herman's way too strict, but that child's sure got a talent for pouring kerosene on a hot fire."
>
> I watched her pour Herman a cup of punch with every appearance of daughterly affection and hoped their reconciliation would last a while this time. [p. 16]

By now we have a pretty clear picture of these characters, despite merely one bit of physical data: Annie Sue's age, sixteen. We have to jump twenty-two pages to observe father and daughter again, also in action:

He was growling at Annie Sue when I drove into their back-yard after supper that Thursday evening. Annie Sue was huffed up and sir-ing him in that snippy-polite way teenagers do when they want to make sure you know that their respect is only on their lips, not in their hearts.

"I told Lu Bingham I'd wire our WomenAid house and now he says I can't," she told me hotly, her Knott-blue eyes flashing in the late afternoon sunlight. "He never lets me do anything!"

"She never did a circuit box by herself and she don't have a license," said Herman. From the tone of his voice, I gathered he'd already said that more than once before I drove up.

"Reese hasn't got a license and you let him wire everything by himself."

"No, I don't and even if I did—"

. . . He still had his work clothes on, as if he'd just come in himself. Hot, tired, dirty and probably hungry, too. There was a pinched look on his face. . . .   [pp. 38–39]

Dialogue makes such a strong impression that we're surprised only three references to Herman's appearance occur: his work clothes, being hot, tired, and dirty, and the "pinched look on his face." The only new data we learn about Annie Sue is her eye color. Our imaginations fill in whatever else we need. With no action-stopping description occurring in any predictable way, nothing can later contradict our own early visualization.

FIND & FIX CLUE #9: POISONOUS PREDICTABILITY

- ➤ Find where each of your characters first appears and watch for any predictable patterns in how you describe them, such as how soon, how much, and what kind of particulars.
- ➤ Introduce characters through dialogue and action, not description, except where a later detail could contradict an early assumption.
- ➤ Work the fewest physical details into the action a little at a time.
- ➤ Avoid stopping the action or sidetracking the story's progression.

CLUE #10: DISAPPEARING BODIES

Remember breathless Jack, whose high-anxiety middle-of-the-night visit to Jill stops abruptly for description? Remember how a dastardly description of Jill interrupts her reaction to his visit, and how both descriptions occur with the same poisonous predictability?

That kind of amateur writing is predictable in one other way: no details from the initial description relate to what comes after. Though the same characters reappear in later scenes, the writer mentions no previously described detail to help us visualize how they carry out these later actions.

If Gertrude Stein were reading that scene, she might say there's no *there* there.

One-time description dumps are quickly forgotten. Readers become overwhelmed by the amount of information presented, yet receive no indication of which details are worth remembering or which characters might later emerge as important players.

Although TV viewers could *see* Big Jack looking down at petite Jill, readers need a little help. Why make him 350 pounds on the page if no action of his is affected by his size? His description serves no purpose if nothing reflects his exertions in climbing a hill, or laboring to catch his breath after fetching a pail of water.

When a character's presence fades and his or her actions become indistinct, a feeling of disconnectedness sets in.

Readers have three options:

1. Page back and hope to find a memory refresher.
2. Plod ahead and hope to piece things together from the context.
3. Stop reading.

If the disconnected reader is a busy screener, forget options 1 and 2.

HAVE A PURPOSE

If you don't follow through on the features you assign, why assign them? If Jack's clothes are not mentioned after his initial introduction, are we to assume he wears the same old thing every day? To counteract that assumption, a daily fashion update would be in order. But that would give far more importance to Jack's wardrobe than it merits.

Okay, you wouldn't waste ink on such things. But what you *do* choose to show in a description may need some later reference to keep dialogue and actions from becoming disembodied. So think through your descriptions not only for their effectiveness but also for their use in successive situations.

In an interview in *Newsweek*, Janet Evanovich calls herself a slow, "reductive" writer. She uses the cooking term "reduction" to compare writing to making gravy, in which a big pot of ingredients is boiled down to "a little pot of stuff, which is the essence."[34]

Here's a dress-for-successive lesson: select details that you plan to carry forward. If you sit a pair of glasses on Jack's nose, show him wiping them when you bring him in from the rain. That's not all. Choosing to outfit him with wire-rimmed glasses means you cannot show him slipping them off, giving them a wipe, and slipping them on again without also showing the careful handling that distinguishes wearers of wire-rims from wearers of horned-rims. Think through the implications of your choice of detail to keep from losing credibility.

We're going to say good-by to Jack and Jill now, recalling that at no time did their descriptions give us any reason to remember them or relate to them as real people. Their author's choice of clothing and features served no story purpose whatsoever. The only function this odd couple filled was to give me an opportunity to illustrate a few dos and don'ts:

- Do have a purpose for selecting details, such as using them to contribute to characterization or plot.
- Do select features that you intend to make use of again.
- Do recharge your powers of observation, especially when bringing a bespectacled character in from the rain.
- If a descriptive detail is worth mentioning the first time, it's worth doing something with a second time.

CREATE EMOTION

In a romance, the hunk gently loosens the woman's hairpins and says, in a husky voice, "I've wanted to do this since I first saw you." He lets her dark, silky tresses fall seductively over her shoulders, then over his chest, and over his—. Ahem. We're talking technique, now: how to use a common physical feature—hair—and make uncommonly good use of it by referring to it more than once. The next three authors show you how.

Dana Lyon's first romance novel, *Heart of the Druae,* repeats an archeologist's momentary visions as he excavates an ancient Roman site:

> He closed his eyes and rocked back on his heels. "What is this power?" he whispered. "Why am I drawn here?"
>
> The answer came in an instant, moving from the shadows of his mind to replace the vibration in his body with the smoke of desire.
>
> *A fall of silken hair, dark as midnight, graced the soft curve of a bare shoulder. Above the gleaming flesh, gold beckoned with a wink.*

Add the sense of touch and smell, and note the appeal to feelings:

> Her hair was a cascade of silk . . . dark, yet full of light. Her smell, so fresh and wild . . . was unlike anything he had ever known . . . and yet, oh, so familiar.

A little later, the vision becomes even stronger with the added sense of touch, which foreshadows the archeologist's travel to ancient times:

> The smell of her hair and the feel of her skin were like nothing he had ever known . . . and yet it was so sweetly familiar. He brushed her hair aside to expose the curve of her neck. Tangled loops of gold lay against her skin, entwined with the dark silk of her hair. He kissed her neck, and against his lips, the gold was warm—

Hair: a recurring feature, plot-related, and enriched via sensory imagery. This is a model for the effective use of a single physical feature.

The same is true for a very different application of the same feature used by Susan Dunlap in *Death and Taxes,* her seventh Jill Smith mystery:

The patrol car was still half a block away but I could make out
a blond officer bending over a man.

The street was dark there. . . .

. . . Pereira was on the far side of him, feeling for a pulse.
The red pulser atop her patrol car turned her tan uniform an
odd shade of army green; her blond hair danced in the light and
disappeared in the darker darkness that followed.   [p. 8]

. . . Her blond hair hung limp over the collar of her tan uniform
jacket. Under the streetlights she looked washed out, ex-
hausted.   [p. 22]

"So," I said, "what's your great surprise?"
"A coup, Smith." Pereira's grin grew wider. Her blond hair
nearly twitched with smug.   [p. 57]

Each reference to Pereira's blond hair reflects a change in her feelings
over the course of her investigation. Effective technique. Creates density.

DEEPENING IMPRESSIONS

Carolyn Wheat, two-time Edgar nominee, also knows how to keep her
characters vivid by selecting and repeating key features. In *Fresh Kills,*
Wheat's third mystery novel featuring attorney Cass Jameson, Cass recognizes the voice of another attorney in a courtroom in Brooklyn, N.Y.

"Anyone here a notary?" The voice was unmistakable, though
it had been a while since I'd heard it. East Bronx Irish, loud
enough to cut through the din of legal chitchat but not so loud
as to render the speaker unladylike.

Marla Hennessey. Sometime friend, sometime rival, sometime bitch. Which of her multiple personalities would be out
today?   [p. 6]

So far, Marla's voice and a little narrative give us a quick impression of
the woman. Two paragraphs later:

"Can you come out in the hall for a minute?" Marla's green
eyes had a calculating look I knew all too well.

"I don't dare miss the first call," I whispered back. "I'll be in

> this damned courtroom for the rest of my natural life as it is."
> . . . "Cass, don't bullshit me." Marla was one of the few
> people I knew who could shout in a whisper. . . .   [p. 6]

Though Carolyn Wheat has not yet mentioned what Marla looks like, other than one indirect reference to her green eyes, the author has already created a stronger, more distinct impression of this character with dialogue and with the sound of her voice than most writers do with pages of detailed description.

Two more paragraphs go by before readers learn of Marla's physical appearance. Nothing is lost by delaying that description. In fact, Wheat has written this character's dialogue and actions to make us so interested in Marla that we are now ready to absorb the few descriptive details that complete the picture:

> . . . she lit a cigarette and began waving it in her hand, her huge
> hammered-silver bracelet riding up and down on her wrist.
> She'd put on weight. She'd colored and cut her hair, wearing
> it in a platinum pageboy that fitted her head like a cap. Her
> clothes were silver and mauve, flowing garments that gave an
> illusion of soft femininity. As I listened, I reminded myself that
> it was only an illusion. Marla was as armored as if her clothes
> and hair were made of stainless steel.   [p. 7]

Appreciate the symbolism of Marla's huge hammered bracelet in motion, her armored clothing, her weight that she keeps throwing around (metaphorically), and her stainless steel hair. Wheat's choice of "platinum" for hair color is also a metal. And *illusion* is mentioned twice.

Most of these details live on in later scenes, from Marla's clothing and jewelry to the sound of her voice. Each additional image reinforces and amplifies the character and anchors her in her surroundings.

For example, the next three passages refer to Marla's shoes and how they make an impression—a sharp, deep, literal impression:

> "Jesus" was all Marla said, but she slammed the car door hard
> and walked quickly, the heels of her shoes making little holes in
> the grass as she took the straightest path to the door, disregard-
> ing the curved flagstone path.   [p. 16]

She then swept out of the car in a cloud of expensive perfume. I followed, racing to keep up even though the heels on my shoes were half the height of the bronze pumps Marla wore. Did the woman ever *walk?*   [p. 45]

She dropped her cigarette to the floor and crushed it with her silver pump. . . . Marla's eyes held a malicious glint as she shot back, "What conversation, Cass? It's your word against mine." Her heels clicked on the pavement, and she swung the courthouse door open with a wide flourish.   [p. 82]

Whatever genre you write, study the techniques of Wheat, Lyon, and Dunlap shown here as therapy for cases of arrested development. Get beyond the dastardly description, poisonous predictability, and disappearing bodies (CLUES #8 through #10) that sabotage the average submission.

FIND & FIX CLUE #10: DISAPPEARING BODIES

- Examine how you describe your major characters to be sure you know the purpose for every detail you choose (please review WITH PURPOSE AFORETHOUGHT in PART II).
- See that your descriptive details contribute to characterization.
- Verify that the attributes you assign to your characters continue to be reflected in their actions, wherever appropriate.
- Replace details that offer no opportunity for follow-through with details you can use again to expand or deepen your portrayals.
- Confirm that your selections:
    - do double duty
    - are worth repeating
    - contribute to enriching your writing style.

PART VI: CHANGE OF VENUE

"The way manuscripts are thrown into the Rejection
pile on the basis of early mistakes is a crime."
Pat Holt, former *San Francisco Chronicle* book reviewer [35]

CLUE #11: SHIFTY EYES

With publishing's emphasis on novels that are more character driven than plot driven, selecting an effective point of view is one of your most important decisions. Each POV offers a different advantage. Because the literature on this subject is considerable, I'd like to believe you researched your options carefully before deciding on the character through whose eyes you want readers to experience your story.

This CLUE helps you evaluate the results of your choices and understand the POV problems that frequently sabotage a submission.

FIRST-PERSON POV

Let's suppose your story is told from your protagonist's first-person POV. You write: *I parked at the branch office and did a quick check in my rearview mirror: short red hair, green eyes, freckles—*

Oops! The reflection-in-the-mirror self-description is a cliché typical of the average writer. More imaginative alternatives appear on the next few pages. Meanwhile, back at the branch. . . .

Before I could knock on the manager's door it flew open, and I found myself face-to-face with a man who glared at me, wanting me to get lost.

Whoa! A first-person narrator cannot know what others want, think, or feel, only what she wants, thinks, and feels, and what her own five senses tell her about others. Your job is to report the objective data that lets your character and your readers reach their own conclusions, such as:.

He glared at me (sight), *poked me sharply on the shoulder* (touch), *and growled, "You again"* (sound), *his onion breath nearly knocking me over* (smell). Sensory data produces conclusions—stated and unstated.

Okay, let's try this once more. *The front of his tee-shirt read "Builders do it with . . ." and the back bore the words—*

No, no! When two people come face to face, Ms. First Person cannot see the other person's back. Or what's behind her, unless she's gifted with a third eye. You know the one—in the back of your mother's head.

One manuscript I saw had the main character describe two women having lunch in the booth behind him. He never met them nor saw them; they sat down after he arrived. Yet he told us what Rhoda, a music teacher, looked like, as well as Heidi, a conference planner. How could Mr. First Person narrator know their names and occupations and what they looked like? He couldn't. He was a victim of the author's shifty eyes.

Review your writing for slips like these, which pull observant readers right out of a story. One clumsy slip, slide, or shift in POV is enough to cause a busy screener to slip a submission onto the "no" pile.

LOOK MA, NO MIRROR

If you want to include a description of your first-person narrator, you need a more original device than the amateur, clichéd reflection in a mirror or store window. In this scene from *Death and Taxes,* author Susan Dunlap has a fresh take on a familiar source of I.D.—the driver's license that officer Jill Smith produces for a cautious homeowner:

> As she looked from my license to me, her finger moved
> across it from *Brn* (hair) to *Grn* (eyes) to *5-7.* (I had the feeling
> she knew I'd stretched the truth there, but maybe that's just the
> paranoia of the shortest officer in Detective Detail). . . . [p. 26]

Self-deprecation works for Dunlap's officer and for the next several examples. After all, who could pull off a flattering self-portrait without sounding insufferably conceited? Here's a fresh take by Denise Dietz from

Footprints in the Butter, the first title of her second series. Protagonist Ingrid Beaumont experiences a fumble at a football game:

> The Broncos blitzed. The Cowboys fumbled. The Broncs recovered. I roared my approval, then performed a high-five with the fat man sitting next to me. He fumbled for my breast, I don't know why. I'm not a ravishing beauty, quite the opposite, yet men always try to ravish me. I've been told I look like Bette Midler. When people tell me this, they usually stare at my bust, then, embarrassed, raise their eyes to my slightly crooked front teeth, which are frequently clenched.   [p. 2]

John D. MacDonald makes Travis McGee charming and disarming when describing himself in *The Deep Blue Good-By.* This is the first book written in the long-running series, though not the first published:

> "Mrs. Atkinson? My name is Travis McGee."
> "Yes? Yes? What do you want?"
> I tried to look disarming. Am pretty good at that. I have one of those useful faces. Tanned American. Bright eyes and white teeth shining amid a broad brown reliable bony visage. The proper folk-hero crinkle at the corners of the eyes, and the bashful appealing smile, when needed. . . .
> So I looked disarming. When they give you something to use, you use it.   [p. 33]

Peggy Ehrhart's first novel, *Sweet Man Is Gone,* features Maxx Maxwell (first name Elizabeth but she doesn't like it). In this scene, Maxx, the leader of a blues band, has just entered a rehearsal studio:

> . . . A bunch of guys with assorted tattoos and facial piercings are perched on the folding chairs strung out along the back wall. One of them whistles at me.
> In my mind I'm still a skinny chick nobody'd look twice at, but I got my nose fixed before I went off to college—not that I stayed there long—and I went blond when I hooked up with my first band. And it's amazing how a push-up bra can help you fill out a T-shirt.   [p. 14]

Note the variety of situations that authors create to facilitate their characters' self-descriptions. In *Milwaukee Winters Can Be Murder* by Kathleen Anne Barrett, the protagonist's intention to look for a murderer causes this argument with her friend Emily—and leads to an exceptional description:

> "What are you going to do," Emily said, "wrestle the guy to the ground when you catch him? You don't even weigh enough to donate blood, for Pete's sake. I mean, you're even smaller than my nine-year-old niece. . . . my dog sat on you once and you couldn't even get up, do you remember that?"   [p. 322]

If you prefer a simpler approach, here's how Lorie Ham has Alexandra Walters describe herself in *Murder in Four Part Harmony:*

> Daddy told me my best features were my green eyes and long blond hair that fell just past my shoulders, features I'd inherited from my Grandma Walters.   [p. 1]

How original is your first-person narrator's self-description? How unique is the situation that prompts the description so it seems to occur naturally?

MORE FIRST-PERSON PITFALLS

First-person POV may seem the easiest, most natural way to tell a story, but it's not as simple as it looks. Inviting us into your character's consciousness means playing fair with your readers, not withholding information the protagonist knows or learns in the course of the story.

However, nothing prevents you from underplaying a clue, disguising its significance, or intentionally diverting attention, as with a red herring.

One limitation of first-person is that the protagonist-as-narrator must be present in every scene. If your plot makes this impossible, you don't want to discover it three-quarters of the way through your first draft. I've seen too many first-person submissions that attempt to adjust for later point-of-view problems by awkwardly manipulating the plot, or by making the main character merely hear about important events from other characters after these occur offstage.

Second-hand action is weak and cancels the value of a first-person you-are-there POV. No matter what genre you are writing, dramatize key events so your readers experience them directly. Ixnay on the hearsay.

Other issues with first-person are that the writing tends to mingle the voice of the narrator with that of the author, to rely on internal thoughts when dialogue could do a better job, to ramble, and to rehash the same thoughts. In first-person POV more than any other, your main character should be so interesting, quirky, and insightful that readers want to see the world through her eyes for an entire novel.

Beware of observations such as *A shadow crossed my face* and *The lines in my forehead deepened.* Not possible for a first-person narrator to see, even with a mother's third eye.

If your fiction reveals any first-person weaknesses, fix them or change to a more versatile, flexible point of view.

THIRD-PERSON POV

The most versatile, most popular narrative mode is third-person. The narrator is not a character in the story. Cast members are *he* or *she;* there is no *I,* except in dialogue. Not every scene requires the protagonist's presence, though whenever she does appear she should be the viewpoint character. Third person comes in two flavors, limited and multiple.

Limited, also known as *close* or *tight,* sticks to the viewpoint character throughout a scene, as first-person does, and it imposes some of the same limitations, such as not letting the protagonist know what others are thinking.

A major advantage of third-person limited is that it is both subjective and objective: readers learn the protagonist's internal thoughts and feelings as well as what the external narrator tells us and shows us.

Doris Betts, award-winning author of short stories and novels, advised a writing class that in a tight point of view, the way your character "sees" a sunset should not only create the picture but also reveal something about the character.

Multiple expands the number of heads the narrator is able to access. Not more than one head per scene, though. When changing viewpoints, start a new scene. Among the plusses of multiple is the opportunity to leapfrog: to open a scene in the POV of a different character from the one smacked by the plot twist at the end of the preceding scene.

Because leapfrogging does not take readers where they want to go—at least not for another scene or two—the technique prolongs suspense.

Leapfrogging also lets you braid separate story lines until you are ready to show how they all come together.

Caution: too-frequent POV switches can leave readers feeling detached from the protagonist. Caring about one character engages the reader more effectively than attempting to care about a group of characters.

Within a scene, keep the same viewpoint. Each time the POV does switch:

- Open the new scene with a hook, thereby reducing the chance that readers will lack interest in the new viewpoint character.
- Let readers know right away whose viewpoint they're in.
- Establish the identity of each new viewpoint character by using action and dialogue, not the slower thought mode.
- In braiding scenes, take a detail from the end of the earlier scene that left readers hanging at its end, and refer to it at the start of the later scene to immediately pick up the same plot thread.
- Maintain a fairly consistent pattern for alternating scenes and POV, so you don't change viewpoint characters for the first time after a hundred pages of going steady with the same character.

Scenes in *More Than You Know* by Meg Chittenden alternate viewpoints, showing Nick and Maddy collaborating on their mutual goal of learning the truth about Maddy's husband. Yet they remain wary of each other because their motives are different. Nick's third-person POV opens the book and continues through Chapter 2, Scene 1. At the start of the next scene it shifts to the third-person POV of Maddy, whom Nick has been following. The change in viewpoint causes no break in continuity.

Dramatic irony and tension build as Nick and Maddy become romantically attracted to each other while hiding their motives from each other.

OBJECTIVE DISTANCE

Whether limited or multiple, third-person permits *distance,* as shown by this excerpt from *Blood Lure,* ninth in the Anna Pigeon, park ranger, series by Nevada Barr, an Agatha and an Anthony winner:

> "I see you've made yourself at home," Harry said acidly.
> "Yeah." Anna was too absorbed to notice the intended reprimand. "So the army jacket Carolyn was wearing wasn't hers?"

> [Harry] shook his head disgustedly. Since Anna'd not been
> aware of his implied rebuke, she also missed its annoyed
> follow-up at her obtuseness and took the headshake as a
> negative about the jacket.   [p. 178]

Because part of Anna's characterization is her singlemindedness, she is
unable to see herself as others see her. For that reason she would be an
unreliable first-person narrator. Third-person gives Barr a greater opportunity to control how much objectivity and distance to maintain in effectively portraying her series character.

THIRD-PERSON LIMITED SUBJECTIVE

Analyze how Peter Abresch uses POV in his Elderhostel mysteries featuring James P. Dandy (yes, that's Jim Dandy, to his frequent consterna-
tion). From the opening line of *Bloody Bonsai,* first in the series, Jim is
grousing about going on his first solo junket after his wife's death:

> *You'll have a really good time,* they said.
> *You'll learn lotsa stuff,* they said.
> *You'll meet people,* they said.
> Yeah, right.   [p. 8]

Jim brings his anxiety with him, along with a suitcase-sized chip on his
shoulder. That attitude immediately introduces a conflict and quickly establishes his character and his voice:

> Shouldn't have come.
> Uncle George's fault. . . .
> Or maybe it was Ceecee's fault.
> "Go Dad, you already paid your money." It went on for two
> months. Getting her brothers to gang up on him. "You need to
> get away. You haven't gone anywhere since Mom died."
> Did any of them ever wonder that maybe he hadn't wanted to
> go anywhere after Penny died? And on top of it, two to a room,
> he would be paired up with a stranger for a roommate.
> Great, really great.   [pp. 9–10]

These passages suggest a first-person viewpoint—until you glance at
the lines I omitted. Directly after Jim's opening grumble *(Yeah, right),*

Abresch orients us in the scene: *Jim's two-year-old blue Lincoln. . . .* Jim's sarcastic riff on bunking with a stranger *(Great, really great)* is followed by: *He climbed out of the car, got his bag from the trunk. . . .*

This is third-person limited subjective. Gone are the usual third-person *he thought-felt-wondered-realized* tags that impose a filter between narrator and character and increase the distance between them. Instead, thought blends seamlessly with the narrative. The form could almost (not quite) be generated by writing in first-person, then changing pronouns.

MULTIPLE SUBJECTIVE

For third-person multiple subjective, look at Nancy Means Wright's *Mad Season,* first in the series of Vermont mysteries featuring Ruth Willmarth, whose husband left her. Ruth runs their dairy farm and rears the two children still at home. When elderly neighbors are assaulted, the ten-year-old tells her that at one time he'd accidentally seen where the neighbor kept a wad of money. But the boy had said nothing at the time—he was afraid.

> "Afraid of what?" She clasped her knees. She saw how thin Vic was. He'd been losing weight and she was only just aware of it. She was too busy, she was a terrible mother, she couldn't keep up with farm and family. The fear of losing her children crept over her again and she held out a finger to touch Vic. But he shrank away.   [p. 20]

Wright lets us experience the mother's angst as powerfully as if the narrative were first-person. It almost is; such intimacy is what subjective third-person can do. Ruth's interior voice becomes one with the invisible narrator's, producing *close* or *tight* POV, the opposite of *distant.* Occasionally Wright switches to third-person multiple to present the thoughts of a few other characters—but always within their own scenes.

In my opinion, *limited subjective* combines the best of all worlds: the flexibility and control of third-person and the intense closeness of first.

This technique is not to be confused with omniscient POV, which lets the narrator enter the thoughts of any and all characters any old time. The lack of boundaries can keep readers from bonding with important characters. Moreover, omniscient is difficult to pull off effectively, so I don't recommend it for the developing novelist.

THIRD-PERSON PITFALLS

Because third-person gives writers the freedom to enter the thoughts, feelings, and fields of vision of different characters, a frequent mistake is to present too many viewpoints. Doing so fragments your readers' focus and keeps them from feeling close to anyone, including the main character. In some novels it's hard to tell who the main character *is*.

Another pitfall is *head-hopping:* visiting the minds of different characters in the *same* scene, which weakens the impact of the scene's events on the character most affected by them. Head-hopping also disorients readers and marks the writer as an amateur.

Phone calls offer a special kind of wrong number. If you replicate a dual sound track for telephone dialogue, don't include actions and mannerisms for both parties. The viewpoint character cannot see into the receiver.

To show the party on the other end, begin a new scene in his POV—and stay there a while. Don't play ping-pong with your readers.

Lesley Grant-Adamson cautions new writers that the more viewpoints, the more complicated the writing: "Please think very hard about whether you feel ready to tackle a form that presents extra difficulties."[36]

DELIBERATE SLIPPAGE

An experienced writer might intentionally slide into another character's point of view at the end of a scene. In *Desert Heat* by J.A. Jance, Joanna Brady's husband has been fatally wounded. Joanna grieves during the long ride to the hospital in Tucson, then composes herself and handles the admitting procedure with the efficiency of an insurance agent, which she happens to be.

> "One of the forms is missing," Joanna said.
>
> Annoyed, the clerk peered at her. . . . "Really? Which one?"
>
> "The organ donor consent form," Joanna answered firmly. "His heart's already stopped once. I want to go ahead and sign the form now, just in case."
>
> The clerk frowned. "That's not a very positive attitude, Mrs. Brady," she sniffed disapprovingly. "Our surgeons are very skillful here, you know."
>
> "I'm sure they are, but I still want to sign it, if you don't mind."

After the form is produced, signed, and witnessed, Joanna asks if she could see her husband before surgery.

> "I doubt that," the clerk replied coldly. "I doubt that very much."
>
> Actually, as far as the clerk was concerned, if it had been left up to her, the very fact that Joanna Brady had insisted on signing the prior-consent organ-donor form would have cinched it. No way would she have allowed that woman to see her husband now, not in a million years.
>
> Women who were that disloyal didn't deserve to have husbands in the first place.   [p. 34]

At the word "Actually," Jance shifts from Joanna's POV to the clerk's. The narrative takes on the clerk's attitude, and we hear thoughts that could come from no one but the clerk. This viewpoint shift introduces a lighter tone following two grim chapters, and it accounts for a plot event in which Joanna does not see her husband before he dies.

As skillfully executed as Jance's technique is, shifting viewpoints within a scene is risky. My advice to the still-developing writer: Don't try this at home.

MIXED UP

Over the years, a great many guidelines have been put forth about point of view, all of which have been disregarded at one time or another by respected authors. Occasionally a break with tradition is effective; occasionally it bombs.

Consider what's known as *mixed* POV. The writer presents certain scenes in first-person, others in third. Some readers admire the technique, some hate it—both sides citing identical novels.

The author with a supportive editor and loyal fans can afford to experiment. Innovation is riskier for mid-list writers with borderline sales, whose options for a career boost include trying a name change and finding a new agent and publisher. For writers who have yet to find either one, embracing the unconventional could mean sabotaging their submissions.

Dawn Cook's debut novel, the fantasy *First Truth,* originally used first-person for the protagonist, Alissa, and third-person wherever the tension benefited from the reader's knowing more than Alissa was able to know. Cook's agent advised that a consistent POV would more readily meet the preferences of publishers for a first novel. Cook weighed the need to sustain the story's tension against the potential loss of first-person punch, then began her extensive revision.

> "One must be drenched in words, literally soaked in them, to have the right ones form themselves into the proper pattern at the right moment."
>
> Hart Crane

In its published form, *First Truth* is compellingly told throughout in third-person.

Despite growing acceptance for mixed POV, even experienced writers get mixed results. One famous author presents the first four chapters of one of his novels in his protagonist's first-person POV, then opens Chapter 5 with a jarring third-person "he." We discover we've been unexpectedly plunged into backstory, learning about an unnamed individual's first assignment as a cop.

Who is it?

Readers new to the series might think this is still the protagonist talking. Maybe this no-name rookie who's reliving his early days on the force is the friend who visited the protagonist in Chapter 4. A page and a half into Chapter 5 we learn what's-his-name's identity, but until then we continue wondering who "he" is—a state of limbo that prevents our fully engaging with this character or becoming interested in his backstory.

Any time a reader tries to figure out who is speaking, wondering produces wandering attention. That's when we stop reading.

Famous or not, this author violates two fundamental principles:

- ➡ to always keep the reader oriented, and
- ➡ to always identify the new POV character right after a switch.

By comparison, J. A. Konrath in *Whiskey Sour* uses both first and third in a fairly consistent pattern of alternating chapters. Readers quickly adapt to the pattern of POV shifts and look forward to them. The techniques of contrasting verb tense and gender help, too. Chapters featuring Lt. Jacqueline "Jack" Daniels are told in first-person past tense. The killer's chapters use third-person present tense—techniques that make the antagonist's actions appear more immediate and therefore more menacing.

Mixing first and third can nevertheless be hazardous to the health of an unsold manuscript. For every choice you make, let your reason be that no other point of view could be as effective.

Whether you choose first- or third-person viewpoint, keep these realities in mind: when one character turns her back on another character, he cannot say she's scowling. And when two cars of similar size stop alongside each other at a red light, the drivers can flirt with each other all they want to, but neither of them may describe what the other is wearing below the line of sight that each car's window permits.

> "Rewriting is the whole secret to writing."
>
> Mario Puzo, author of *The Godfather* (quoted online)

FIND & FIX CLUE #11: SHIFTY EYES

- When revising, identify the point(s) of view you use in every scene and review for consistency.
- Double-check each scene to verify that its viewpoint character does not know what other characters think and feel except through personal experience, such as by observing body language and hearing dialogue.
- With first-person POV, confirm that your narrator is physically present in all scenes.
- Verify that first-person does not ramble, overuse interior thoughts, or unnecessarily rehash the same thoughts.
- Be cautious about mixing first- and third-person POV in the same novel, but if you do, establish an early pattern for switching viewpoints before readers learn to anticipate some other pattern.
- See that any scene introducing a shift in POV identifies the new viewpoint character promptly and keeps the reader oriented.
- Confirm that even though POV might shift from time to time, your main character remains the story's focus.

D.O.A.

CLUE #12: UNSETTLING SETTING

What's the first thing a movie or comic book character is expected to say upon coming to after being knocked out? *"Where am I?"* We humans have a primal need to feel oriented in our surroundings. A story that neglects to instill a sense of place from the outset leaves readers feeling unsettled and *dis*oriented.

Make one editing pass through your manuscript solely to verify that each scene establishes its setting right away. This does not mean beginning each scene with a full-blown description; it means letting readers have a quick, general sense of where the action is taking place—in hospital admissions, or "out back" in the garden, or downstairs from "that front bedroom where you sleep, Ashley dear."

One manuscript I edited opened with the narrator describing a public figure holding a press conference outside a government building. I visualized the narrator standing in the crowd, until the next paragraph made clear that our observer was sitting at home watching the press conference on television. That manuscript needed a buckle-your-seatbelt warning.

Occasionally a setting is mere orientation and backdrop—just another pretty place. When most effective, a setting may reflect a time and a culture, evoke the mood of a story, underscore its theme, or add depth to the characters and their behaviors. Setting often unifies a story. In some fiction, it plays a role as significant as that of a character.

When setting is *not* used effectively, some or all of the following unsettling signs become quickly apparent:

- The story's location is so indistinct that events could be taking place in Anyboro, USA.
- Details are put forth all at once, not interwoven with the unfolding action.

- ◆ Description is little more than an inventory of commonplace features devoid of the location's uniqueness, with quantity of detail trumping quality.
- ◆ Locational information is more detailed than necessary: "The path split after five minutes, so I took the right fork, walked about ten yards, and off to my left about a quarter of a mile farther. . . ."
- ◆ Once described, setting is never mentioned again, never reestablished, unless a later scene switches to a different location.
- ◆ Mood may be set forth once during the initial scene-setting, but it soon evaporates because the writer does zilch to sustain it.
- ◆ Nothing about the setting appears related to the story, its theme, its characters, or their actions and emotions.

For submissions with these qualities, the setting is the "no" pile.

In addition to aesthetic value, a novel has potential market value if it offers a fresh locale that depicts a previously untapped regional, ethnic, or interest group. A compelling sense of place rich in local color and history can make a well-written manuscript stand out among the hundreds of others set in faceless places.

FAMILIAR SETTINGS

Even an often-used location such as Miami, Chicago, the Big Apple, or La-La Land can make editors take notice of a new writer who presents it with originality.

Michael Connelly received an Edgar award for best first mystery for *The Black Echo,* which introduced Harry Bosch, LAPD homicide detective. In the scene opener that follows, the first sentence puts forth the type of descriptive detail usually associated with setting. But the three sentences following it deepen the relationship between the location and Connelly's theme:

> The setting sun burned the sky pink and orange in the same bright hues as surfers' bathing suits. It was beautiful deception, Bosch thought, as he drove north on the Hollywood Freeway to home. Sunsets did that here. Made you forget it was the smog that made their colors so brilliant, that behind every pretty picture there could be an ugly story.   [p. 70]

Would the idea of a beautiful deception hold as much meaning if the story were set somewhere other than a city known for creating illusions?

Echoes of this theme resonate in the Edgar-nominated *Offer of Proof,* by Robert Heilbrun. Chapter 8 opens with the protagonist, a New York public defender, on his way to Rikers Island to interview the prisoner he is about to defend:

> I saw the New York skyline glowing like gold in the crisp blue sunny air. From a distance, it looked like beautiful science fiction, created on a scale no one could believe. This was real talent. You could almost forget that there was no design to it at all, that up close, it was a big mess. But the illusion never lasted more than a few minutes anyway. Then the endless gravestones in the cemeteries along the highway told the story again of the human anonymity that was the price of the glittering city.   [p. 55]

Heilbrun selects contradictions to build this illusion of New York City. Of Rikers itself, the largest penal colony in the world, he uses a comparison that resonates meaning on several levels:

> . . . acres and acres of fenced-in land, more like some kind of third world plantation than an American prison.   [p. 56]

PERVASIVE SETTINGS

Settings that are said to play a role as significant as a character are those that affect the existence, sensibilities, and behaviors of an area's inhabitants. A small English village offers such a setting for Val McDermid's first standalone novel, *A Place of Execution,* winner of many awards including the Barry for best British mystery:

> Scardale wasn't just a different world from the bustling market town where Swindells lived and worked; it had the reputation of being a law unto itself.   [p. 10]

The details McDermid selects capture the insular quality of this unusual village, and she presents them in the way that Detective Inspector George Bennett experiences them as he approaches the village for the first time:

. . . In the eerie light of the moon, George could see fields of rough pasture rising gently from the road that bisected the valley floor. Sheep huddled together against the walls, their breath brief puffs of steam in the freezing air. Darker patches revealed themselves as areas of coppiced woodland as they drove past. George had never seen the like. It was a secret world, hidden and separate.   [p. 22]

Settings in genre fiction are usually brief and not as all-encompassing or as pervasive as Scardale is in *A Place of Execution*. Nonetheless, choose your details just as carefully as McDermid does—for their effect on your readers as well as on your characters.

CONSIDER ALLUSION

Brevity in a setting means more than short; it means sharp, concise. For a specific image with the fewest words, consider the benefits of *allusion*. Note how John Ramsey Miller uses the technique in *Side by Side:*

Fast-moving clouds were mirrored in the puddles of standing water left by a late afternoon rainstorm. Halogen fixtures set on tall poles spaced fifty feet apart painted the landscape an unholy orange-blue.
A solitary figured dressed entirely in black slipped through a vertical slit in the tall hurricane fencing topped with loops of concertina wire. The fence surrounded a forty-acre lot beside a train yard where several hundred steel containers had been stacked and ordered with Mondrian-like precision.   [p. 1]

Miller's alluding to the style of a well-known cubist painter instantly creates a sharp image, condensed, efficient. No further description needed.

SMALL-SCALE SETTINGS

Almost any interior—a house, car, garden, or place of business—can be made to do double duty. Besides setting the scene, an interior can reveal what its occupant is like. Avoid getting carried away, as some writers do, by devoting a great deal of attention to describing an interior that belongs to a minor character. Balance the attention you give to a setting with its significance to your story as a whole.

In addition to maintaining a balance, maintain the *perspective* of your viewpoint character. I've read more than one submission in which the first-person narrator, having entered a house for the first time, proceeds to tell us from the vantage point of the front foyer all about the rooms in the house, including down the hall and off the kitchen behind the garage.

If you're writing science fiction your characters might "see" locations beyond their line of vision, but for all other fiction, ixnay on the x-ray.

Instead, weave description into your action and stay with the perspective of the viewpoint character, as demonstrated in the next two examples. Present information in a sequence that your character would logically experience. As always, be selective. Offer a few carefully chosen details and trust your readers' imaginations to fill in the rest.

SETTING AS ACTION

S. J. Rozan creates a vivid impression of both a setting and its occupant in this passage from the Edgar and Macavity award-winning mystery *Winter and Night*. Bill Smith, one of Rozan's two lead characters in her Lydia Chin/Bill Smith P. I. series, drives to an address in search of information:

> . . . I turned in, parked behind a rust-pocked Olds Cutlass that was probably as surprised as anyone every time it found itself running. Mud clutched at my shoes as I walked to the porch, and the steps creaked as I climbed them. . . .   [p. 209]

All description proceeds from Bill's experiencing the setting, from his turning in and parking to walking to the porch and entering the house:

> I wiped my feet on a worn mat, followed Beth Adams and the dog through a dank hall to a sticky-floored kitchen. I took the can of Bud she handed me, and then followed again into a living room sloppy with old magazines and *TV Guides*. . . .
> The cloud of dust I raised when I sat on the broken-down couch danced in the sunlight.   [p. 210]

Examine what makes this writing active, not passive: no yard *was* muddy, mat *was* worn, or floor *was* sticky. The room did not *have* old magazines.

Another setting shown through action occurs in *Sinister Heights* by Loren Estleman. When Amos Walker, P. I., comes to the home of a wife-abuser, he has to defend himself against its inebriated owner, Glendowning. Chapter 6 ends with Amos knocking his assailant unconscious on the front stoop and dragging him inside; Chapter 7 opens without missing a beat:

> We went down a step into a sunken living room that smelled as if it had gone down with the Armada. It was carpeted in deep pile from which Glendowning's heels dragged up dust and strips of cellophane from cigarette packages past as I hauled him backward toward the nearest chair. This was a fat gray recliner that went into its act when I dumped him into it, stretching its spine and swinging up its footrest. . . . If there was an ashtray under the bent cigarette butts on the end table by the chair, or for that matter an end table under the squat brown beer bottles, I would have needed a shovel to find them.   [p. 53]

Estleman reveals this setting in the context of having Amos smell, haul, dump, and mentally shovel it. The action characterizes both the slob who lives here and the protagonist, Amos Walker.

EATING AGAIN?

Now that we've come indoors, I'd like to make you aware of one type of setting that's frequently misused and overused: the restaurant or bar. Granted, your characters have to meet with each other during the course of the story, and convenient places for doing so can range from a five-star French restaurant to a pancake franchise.

Anything wrong with that? Depends. Action is conflict. Busy manuscript screeners want to see it and feel it. Action is also tension that arises from *anticipated* conflict. But meeting is not action, and seating two people at a table to exchange information only weakens a scene already at risk.

Writers often make up for a lack of table action by occupying their characters with sipping a drink, looking at a menu, placing an order, taking a bite, having another sip, stirring, cutting, chewing, and swallowing.

That's not action, it's activity, and essentially meaningless. Activity without conflict or tension does not make a scene *a scene*. Nor does tension come from looking at a menu—unless the prices are criminal.

Although the information that characters exchange might produce a little tension, dialogue that tells about an off-stage event rarely has the emotional impact of parading an on-stage event before the eyes of an audience.

Conflict merely talked about falls flatter than a franchised pancake. So here are two ways to energize a static, action-deprived table setting. One is to create a reason for your characters to disagree. Maybe they are trying not to be seen together in public. Maybe they dislike each other.

Even best friends argue. The friend might have to get home so the babysitter can leave on time. That's tension. Maybe the friend has no patience for more than a quick drink and a quicker news briefing—not the discussion that her close friend wants to pursue. That's conflict.

Friends may share the same values and goals but not the same priorities at the same moment. Making sure they don't is up to you.

SWITCH SETTINGS

A second technique is to borrow tension from another situation by moving your characters to a setting that offers conflict of its own. A hockey game, perhaps, or a long, hot line for a sale. Get your characters arguing. Plant some earlier mention of their interest in the activity so their time engaged in it becomes believable. Different settings offer different possibilities for cranking up conflict.

Suppose Mary Jane wants to sound out her theory of a crime with her best friend, but Best Friend plans to spend a quiet Saturday fishing. So M.J. invites herself along, and their quiet day on the water is anything but. One focuses on catching a carp and the other keeps harping on catching a criminal. When a whopper of a fish gets away, B.F. blames M.J. and retaliates by poking holes in her theory. Then M.J. begrudgingly revises her thinking, and the plot takes a new direction—as it should, frequently.

Whenever or wherever feelings run high, almost any setting will do. Use one that doesn't appear in everyone else's novel.

True, everyone has to eat, and people do arrange to meet for dinner and drinks when they want to talk. Yet too many fictional tête-à-têtes are staged in restaurants and bars for no reason other than the setting's having come easily to mind and needing no research. Convenience food.

RELEVANCE

For writers who make an eatery or night club part of their main character's life, that setting plays a continuing role in the story. But for characters who do not work around food and drink, what other ways might a restaurant or bar provide a logical, relevant setting? Perhaps. . .

- if the weapon of choice is poison or knockout drops administered in a Shirley Temple. . .
- if the plot establishes that a suspect or witness is known to hang out at Wookie's Nook. . .
- if a clumsy waitperson spills the soup, causing Eliza Dewmore to make an unscheduled trip home to change clothes, where she walks in on. . . .

You get the picture. After all, you don't have your characters meet at the airport if no one is taking a trip or opening a storage locker. So instead of staging a meaningless meal, think about having your characters rendezvous at a racetrack, dialogue at a dog park, or kibitz at the car wash.

I'm not saying put your characters on a diet and keep them out of the bars. I *am* saying don't pick a place from force of habit or lack of imagination. Choose each setting for its relevance to your characters and plot, and for its potential in heightening interest, tension, and conflict.

Is a racetrack or dog park where your characters should exchange their information? Only if it works for your story. If the best spot for the action you need is Chez Café, go ahead and take everyone out to eat. But please, put a lid on all that sipping and chewing. After a while it's hard to swallow.

FIND & FIX CLUE #12: UNSETTLING SETTING

- Evaluate how you establish a sense of place, then maintain it.
- Determine whether your characters are affected by their environment and, if so, how much attention you want to give it.
- See if details in your settings are presented as part of the action.
- Check your interiors to see if they characterize their occupants.
- Balance the amount of attention you give to describing a setting with its importance to the story.
- Consider changing a scene's location to one that adds tension of its own.

D.O.A.

CLUE #13: INSUFFICIENT GROUNDS

New writers, like new parents, record every detail of their novel's first setting but neglect those that follow. When a later scene opens in a location previously described, the new writer adds a meanwhile-back-at-the-ranch kind of reference without reinforcing the unique imagery of the setting or reestablishing the desired mood.

Sorry, Charlie, characters and their actions need periodic grounding or anchoring. Once is not enough. Your fictional people and places are real to you but mere illusions to your readers, who need visual props and other sensory data to ground your characters in their places in space. Fictional folk who are not reconnected to their surroundings from time to time revert to the illusions they are, their actions and dialogue fading and breaking up like cell phones in the Rockies.

In the same way that a story without a sense of place can make us feel disoriented, a scene with insufficient grounding can make us feel adrift. Keep the spatial dimensions of your scenes intact and your characters grounded. Once in a while repeat a reference to some tangible aspect of the setting—like Estleman's bent cigarette butts and squat brown beer bottles (CLUE #12). Watch how the next three pros do it.

SPATIAL GROUNDING

In *Lethal Genes* by Linda Grant, one scene takes place on a ferry crossing San Francisco Bay. The protagonist, Catherine Sayler, P. I., had agreed to go to dinner with a colleague, Kyle, in exchange for his getting information for her. The scene's tension comes from Catherine's trying to figure out the significance of what he tells her, and from rebuffing his advances.

Periodically, Grant repeats details of the setting to ground or *re*-anchor her characters in the scene. To help focus your attention on those techniques, I omit from the following examples all talk of the criminal investigation as well as all sexual innuendos. (Disappointed? Read the book.)

133

"Can I get you wine or something harder?" he asked as the ferry pulled away from the dock.

"White wine would be nice," I said. "I'll be out on deck."

It was a mild evening, but the wind was still brisk and cold. I was glad I had on a warm jacket. Still, the view was worth the discomfort. San Francisco was a city of lights, the buildings just dark shapes against the darker sky, their lit windows like cutout peepholes into a hidden shining world.

Near the dock they loomed over us, close enough that you could actually make out some of the features of the lighted rooms. As we pulled out into the bay, they shrank and became a spectacular backdrop.

Kyle joined me at the rail. . . .   [p. 177]

We know where we are, what time of day it is, what the air feels like, and what the eye can see—a vivid setting able to sustain the full page of dialogue that follows it, after which Grant briefly reestablishes the setting:

. . . We were far enough out into the bay so that the wind was stronger and I shivered inside my jacket. But looking back at the sparkling city and the strings of lights that outlined the Bay and Golden Gate bridges, I wasn't about to go inside. [p. 179]

Next comes a page of Catherine's thoughts about the case, then:

We were past Alcatraz now. . . . A gust of wind peppered my face with drops of briny sea spray.   [p. 180]

Note how each reference to the setting becomes progressively briefer yet supports longer passages of dialogue and action. After another full page about the case, one final grounding takes place aboard the ferry:

Kyle straightened up, turned, and leaned his back against the rail.   [p. 181]

This scene's most striking aspect is its sense of place. However, what I want to call your attention to is Grant's pattern of anchors to reestablish that sense of place. The following five lines of nearly inconspicuous business do double duty by positioning the characters in relation to their surroundings and to each other:

1. he asked as the ferry pulled away from the dock.
2. "I'll be out on deck."
3. Kyle joined me at the rail and handed me. . . .
4. looking back at the sparkling city and the strings of lights that outlined the Bay and Golden Gate bridges. . . .
5. Kyle straightened up, turned, and leaned his back against the rail.

Try an experiment. Take the five lines above, change the nouns to fit your own story, and see how you might incorporate Linda Grant's locational references into one of your own scenes. Then compare the next six anchors with your scenes. Though your sensory details do not have to be as abundant as Grant's, see if they are as clear and strong:

6. wind was still brisk and cold. I was glad I had on a warm jacket.
7. the view was worth the discomfort.
8. Near the dock they loomed over us, close enough that you could actually make out some of the features of the lighted rooms. As we pulled out into the bay, they shrank.
9. the wind was stronger and I shivered inside my jacket.
10. But looking back . . . I wasn't about to go inside.
11. A gust of wind peppered my face with drops of briny sea spray.

Strong sensory data like this lets readers experience a setting subjectively, as the character does. Instead of the author's objectively reporting that the wind covered the deck with drops of sea spray, she has Catherine say that the wind peppered her face with it. Who doesn't feel *that?*

And who never watched a building "shrink"? Physically impossible, of course, but having Catherine observe the phenomenon puts us inside her perspective, exactly where we should be.

SATISFYING NEEDS

Whether your setting is a castle or a cave, choose descriptive details you can mention again as your action unfolds. Don't depend on dropping anchor once and assuming it will hold throughout the ups and downs of each scene's action. Readers have a hankering for anchoring.

How often anchoring or grounding should recur varies with the tempo or pace you desire and the kind of action involved. Grant's leisurely paced ferry scene uses all eleven of the aforementioned anchors within four pages.

From the manuscripts I see, not all writers are aware of pacing. Some interrupt action haphazardly, inserting locational reminders or beats at random. Some do the opposite: inserting beats with numbing regularity. One manuscript showed a gesture for every two lines of dialogue, producing a tiresome, predictable rhythm that flattened momentum and prevented the build-up of tension.

Norman Mailer observes that the sole virtue of losing short-term memory is that it frees you to be your own editor.[37]

Unlike a soap opera's installments, there's no written formula. In general, re-anchor your characters shortly after the initial scene-setting. Make each subsequent anchoring briefer and farther apart. As the action builds, the interval between anchors grows. To slow the pace, interrupt the action with increasing frequency.

Novelists refine their pacing by practicing it and getting reliable feedback on their writing. Especially instructive is reading to analyze the techniques of others and to enjoy the sound of their rhythms.

ANALYZE THIS

For another grounding pattern, look at Ruth Birmingham's technique in the following scene from *Atlanta Graves*. The situation is a staple in the mystery genre: interviewing a suspect.

The setting is the home of art dealer Charlie Biddle. A painting has been stolen from her gallery, and she is about to be questioned for the second time by the series character, Sunny Childs:

> Charlie Biddle was wearing sweat pants and had her hair up in a ponytail when I got to her house, an ugly brick ranch in the not-especially-swank Atlanta suburb of Doraville. I'd expected her in some charming Inman Park Victorian—but I guess Doraville's cheaper. The inside of the house, though, was pleasant and warm and lived-in, with books scattered around the living room and nice paintings on the walls.
> She gestured wordlessly to a chair, then flopped down on a big white couch and lit a cigarette.   [p. 196]

The scene is set, and now the dialogue begins. Sunny opens with a question about the case. That is followed by a paragraph of Sunny's thoughts and four paragraphs of dialogue. Then comes the first re-anchoring:

> [Charlie] stood up. "Can you hold on a second?"
>
> She was gone for a minute or two and I could hear noises coming out of the kitchen. She came back with a bowl of Froot Loops, started eating them with relish, cigarette held in one hand, spoon in the other.   [p. 197]

Sunny brings the subject back to the theft and states one theory of how Charlie might've done it. Charlie agrees, hypothetically.

> She dug into the bowl of cereal. When she was done, she stubbed out her Marlboro in the film of milk in the bottom of her bowl.   [p. 197]

That brief anchor sustains the next two pages of dialogue about the case, accompanied by the occasional *she said* or gesture-type beat. The next regrounding is, *She lay back on the couch and looked up in the air through the cloud of smoke over her head.* That line sustains three more pages of dialogue. The seven-page scene comes to an end when the art dealer discloses something that takes Sunny by surprise, and she:

> . . . sat there in a stupor for a while.
>
> "So am I going to lounge around here smoking all morning while you meditate?" Charlie said after a while. I noticed she was on her third Marlboro.
>
> "Nope," I said. "I think this will get me started."
>
> I left her to her lounging and her Froot Loops, and walked out without saying another word.   [p. 202]

Here's a quick review of the author's pattern of grounding the characters in their space while also building a steadily increasing pace:

- ➡ 1 paragraph of detailed scene setting, then 3 paragraphs of dialogue.
- ➡ 1 brief reference to setting, then 4 paragraphs of dialogue.
- ➡ 1 reference to the kitchen and to 2 props (cigarette, cereal), then 1 paragraph of dialogue.
- ➡ 1 reference to cereal, then 21 short paragraphs of dialogue.
- ➡ 1 reference to the couch, then 38 short paragraphs of dialogue and 1 final reference to cereal.

The third mention of Froot Loops unifies the scene and ends it.

ACTIVE V. STATIC SETTINGS

To show how writers divorce action from its setting instead of blending them, I rewrote the bookshop scene from Orwell's *Nineteen Eighty-four:*

> *As* Winston *went up* the stairs to the room above Mr. Charrington's shop, *in his hand he carried a brief case.* The room *had* a window, *which* he opened. *There was also* a dirty little oilstove *and an* armchair.

My parody separates the setting from Winston's interaction with it. The result is wordy, uninteresting, and static—but common: *In his hand he carried . . . There was also.* The only movement is *He went up* and *he opened.*

Yawn. Adolescent exposition. Static properties. Monotonous construction. Compare my parody with the scene as Orwell wrote it (CLUE #5), to see how his verbs reflect what Winston *does:* climbed, opened, lit, put, and sat. After only one paragraph, Orwell's first re-anchoring occurs, adding four details to reinforce the setting and its relationship to the world outside:

- ➤ the air *played* against his cheek
- ➤ the shouts of children *floated*
- ➤ Winston *settled deeper* into the armchair and
- ➤ *put his feet up* on the fender.

Orwell presents each detail with a verb of motion, creating sufficient grounds for the reader to experience the scene.

FIND & FIX CLUE #13: INSUFFICIENT GROUNDS

- ➤ Select scenes from your work at random and highlight all instances of scene-setting and grounding of the characters in that setting.
- ➤ Look for patterns in frequency, length, and spacing of references to setting, and see if those patterns enhance the pace you desire.
- ➤ Review the sensory details that help readers feel they are experiencing the setting in every chapter—as a character would.
- ➤ Examine your verbs and integrate description with action.
- ➤ Be sure every page offers something to visualize.

D.O.A.

PART VII: THE USUAL SUSPECTS

"One of the first things you learn about writing is that if you
come across a passage that you've written and you're struck
by how wonderful it is, you cut it, leave it on the cutting-room
floor because (writing) is not self-indulgence."
Fred Chappell, Poet Laureate of North Carolina 1997–2002 [38]

CLUE #14: SLOW DEATH

When details are too few, a story is hard to follow. Often, what's missing is the effect without a cause. That is, we witness a character's reaction, but the action that produces it is missing. Jack Bickham says for everything a character does, show an immediate, physical cause for it, not "merely a thought inside his head."[39]

However, when details are too numerous, the weight of it all drags the story to a slow death. If your manuscript suffers from overwriting, forget what might be missing. The busy screener won't read far enough to notice.

Luckily, the symptoms of word diarrhea are easy to find and fix.

New writers tend to connect every dot in a sequence of steps, even when the sequence is familiar or obvious—such as leaving one location, driving to another, arriving, and walking to the door. Don't underestimate the reader's capacity for anticipating the familiar and the routine. Over-explaining is irritating.

More leaving, walking, and arriving goes on in unpublished fiction than at Los Angeles International Airport. Slow death.

TRANSITIONS AWAY

Think about the steps Patricia Highsmith omits from this passage in an early mystery novel, *The Blunderer.* Walter Stackhouse, the central character, has telephoned a woman he wants to see again:

> . . ."Maybe I can help you," he said. "Can I come over? I'm not far away."
>
> "Well—if you can stand a mess."
>
> "What's the address?"
>
> "Brooklyn Street, one eighty-seven. The bell's under Mays. M-a-y-s."
>
> He rang the bell under Mays. . . .   [p. 76]

Are you confused because the scene shifts without a break, and Walter is not shown hanging up the phone, driving to Brooklyn Street, and walking into the apartment building? Surprised, maybe; confused, no. The author's omissions are understood because the connections for the leap in time and place are routine. What she omits is not action, it's housekeeping.

One way to see the difference is by reading a great many works of fiction and noting the techniques of others. Look for examples of transitions without wordiness. You know the old saw: If in doubt, leave it out.

A clear leap in time and place occurs in Linda Grant's *Lethal Genes* at the end of the ferry scene (CLUE #13). When last we saw the lights of San Francisco, Kyle had just:

> . . . turned, and leaned his back against the rail. "Doesn't make sense," he said. After a couple of minutes of silent thought, he added, "I need more fuel. You want another glass of wine?"
>
> We had a wonderful dinner of mesquite-grilled shrimp at Guaymas in Tiburon. The restaurant sits on the water, near the dock, and we had a table next to the window so that we looked out across the dark bay at the lights of San Francisco in the distance.
>
> Anyone watching us would have seen a couple so intensely involved in conversation that they seemed unaware of food,

> wine, and even the shimmering beauty of the view. They would probably have assumed that a great love was flowering. They'd have been wrong. What animated our passion that night was not romance but murder.   [p. 181]

End of chapter. Do you feel on edge because Kyle isn't shown returning with the wine? Maybe you'd hoped to watch the ferry tie up at the dock. Nice touches, but unnecessary, because the scene does all it needs to. There's no reason to prolong it once Catherine's goal is met. The information she learns from Kyle influences the direction of the investigation from this point forward. All scenes should produce some new insight, angle, or other development to continue propelling the plot.

With Catherine and Kyle at dinner looking "out across the dark bay at the lights of San Francisco in the distance," Linda Grant brings full circle the imagery that runs throughout the scene. The unity brings closure, and "they'd have been wrong" evokes a theme inherent in much genre fiction, especially sci-fi, mystery, and fantasy: things are not what they seem.

More manuscripts would benefit from scenes as purposeful, unified, and grounded as these examples. However, if you're uncomfortable omitting routine transitions from your own writing and long for a bridge to cross small gaps, here's a technique made for you. Before the transition, end the scene, skip a line, and open a new scene in the new location. On the skipped line, centered, type the symbol for a scene break, like this:

or   * * *

One contribution a transition makes is to slow a story's pace and provide a breather after a fast-moving action scene. If you remain aware of pacing, you can use the driving or walking time between scenes for your protagonist to ponder the latest developments and plan the next step.

Most of the admonitions we hear about transitions have to do with their absence, which can disorient readers whenever time or place changes. So if you remain uneasy with such a quick change to "He rang the bell under Mays" or "We had a wonderful dinner . . . in Tiburon," you can always add a few words such as: "An hour later he rang the bell. . . ."

Or start a new scene, as you would do when changing to a different viewpoint character. Please don't include every step in the journey. My own admonition is to prevent superfluous, wordy bridges, as if the writer felt compelled to record the character's every thought, word, and deed enroute to the next action. That compulsion leads to a slow, painful death.

BLOAT

Techniques are available to slow a novel's pace. Wordiness is not one of them. A writer in control draws out a scene to produce a planned effect. A writer not in control connects every step, unaware of the effect.

What moments would you cut from the following?

> Wally Bloat put down the phone and noticed the clock on the wall showing a quarter to five. He walked to the coat rack in the corner of his office, put on his brown overcoat, and picked up his briefcase with his right hand. He was finished for the day.
>
> As he walked through the outer office he called to his secretary, Lotta Thyme. "I'm leaving now, Mrs. Thyme."
>
> "Looks like you're taking work home again, Mr. Bloat," she said.
>
> "Yes, I am, Mrs. Thyme. Goodnight."
>
> "Goodnight," she replied.
>
> Arriving at the elevator, Bloat punched the down button to go to the underground garage where his car was parked. While waiting for the familiar "ding" he took his car keys from his pants pocket. When the doors opened he. . . .

Okay, okay, I'm exaggerating, but not as much as you think. Plenty of writers seem to have learned little from reading other authors. Unsure of what to include in their own writing to promote understanding, they connect every dot. For them it's a form of insurance. I consider it malpractice.

Showing someone grabbing his coat at a quarter to five sends a pretty clear message that he is "finished for the day" and is "leaving." Whether the coat is brown or the briefcase is carried in the right hand doesn't matter unless it matters to the *story*.

Mentioning every step in an ordinary, familiar sequence is different from the legitimate need to account for every step in the solution of a crime. But anything as plodding as Wally's leaving his office is itself a crime.

When I point out unnecessary details to writers, a few defend the method as adding realism. Careful here, because realism is a means to an end, not an end in itself. Busy screeners have plowed through enough submissions to know that overwriting on page 1 foretells overwriting throughout. They don't have to witness a manuscript's brain death before pulling the plug.

PURPOSE OF DETAIL

If advancing the plot were a scene's only function, entire books could be written in thirty pages. They'd read exactly like a synopsis.

As you revise, be guided by your purpose for each scene. You may be justified in drawing out the wait for an elevator if slowing the pace sets up the reader for a surprise—such as a stranger's stepping out of the shadows and into the elevator with Mr. Bloat as the doors close.

What about the set of keys Mr. B. takes from his pocket? Superfluous detail or legitimate clue? Again, be guided by your purpose. Let's say this fellow is found a week later floating in the Gowanus Canal, as bloated as some writers' prose.

If the victim happens to be your protagonist, your story is dead in the water anyway—not the first to self-destruct by killing off its lead character.

If the keys serve no purpose affecting the story, lose them. But what if they turn up in one of Bambi's bureau drawers tucked under the pink panties? That could be a red herring.

Or the keys might be real evidence. If so, show them in the victim's possession before he disappears, without drawing attention to them. Thus, the waiting-for-the-elevator scene may be necessary after all, if for no other reason than to plant those confounded keys.

To plant an object, be subtle. Use humor, which distracts, or show it among other objects. To disguise a behavior, show it among other behaviors. Thus, Mr. Bloat should be seen doing more with his hands than reaching for his keys. Perhaps he repeatedly pokes the "down" button or jiggles his pocket change. Whatever details you decide to show or withhold, evaluate how those decisions affect the scene's purpose and pace.

There are two reasons for planting a clue early. One is that readers are less likely to realize its significance at the time. The other is to avoid making its later discovery seem too convenient.

Whereas a twist of fate might set in motion a situation at the start of a story—as with a stranger's picking up the wrong briefcase —a coincidence should not be used later to get a character out of an awkward situation. Solutions should come from the insight of your main character.

What's more, unless a paranormal element is present from the start, never, for heaven's sake, have a solution materialize through divine intervention.

REPETITION

Assuming you have no *story* purpose for dramatizing Mr. B's elevator scene, how many lines can you slice from his leaving-the-office extravaganza on page 142? Here's one version to survive a severe edit:

> Wally Bloat hung up, grabbed his coat and briefcase, and called goodnight to his secretary. When he stepped off the elevator at the underground garage. . . .

Other versions are possible, of course. The object of editing is not shorter but sharper. How sharp is this next passage from a published short story?

> She was brutally murdered, her face and neck stabbed ten times with a butcher knife.

Ouch. Ten body piercings is sharp indeed. Umm, wait a moment—a second look reveals that the words "brutally murdered" provide a summary of the more specific, graphic fact. Redundant. Not so sharp after all. However, in this case repetition might be forgiven because it reinforces a dramatic effect, and it is brief enough not to annoy.

Not so for the following redundancies. They come from an otherwise well-written manuscript, though I changed the details:

> When the detective told us how the mine owner had been murdered, Evan and I exchanged glances, recalling that the brother of the trapped mineworker vowed to find and kill the owner. Evan turned to the detective and said, "I didn't take this seriously at the time because it was right after the accident, but the brother of one of the miners threatened to kill the owner."

Repeating information adds nothing but extra words. Which repetitions above should be cut? Keep the dramatic action *(exchanged glances)* and the dialogue *("the brother . . . threatened")*. Dump the exposition that explains why they exchanged glances *(recalling that the brother . . . vowed)*. The glances are effective; the *why* is evident from the context.

When the original scene occurs recently enough for readers to recall it, a more efficient way of referring to old news is to paraphrase it:

> Evan and I exchanged glances. Then he told the detective about the brother's threat to kill the mine owner.
> "I didn't take it seriously at the time because it was right after the accident."

However, when the original dramatization occurs so early that readers are unlikely to remember its details, an effective technique is to have the paraphrase remind us of the *setting* in which the event occurred:

> Evan and I exchanged glances, remembering our run-in at the funeral parlor with the brother of the trapped mineworker. Evan told the detective about the brother's threat to. . . .

Looking at old events in a new way is itself new information. Repeating the same information is not.

PARAPHRASE

The most succinct paraphrase I've ever seen occurs in *Killer.app* by Barbara D'Amato. Detective Jesus Delgado is asked to tell the police superintendent about events that readers already witnessed in earlier scenes. D'Amato writes:

> Rendell said, "Tell the superintendent."
> Jesus told.
> When Jesus had finished with the details. . . . "   [pp. 179–80]

D'Amato does not subject her readers to a recap of familiar information. Instead, she focuses on the superintendent's subsequent reaction to it—a reaction that takes the investigation forward in a new direction.

ONCE MORE WITH FEELING

When a scene you've written call for more than a trim—it needs a full buzzcut—you may find it hard to know what to keep and what to sweep out the door. Keep action that creates emotion in the reader. And except where the plot says otherwise, have the triggering event precede, not follow, your character's reaction to it. Cause first, then effect. Stay in sequence.

The next example evokes two contrasting feelings: empathy for a protagonist shocked by finding her first dead body, and amusement over the police officer's behavior. Humor keeps the pathos from turning into bathos in this scene from *An Eye for Murder* by Libby Fischer Hellmann:

> When the cops arrived, I was on the porch steps taking big gulps of fresh air. One of the cops was young, with a leather jacket, crisp uniform shirt, and a pencil-thin mustache that looked pasted on. His partner, older and more rumpled, wore an expression that said he'd seen it all.

Ellie Foreman, the protagonist, is then asked a few questions:

> The younger cop dug out a cell phone and started tapping in numbers.
>
> The older cop grabbed it away from his partner. "Don't waste your minutes." He yanked his thumb toward the house. "Use hers. She won't be needing it."
>
> The younger cop slipped his phone into a pocket and headed inside.
>
> "Is she. . . ?" I asked shakily.
>
> The older cop, whose shield read Mahoney, nodded.
>
> I gripped a stake on the porch railing. "But I was just with her an hour ago, and she was fine. What happened?"
>
> Interest flickered on Mahoney's face. "You were here earlier?"
>
> "I left around three."
>
> "Powers. Get back out here." The younger cop reappeared. "Why don't you tell us about it?"
>
> Midway through my first sentence, the older cop raised a hand, cutting me off. "Notes, Powers. You gotta take notes."
>
> [pp. 29–30]

At this point, paraphrasing begins:

> . . . He wrote furiously as I told them how I'd come down to Rogers Park at Mrs. Fleishman's request. How we went through Ben Sinclair's things. How she persuaded me to take the boxes and how, when I came back, she was on the floor.

Repeating Ellie's actual dialogue would capture all her words, but the reader already experienced the earlier events she now paraphrases. A verbatim playback would be insufferably repetitive. Paraphrase minimizes, summarizes, and reminds without repeating.

The techniques shown in the above scene serve multiple purposes by balancing dramatization with paraphrase and leavening Ellie's shock and grief with the humor provided by the older cop.

DIGRESSION AND DISCOURSE

Patricia Highsmith admits to occasionally digressing. She describes it in *Plotting and Writing Suspense Fiction* as "writing elaborately about small matters." But by stepping back and looking at the whole, she was able to see when a book of hers was no longer in proportion.[40]

Do lots of research; use little of it.

Isabel Zuber, author of the historical novel *Salt,* explains what throws a story off balance:

> An author has learned so much in the search for information on a particular topic, often about how to do or make something, that an obsession sets in and all that has been collected gets included instead of parts being integrated into the plot, or only summarized or suggested. . . . [T]he action of a story can easily slow to a crawl.[41]

Suppose you decide to do away with a certain Mr. Throckmorton. Your weapon of choice is poison. You spend weeks researching every potent possibility before deciding which one the killer shall stir into Mr. T.'s tea. How do you include all that fascinating information?

You don't.

As a fiction writer you are primarily an entertainer, and that supersedes a desire to educate, persuade, or show off. If you supply more information than your story needs, you interfere with its dramatic flow. Whether you call it digressing, obsessing, or going off on a tangent, it's self-indulgent—which is rarely entertaining to others.

If a digression offers data that readers need for understanding some technical aspect of your story, you have options for presenting it without knocking the story off balance. One is to slice, dice, and splice the essentials in with the dramatic action a little at a time.

EXPERT TESTIMONY

Another alternative is to invent a character whom the protagonist contacts for specialized information, someone who functions as a subject matter expert (what tech writers call an SME). Beware of the expert who so loves discoursing on his favorite topic that he's only too happy to help. The result is not a dialogue, it's a lecture, slow death for sure.

Talk designed to educate runs the risk of talking down to readers or going over their heads. It can take on a moral tone, boring some, offending others. Besides, lecturing lacks action. What some writers think of as action is more like mannerism or gesture, and is no closer to real action than the taking-another-bite and having-another-sip busyness that goes on in poorly conceived restaurant scenes—themselves thinly disguised data dumps.

> "Thou shall not fall in love with thine own words."
>
> Ellen M. Kozak,
> literary arts attorney
> and author [42]

I've seen manuscripts in which the main character's role is reduced to that of passive listener ("Do go on"), mere questioner ("What happens after that?"), and helpful summarizer ("I see, so what you're saying is Colonel Mustard couldn't possibly have been in the conservatory with a knife").

Action, which is conflict or anticipated conflict (tension), comes from resistance and opposition. Dialogue with a cooperative expert offers little opportunity for conflict to raise its argumentative little head. Consider giving your protagonist one more hurdle to overcome by making your expert less obliging. Turn the scene into a verbal fencing match, and include essential bits of information with each thrust and parry.

What if the two characters already have a feud going about something else? Goody! That means more conflict. Use shorter sentences, faster dialogue. (See CLUE #16 for more about dialogue.)

TAKE SHORTCUTS

In her short story "Do Wah Diddy Die Already," Pauline Baird Jones tells us about a young woman, newly hired at a bed and breakfast. She replaces Louise, under whose tenure—well, you can guess what happened from the context. Here is one tightly packed paragraph so effectively presented that from it we learn, indirectly, a great deal of information:

> [The B&B] had been open for three months now and, con-
> trary to [a character's] expectations, no one had died—not even
> of food poisoning. That was probably because Luci had hired a
> new cook-cum-housekeeper-cum-au pair, though she still
> missed Louise. Saffron talked. *A lot.* Of course, she hadn't
> killed anyone either, and Luci's three-year old adored her—so
> much so, she wanted to have multi-colored hair, too.

Indirectly we learn the young woman's name, Saffron, and her multiple roles. We learn that her cooking is safe (so far), that she's talkative, and that she's adored by a child. And we learn the color of her hair without being told of it directly. The author's indirect method of getting information across is both efficient and effective. Study her technique.

If you don't have an ear for condensing your writing and ridding it of excess, read more well-written books and analyze how skilled writers create their effects. Or have an editor show you how to tighten and sharpen your work—a process by which you develop a keen eye and ear of your own and learn to *self*-edit more effectively.

> "Never miss a good chance to shut up."
>
> Will Rogers

MAKE ASSUMPTIONS

Also teach yourself to listen for what's *not* there when you eavesdrop; that is, what people omit from their dialogue because they assume, rightly or wrongly, that they know what others are about to say and charge ahead without giving them a chance to say it.

Conversational shortcuts help you construct dialogue that leaps from one speaker's assumptions to another's, leaving out the easily understood connections. Once you become comfortable taking shortcuts from A to C, you can avoid passing B and collecting 200 extra words.

In *One for the Money*, Janet Evanovich's first Stephanie Plum mystery, the following exchange offers a good example of shortcuts based on as-sumptions. Both Stephanie and her mother assume, correctly, that each knows what the other is thinking. Undoubtedly, similar conversations have occurred between these two before:

> "I hear Loretta Buzick's boy is separated from his wife," my
> mother said. "You remember him? Ronald Buzick?"

I knew where she was heading, and I didn't want to go there. "I'm not going out with Ronald Buzick," I told her. "Don't even think about it."

"So what's wrong with Ronald Buzick?"   [p. 9]

As rapidly as this passage moves, it would speed up even more without the line: "I knew where she was heading, and I didn't want to go there." But I relish that line because it expresses a principle I'd like you to remember when you self-edit:

Readers know where I'm heading and don't need to go there.

I nominate these words as the mantra for writers who like to write too much.

FIND & FIX CLUE #14: SLOW DEATH

- List your purpose for every scene and confirm that each achieves the purpose you intend it to.
- Omit or condense transitions and routines that are familiar to the average reader—except where drawing out a transition achieves an intended benefit, such as slowing the pace.
- Get rid of unnecessary repetition.
- Decide what material is better presented via paraphrase.
- Sharpen, tighten, and delete overwriting, whether that means killing words, sentences, paragraphs, whole scenes, or characters.
- Never lecture; remember that the industry's primary interest in publishing category or genre fiction is to make money through entertainment.
- Consider getting a pro to show you how to sharpen and tighten your writing.
- End a scene once it serves its purpose—which requires defining its purpose (or purposes) before you write it.

D.O.A.

CLUE #15: BURIED AGENDA

Mention the word "motive" and people think of the whydunit behind the whodunit. Yet motivation goes far beyond a villain's reason for performing villainous acts. The good guy, especially in genre fiction, has to show just as much motivation, even if that springs from a wish for life to return to normal. But life is always eventful in fiction, and those events increase everyone's motivation. Often missing is a clear, overt expression of what each major character wants.

> "Well, whoever did this, he won't get away with it," Destin vowed. "I plan to look into his murder starting tomorrow. I need to clear my name. And most of all, I owe it to George." [p. 31]

Congratulations to N. L. Williams for making sure readers know what Destin wants, and why, in *A Matter of Destiny,* a first novel.

Praise to Radine Trees Nehring, too, for having Carrie tell us what she wants, and why, in *A Wedding to Die For,* third of five mysteries (so far):

> "Henry wants to go to the court house but I never had a real wedding, and, and . . ." She heard her voice saying the words, rushing through them: "And I'd like a minister, a dress, and flowers, and a cake, and friends, and a Christmas wedding, and all of it. . . ." [p. 17]

In a well-developed novel, as in life, every character wants something (a goal), has a reason for wanting it (a motive), and harbors some notion, realistic or not, of how to get it (a strategy). In short, everyone has an agenda.

Compared with the life-and-death issues that drive the protagonist and antagonist in a novel of suspense, the agendas of secondary characters are of little importance. *But not to them.* The writer who treats characters as if they have no wants of their own robs their actions of purpose and direction.

I'm not talking about internal goals (not yet, anyway) but about external circumstances that your characters are consciously motivated to change or set right again.

When readers are made aware of a consciously pursued agenda, we are able to root for the protagonist's every step forward, grow anxious over each new setback, and anticipate the potential for conflict. Anticipation creates tension, builds suspense, and maintains our addiction to adrenalin, all of which keeps us turning pages.

Gary Provost's writings point out that once writers understand the concept of character goals and the value of letting readers in on them as soon as possible, "it's surprising how easily some boring scenes can be made compelling."[43]

If you bury the agendas of your characters you weaken the potential within every role for obstructing the agenda of another character. Obstructions are good; they spread conflict and incite rebellion.

All genre fiction is based on conflict. Without an agenda in play there is no conflict, no tension. Without conflict there is neither progress nor setback; consequently, no *scene.* A manuscript without a sequence of goal-obstacle-outcome scenes does not a novel make.

EXPLICIT AGENDAS

You may have heard that novels of suspense should have conflict on every page. Does that mean you are expected to stage an argument, fist fight, or car chase on every page? Certainly not. Think instead of putting *tension* on every page. Tension comes from the anticipation of conflict.

At the high-powered end of the conflict continuum are the high-stakes issues that pit your primary characters against each other and drive your main plot. At the low end of the conflict continuum are any issues, irritations, or doubts that worry your characters and make readers feel some degree of anxiety.

At every point in between, tension idles, ready to accelerate and shift into high gear. The ever-present potential for conflict produces continuous anxiety and tension. For readers to feel the tension, writers need to keep readers aware of competing wants, motives, and strategies.

Make your characters' agendas known by what they do and say, and by what others say about them. Here's how Lonnie Cruse achieves that in the opening scene to *Murder in Metropolis,* her first full-length mystery novel:

> Sheriff Joe Dalton plunked his boots on top of his desk, leaned back in the protesting chair, snapped open the newspaper, and reached for his coffee.
>
> Before he could down a swig, the intercom buzzed, forcing him to wade under a stack of files and push a button.
>
> "Yes, George?"
>
> "We've got a situation outside on Market Street, Sheriff. Guess you'll have to handle it," the elderly dispatcher informed him. "Morning shift hasn't arrived yet, and the night deputies are still at that big accident scene over on Highway 145."
>
> "Would the situation outside be Big Ed Simmons?"
>
> "Yes sir, drunk as they come and singing fair to wake the dead."
>
> "Where is he? On the courthouse steps again?"
>
> "Nope, this time he's on the steps at Lipinski's Appliances. Miz Lipinski says if we don't shut him up, she will, with that old pistol her husband kept in the store. Though what an eighty-year-old woman with crippling arthritis is doing with. . . ."
>
> "I'll get right on it, George. We don't need Mrs. Lipinski shooting up Market Street at day break."   [pp. 1–2]

How many individual agendas can you find in this opening scene? The sheriff's newspaper, coffee, and boots on the desk are clues to his immediate goal, which takes precedence over the piles of files on his desk. But as soon as he learns of a "situation," his priorities shift, and his long-range goal of serving the public good reasserts itself at the top of his to-do list.

The agenda of the elderly dispatcher, George, is to perform his job by promptly handing off every new assignment to the work detail next in line.

Based on what George and the sheriff say about Mrs. Lipinski, we understand her goal is to get the drunk away from her store. An old pistol affords a clear and present strategy. Her motivation? The sheriff's action indicates we'll learn it soon enough.

From what is said about Big Ed Simmons, although we don't know his motivation for doing what he does, we're sure we'll soon learn that, too.

All told, Cruse's opening scene is brimming with explicit, overt actions and implicit possibilities. The immediate agendas of four characters set us up to anticipate several collisions ahead.

WHAT'S AT STAKE?

You may be thinking, "How do I maintain suspense if I let readers know what every character is thinking and planning?" The more useful answer comes from asking yourself a different question: "What part of each character's agenda must I conceal for the time being?"

Suspense is tension magnified. It needs the expectation of something about to happen. For readers to feel anxiety, tension, suspense, or anticipation, we need information, not its absence. If we're unaware of the relentless descent of a razor-sharp pendulum, we have no reason to feel anxiety for the condemned man strapped directly beneath it.[44]

Anxiety increases in relation to our awareness of how improbable escape seems, how drawn out the approaching danger is, and how high the stakes are. Suspense comes not from ignorance but from knowledge: from the certainty that something—usually bad—is about to happen.

"When anticipation ends, the story is over."

"Suspense," in
Mystery Writer's
Handbook, 1956 [45]

To illustrate the value of letting readers in on all or part of a character's agenda, imagine this scenario. Time and place: early one morning on a city street. Action: a young woman is searching for a place to park. We'll call her . . . oh, I dunno . . . Ms. Parker. We watch her battered Ford Pinto starting to circle the area for the third time. Do we care? Not really. Not until the writer lets us know she will be fired if she's late to work again.

By learning what she has at stake, we share some of her anxiety and begin to care about her—a little.

For us to care a little more, we have to know what losing her job means to *her.* So the writer revises the scene and discloses Ms. Parker's fervent desire to remain independent of her father, who keeps badgering her to stop all this career nonsense and come home to the farm in Cornville.

Should the writer choose to develop this scenario further, we learn Ms. Parker's long-range goals: that the job in jeopardy is with a publishing house *(no kidding!)* and she's in line for a promotion to acquisitions editor *(how about that?).* We discover her ambition is to nurture new writers *(about time someone did),* and her specialty is the erotic romance *(is the sound I hear that of ears perking up?).*

Knowing what a character has at stake makes a difference, doesn't it? Now we're actually rooting for her to park that Pinto, pronto.

TANGIBLE AND EXPLICIT

See if your manuscript makes the goals of your characters tangible and their agendas as explicit as your plot allows. Give the reader an emotional stake in your characters' wins and losses by revealing what penalties they face if their strategies fail. Most strategies *should* fail, because setbacks let you raise the stakes, escalate your characters' desperation, and intensify their motivation to take greater risks.

Perhaps one of Ms. Parker's initial strategies is to set her alarm an hour earlier. Only when that fails to resolve her problem does she become ready for a bigger step, such as changing publishing houses. Or paying higher rent to live closer to work. Maybe she eventually gives up her goal and returns to the farm, where she produces corn, not porn. [46]

You don't need to pursue every agenda to its completion. Minor characters seldom think beyond their immediate objectives. A brief mention of the fate of a secondary character is sufficient to put closure on that role—which you'll end once that role serves your purpose.

What might that purpose be? To create obstacles, of course. To complicate and frustrate the goals of the major characters. The more often you put one agenda in direct opposition to another, the higher your story's conflict quotient. Your antagonist's goal may be to upset the status quo. *Your* goal is to keep readers emotionally involved by putting tension on every page.

REMEMBER THE ANTAGONIST

For a primary character, the stakes must be considerably higher than getting fired. And in suspense fiction, losing or winning should be of life and death magnitude. That's why most mysteries are murder mysteries. (Though contested parking spots have also led drivers to kill each other.)

The novels I see do a fairly good job of revealing the agendas of their primary characters, though some mistakenly treat the antagonist as a minor character. The antagonist's goals are as important as the protagonist's—often more so, for without the strong desire that causes trouble for your hero or heroine, there is nothing to react against and become heroic about.

How do you make the antagonist's agenda known? Some writers reveal it in early scenes that show him justifying his behavior *as he sees it.* Writers who don't reveal an antagonist's thoughts until the climax use other means to make readers aware of his agenda early. Ever wonder why so many thrillers involve anonymous threats left on answering machines, scrawled in blood at a crime scene, or delivered with flowers?

As for the protagonist's agenda, if she is a professional crime-fighter her motivation is understood as part of her job description. Even so . . . .

RAISE THE STAKES

Keep raising the stakes to increase your protagonist's motivation—no matter what your genre. How? Add more personal ingredients. Keep her off balance. Create complications that make her struggle with her emotions. Force her to make decisions that risk compromising her values. Have her wrestle with her inner impulses while also dealing with external challenges.

In *How to Write Romances,* Phyllis Taylor Pianka says to select players who complement and contrast with each other. "That contrast must be strong enough to act as a catalyst for conflict, yet the characters must be similar enough in their personalities to be irrevocably drawn to each other despite their differences." [p. 26]

If your protagonist is an ordinary Jo, not a crime-solving pro, her motivation must be extra convincing. You might strengthen her values by giving her, for instance, a firm commitment to justice or world peace—except that such ideals are too broad and generalized to produce victory by the penultimate chapter.

A winnable goal is one that's *specific* and *measurable*—say, finding the ski-masked sniper who shot Aunt Amelia as she led Sunday's demonstration for world peace in front of the war memorial. Endow your character with certain traits: a streak of stubbornness here, an independent lifestyle there, here a quirk, there a quirk.

Personality traits are preconditions for your protagonist to take ever-increasing risks, but traits alone won't convince an editor that a character who is not a cop would choose to pursue a murderer.

How do you create that kind of motivation? By raising the stakes. It's an element missing from a number of first-time submissions. Check to see where and how your manuscript:

- emphasizes *l'ingrédient personel:* the conviction that your protagonist, or someone she cares about, will be grievously harmed
  if someone or something isn't stopped before a certain time;
- establishes her initial reluctance to get involved;
- shows her exhausting all logical alternatives, such as trying but
  failing to convince others to take her suspicions seriously;
- creates new actions that keep ratcheting up her desperation.

Wasn't it the need for this degree of compelling motivation that put so many personal friends and family members of TV's Jessica Fletcher in mortal danger once a week?

GO SCHIZO

The goals of minor players may be insignificant compared to the life-and-death issues of the primary players, but don't let those goals be invisible. Determine how each member of your cast behaves when his desires are thwarted. Does he become more subtle and cunning? Or angry and vindictive? Examine the profiles or bios you developed for your key characters and identify the following three factors for each:

- what the individual wants—*specifically;*
- how far the character is willing to go to get it; and
- what it takes for him to change priorities and adapt his strategy.

To verify that your manuscript reflects all three for every character, color-code each of their scripts. Start with the antagonist and highlight his words and actions from beginning to end as you live his role and only his role. Repeat the process with your protagonist. Take her role to its end before starting on the neglected agendas of your secondary characters.

As you trace one complete script at a time, want what each character wants and is desperate to get from someone else. Go beyond knowing someone's motivation to *feeling* it, both the all-consuming compulsions and the momentary whims. Take on each cast member's beliefs, attitudes, incentives, and insecurities as if they were your own. Let each character's feelings guide you as you milk every role for its adversarial potential.

In strengthening the script of each character one at a time, also revise the words of the other party to the same confrontation. Later, when you take on the role of that other party, revise again. Make all words and actions sharper and more representative of each character's true feelings.

If you intend someone's words or actions to mislead, present the false agenda with the same degree of clarity and conviction.

Naturally, you want everyone's actions to serve the goals of your story. But characters cannot exist solely for your convenience. They need to behave as if advancing their own agendas. Keep tightening and sharpening their words and actions as if your self-interest were at stake. It is.

INTERNAL CONFLICT

Conflict in a genre novel must be externalized so readers can see the characters acting out their opposition to each other. Whereas early pulp fiction may have taken conflict no further than physical encounters, today's editors also expect a second, more profound form of conflict: internal.

Character development comes from the struggle within. If your protagonist is to work through a dilemma and emerge a better person, you need to show her confronting her internal demons in addition to face-to-face confrontations with her antagonist.

A dilemma is not simply a problem; it's a choice that causes trouble no matter which path is taken. The dilemma's motto is, "You can't have it both ways, and you can't have either without some negative consequence."

In *Relative Danger* by June Shaw, Cealie wants it both ways:

> Gil drove me to the condo. He walked me to the door and stood, gazing at me. "Should I come in?" The overhead light forced a glitter from silver strands in his hair. Gil's eyes looked like new charcoal. A murmur came from deep in his throat.
>
> I touched that area of his neck. My hands stroked his familiar skin. This man was a wonderful lover. Such fun to be with. Did I want to renew our relationship?
>
> I ordered up a vision of mounds of dirty dishes. Hampers of clothes to wash, me waiting around for repairmen. Being stuck in one house. . . .
>
> I moved my hands off him. I adored this man. But now I needed freedom. Self-discovery. "Not tonight," I said.
>
> Then why didn't I move back? Step away from him. I clasped him within my arms. "See you, mmm, later," I said.
>
> Gil backed me through the doorway. "Yes, see you."
>
> "Ummm."   [pp. 299-300]

Fiction's most consistently conflicted hero is Parnell Hall's luckless Stanley Hastings. His job is to sign up accident victims for an ambulance-chasing attorney—a job that ensures many close encounters of the unsavory kind. But Stanley is a coward. In *Murder,* the second of more than a dozen novels featuring this unlikely hero, Stanley realizes who the killer is.

Does cowardice cause our hero inner turmoil and interfere with his work? You bet it does. He tells himself:

> You ought to walk right up to him and tell him you know he's slime and a murderer. Look him in the eye and say, "I know you popped Darryl Jackson."
>
> As I envisioned myself doing this, I got so paranoid I started shaking all over. I had to pull the car over to the side and stop.
>
> Jesus Christ. If just the *thought* of doing it does this to me, what would *doing* it be like?
>
> Not that bad, I told myself. He couldn't touch you in a crowded bar. There's nothing he could do. You'd be perfectly safe.
>
> Yeah, sure. Safe. I'd be safe.
>
> But so what? What did it matter?
>
> The question was academic, anyway.
>
> 'Cause I was a bloody fucking coward, and I wasn't going to do it.   [pp. 183–84]

Does Stanley do it? We know he manages to solve crimes in spite of himself . . . but how?

INTERNALIZING OPPOSITION

Three-time award-winner Vicki Hinze opens her second romantic suspense novel, *Duplicity,* with an external conflict that transforms itself into an internal one within the first few pages. Captain Tracy Keener, a staff judge advocate in the Air Force, learns from her colonel that she's been assigned to defend a captain charged with abandoning his men to die. Hinze does not hide Tracy's motivation or internal conflict:

> . . . Only a sadist would be elated at hearing they'd been assigned to defend Adam Burke. . . .
>
> She had to get out of this assignment. That, or kiss off her career.   [pp. 1–3]

With the same clarity, Hinze reinforces Tracy's position by having the colonel reveal the agenda of the military:

> . . . "The Burke case has tempers running hot and hard up the chain of command and the local media is nearly out of control. Between the two of them, they're nailing our asses to the proverbial wall."
>
> Hope flared in Tracy. If he could see that, then surely he would see reason and assign someone else to the case. "I'm up for major, sir," Tracy interjected. . . .
>
> . . . This was her fifth year in the Air Force. Her first and . . . last shot at selection. If not selected, she'd promptly be issued an invitation to practice law elsewhere, outside of the military.
>
> This was not a pleasing prospect to an officer bent on making the military a career.   [pp. 4–5]

Colonel Jackson adds another of the military's motives: ensuring the accused receives the defense he's entitled to. Tracy agrees but presses on:

> ". . . can't an attorney who already has Career Status defend him? If I lose this case—and we both know I will lose this case . . . I'll be passed over for promotion and for Career Status. . . . If that happens, my military career abruptly ends."   [p. 5]

When Colonel Jackson adds yet another motive—that Tracy is the military's asset with the media—she begins to grasp the complex, contradictory nature of her position. A paperweight symbolizes that complexity:

> . . . She stared at the eagle paperweight, at the dark shadows between the glints of light reflecting off it. As much as she hated admitting it, Jackson and Nestler's rationale made sense. As a senior officer in the same situation, she'd use whatever assets she found available to defuse the situation. Could she fault them for doing what in their position she would do herself?   [pp. 7–8]

Once Tracy understands this, she *internalizes the motivation of her adversary.* Conflict shifts from the opposing agendas of two people to one person's inner struggle between her own loyalties, suddenly incompatible:

> . . . Burke was guilty. Everyone knew it. And while she might be media-attractive, she wouldn't get him off. She didn't want to get him off. But even F. Lee Bailey couldn't get Burke off, or come out of this case unscathed.
>
> . . . She had to handle the case and give Burke her best. Not so much for him, but because it was right. When this was over, she had to be able to look in the mirror and feel comfortable with what she'd done and the way she'd handled the case, and herself. [p. 8]

Hinze's technique deepens the conflict from an external force over which Tracy has no control to an internal struggle that forces her to choose between her principles and her career desires. Demonizing an external power is easy; resolving a dilemma when the power rests in one's own hands is agonizing. In this, Hinze expertly continues raising the stakes.

We haven't even touched upon the conflicts that play out between Tracy and Adam Burke, the man she's required to defend, already despises, but has not yet met in person.

IMPROBABLE CAUSE

Because every character in every work of fiction wants something and no two want precisely the same thing at the same time, *all* interactions—including those between friends and especially those among family members—are ripe for conflict.

Often, negative wants can be expressed more powerfully than positive wants. Here are the opening lines to *Long After Midnight* by best-selling author Iris Johansen:

> "I can't do it." Kate's hand tightened on her father's with desperation. "I don't want to even talk about it. Do you understand? Don't ask me, dammit."

We then learn that Kate's terminally ill father wants her to end his life.

Review each of your own scenes to see that it pushes the agenda of at least one character, raises at least one hurdle to overcome, and ends with some change in the situation that existed when the scene began.

That change might cause a new intermediate objective to emerge, and with it a shift in strategy. Although things might improve a little for your character, in most scenes make sure things get worse—a lot worse—before they get better. If nothing changes, examine your reason for maintaining the status quo.

Progression requires change of some kind.

Beware the motiveless character—one who floats through a novel causing no conflict, getting in no one's way. Symptoms: weak dialogue, aimless action. Probable cause: no agenda. The character exists for your convenience only, without wants or needs of his own.

Test your writing skills through continued revision. If you cannot embrace the desires and sense of purpose of each character, you'll know it's not the agenda that needs corrective surgery, it's the character.

FIND & FIX CLUE #15: BURIED AGENDA

- Maximize your story's potential for tension by placing characters with opposing agendas in encounters with each other.
- Verify that for each scene, readers have been made aware of the goal of at least one character as early as possible, through action, dialogue, or a little narrative.
- Review each scene to see if it presents an obstacle to thwart the main character's goal.
- Identify where and how you keep raising the stakes and increasing your characters' desperation to justify their taking greater risks.
- Revise each script as if you were playing the role of each character, in turn, and want what each wants and for the same reason.
- Confirm that your story creates anticipation and tension on every page.
- See what internal conflicts your protagonist has that force difficult choices, and whether he or she grows as a result.

D.O.A.

CLUE #16: DYING DIALOGUE

Dialogue in genre fiction is not whatever a couple of characters happen to say to each other. That's conversation, chit chat. An exchange that offers no resistance, no characterization, and no meaningful interaction to move the story forward is not dialogue. Neither is a lecture, discussion, or data dump.

Dialogue is a form of action, a potent technique for exposing conflict and revealing character. It is the mightiest power tool on your workbench for making characters come alive. Instead of your stepping in like an overbearing parent to tell us *about* your characters, write dialogue that shows them expressing their own personalities, feelings, and attitudes.

In a manuscript, passages of dialogue look different enough from other narrative forms that a busy screener-outer can skim a few pages and form a quick opinion of your skills based on dialogue alone. If you write snappy, adversarial, and oblique exchanges (more on that soon), the screener reads on. If the dialogue sounds dead or dying, the screener has no reason to postpone the funeral. The submission is buried, unceremoniously.

Sadly, much of what passes for dialogue in the typical submission is little more than chit chat and data dumps. Just because you put quotation marks around exposition doesn't make it dialogue. Effective dialogue is purposeful—the means by which characters reveal themselves as they strive to realize their objectives, act on their agendas, and provoke reactions from others.

To effectively edit your characters' scripts, first unearth their agendas (see CLUE #15). Once their wants and motives are paramount in your mind and theirs, let *them* go at it. But don't let a word pass their lips without your having a purpose for including it. Information is a byproduct of dialogue, not its purpose. Its purpose is characterization, relationships, emotion, story.

To give your submission a fair chance of surviving its quickest screen test, raise your dialogue's conflict quotient.

163

CONFLICT IN RELATIONSHIPS

The relationships ripest for conflict are family relationships, which you can dramatize most effectively through dialogue. Stephen D. Rogers does this extremely well in this opening to his short story "Bodyshop Blues."

Every time I shut my car door, a small pile of debris was deposited on the ground.

"Rust." My brother shook his head. "What you have here is your basic rust. Seems to be a pretty advanced condition."

"I know it's rust. I came to you to ask what I could do about it." My brother was second-shift supervisor at Looking Good Auto Detailing. I'd never come to him for advice. About anything.

He tapped my door with his index finger, a loose semi-circle around the hole. Then he did it again. "Rust."

I resisted the urge to hit him. "So, if you were in my shoes, what would you do?"

He stood, wiping his hand on a rag that hung from his belt. "I wouldn't get rust in the first place. You have to take care of a vehicle, wash it and wax. Touch up the dings and the scratches before rust has a chance to take hold."

"Okay, I'm lazy and I don't deserve to have a car that looks like new. How do I keep this one from continuing to fall apart?"

"Mom said you called last week."

Apparently he wasn't interested in making a long story short. "I try to keep in touch."

He sniffed. "I must talk to her every other day."

"Where do you find time to buff your car?"

My brother pointed his rust-finding finger at me. "Attitude. You need to lose the attitude."

I tried to appear contrite. "What about the rust?"

"Let me tell you something. Rust is like cancer. Once the rot gets into the metal, it just spreads like wildfire."

"So . . . what? Is there some chemotherapy carwash I can drive through once a week until the rust goes into remission?"

He stepped past me and started walking toward his tool chest. "You'd like that, wouldn't you? Nice and simple."

"Actually I'd prefer something I could spray on just once. Then maybe duct-tape the hole. I need to get the car inspected next month."

My brother slid open the top drawer to retrieve something that he hid from my view. He probably had some chemical he could paint on the exposed metal to stop the process but not until he collected his pound of flesh.

He turned to face me. "Mom was right about you."

Three lines suggest that the brother's issues center on Mom. Though the hostility is primarily one-sided, that's enough to make this pointed dialogue leak conflict like a battery leaks acid.

Whatever your characters' relationships, you can increase the tension in your dialogue with the same techniques Rogers uses: innuendo, unmet expectation, unanswered questions, changes of subject, suppressed resistance, and assumptions about the other person's motives.

SOWING DISSENSION

Any amiable question-and-answer sequence can be given an adversarial flavor by having characters interrupt each other, change the subject, answer a question with a question, and give an unexpected response. Even good-natured teasing can cause tension, as demonstrated in the scene from *Snipe Hunt* by Sarah Shaber. (It's excerpted in CLUE #3.)

Kill the words "yes," "okay," and "I agree," even when all is friendly. The sound of any affirmative breeds a congenial, agreeable tone that takes the steam out of most encounters.

Genre fiction is not a meeting place for a mutual admiration society. Whenever possible, create friction and suspicion among your characters. Invent misunderstanding. Facilitate misinterpretation. Add distraction. Use snappy dialogue. All of the above.

Try to avoid direct replies to questions, because they make dialogue *symmetrical,* a pattern that itself suggests cooperation. When symmetry continues too long, the busy screener reaches for another cup of caffeine.

Symmetry in humor is an exception. Humor is often based on conflict. Enjoy the symmetry of the following exchange from *Silent Scream,* a work-in-progress by James Huskins. The dialogue takes place in a limo, and the relationship between the two men becomes clear from the context:

"I want to talk to you about my murder."

"Your murder, sir?"

"Yes."

"I see. Who is going to murder you?"

"No idea."

"When are you planning to be murdered, sir?"

"Anytime in the next few weeks, I s'pose."

"Do you . . . how will you be murdered?"

"Gad only knows!"

"I see. How may I assist in your murder, sir?"

"What an uncouth way to put it, Dunkle. Don't like driving for me?"

"Sorry sir. Of course I meant to say, how may I assist you in *preventing* your murder."

The structure of this passage is symmetrical in that every question receives a matching response. Nonetheless, tension builds because the responses fail to provide the information Dunkle and the reader want.

The difference in the men's social station adds another layer of tension, since the chauffeur is in no position to insist that his employer quit the game play and spill the story.

ASYMMETRICAL DIALOGUE

Conflict more often finds expression through an *asymmetrical* structure, in which questions are sidestepped and responses are unexpected.

Betsy had to restrain herself from gulping and cowering as he advanced on her. Ugh. . . . Betsy lifted her chin. "You must be Lieutenant Fairfax."

"And you must be Betsy."

What impudence.   [p. 29]

The lieutenant addresses Betsy, a married woman, by her first name instead of mirroring her formal use of his title. His informality shows disrespect, especially for the period in which this novel is set, the American Revolution. This passage is from *The Blacksmith's Daughter,* the second in a series of historical novels by Suzanne Adair—whose first book received a literary award from the Florida Historical Society.

My next example of asymmetry comes from *The Bodyguard and The Show Dog,* the second romantic mystery by Christy Tillery French in her Bodyguard series. Natasha's lover, Striker, discovers that she dumped a bag of dog poop on the front porch of an abuser of animals, who then chased her with a loaded rifle:

> Striker stepped toward her. "So you risk your life playing passive-aggressive with this guy?"
>
> "Well, actually, I didn't think he was home and I for sure didn't know he had a rifle."
>
> He studied her for a moment. His eyes widened with awareness. "How many times have you done this?"
>
> She shrugged. "I don't know. A couple."
>
> "A couple? What the hell is wrong with you?"
>
> "Hey, it's the least I can do."
>
> "So what's next? Rolling his lawn with toilet paper?"
>
> "Gee, I hadn't thought of that."   [p. 80]

This passage shows two kinds of asymmetry. Natasha's lines do not match Striker's in that she does not give direct answers to his questions, though she appears to. Second, their emotional levels do not match. His language shows increasing frustration, whereas Natasha acknowledges her actions while remaining nonchalant, shrugging and prefacing her responses with "Actually," "Hey," and "Gee." We don't need to be told that Striker's voice is raised in anger, because the dialogue itself lets us hear it pitched louder, stronger.

Listen again, and you'll hear the difference in volume, too.

Asymmetrical dialogue is also called *indirect* or *oblique,* and a subset of oblique is *implied* dialogue, in which the listener interprets the meaning behind the other's words or presumes to know where the speaker is taking the discussion. The listener then responds to the implied meaning—not to the actual statement—quickly moving the dialogue forward.

Hal Glatzer uses implied dialogue in his second mystery in the Katy Green series, *A Fugue in Hell's Kitchen,* set in 1939 in the section of New York City known by that name. Violinist Katy Green is investigating the death of the head of a classical music conservatory. She asks a reporter if he'd covered the original story months earlier, and he replies:

> ". . . Yeah. I wrote about that. Good local angle, too: she died in the house she was born in. Did you see my story?"
> "No, I was out of town."
> "Did you know her?"
> "What happened, exactly?"
> "Nobody's saying your friend murdered her, if that's what you're thinking."
> "*Was* it murder?"   [p. 163]

The reporter's first line, "Yeah," is symmetrical, as is Katy's "No" to his first question. When she ignores his second question and instead asks what happened, she makes the dialogue jump ahead. Notice how changing the symmetrical pattern gives Katy control of the interview. When the reporter anticipates where she is going and defensively leaps to head off what he infers she is thinking, Katy leaps to another direct question, taking control again. This scene is a model of fast-moving asymmetrical dialogue.

Meredith Cole provides another example of implied dialogue in *Posed for Murder,* winner of the St. Martin's/Malice Domestic award:

> Mama D'Angelo stood watching the coffee maker drip.
> Lydia had never seen Mama stand still for so long, so she knew something was wrong. "Are you OK?"
> Mama turned around and folded her arms across her chest. "I'm worried about my Frankie."
> Lydia was mystified. "Frankie? Is he sick?"
> "Yes," Mama said venomously. "Sick in the heart, sick in the head. What do you know about this computer dating?"
> "Frankie is dating someone?"   [ms p. 88]

Lydia's last line responds to Mama's question with a question that interprets what is implied, not what is said. The result is vigorous and lively.

THREE TYPES COMBINED

A scene from Dennis Lehane's fourth mystery novel, *Gone, Baby, Gone,* exemplifies all three of the dialogue techniques I describe. Lehane's series characters, private investigators Patrick Kenzie and Angie Gennaro, are about to visit a wounded cop in the hospital when they encounter special agent Neal Ryerson in the parking garage:

"He's dead."

We stopped, and I turned back and looked at the guy. . . . He tapped some ash from the cigar, put it back in his mouth, and looked at me.

"This is the part where you say, 'Who's dead?'" He looked down at his boots.

"Who's dead?" I said.

"Nick Raftopoulous," he said.

Angie turned fully around on her crutches. "Excuse me?"

"That's who you came to see, right? . . . Well you can't, because he died an hour ago. . . .

He smiled. "Your next line is, 'How do you know who we're here to see?'" he said. "Take it, either one of you."

"Who are you?" I said.   [p. 334]

At first the exchanges are symmetrical in both structure and sound *(I said, he said)*. Short bursts of dialogue increase the pace and add tension. They also create contrast for the asymmetrical dialogue that follows soon after. Kenzie's "Who are you?" changes the subject, breaking the pattern of seemingly cooperative responses and taking control of the conversation away from Ryerson.

A page and a half of discussion about the case follows before Angie asks the special agent this question:

"So who killed Mullen and Gutierrez?"

Ryerson looked up at the garage ceiling. "Who took the money out of the hills? Who was the first person found in the vicinity of the victims?"

"Wait a sec," Angie said. "Poole? You think Poole was the shooter?"   [p. 336]

Again, the Q&A sequence breaks, this time when Ryerson responds to Angie's question with a series of rhetorical questions. Angie responds to those with another question, one that interprets the implied meaning of Ryerson's words and jumps to a conclusion.

Strengthen your dialogue line by line to increase the number of indirect, unexpected, oblique replies and to make each assumption leap forward.

INFORMATIONAL DIALOGUE

Genre fiction often involves gathering information and deducing meaning from it. Because characters cannot act on knowledge that the plot gives them no opportunity to learn, the writer has to show or otherwise account for who knows what, when, and how they learn it. Dialogue is the main vehicle for the exchange of information.

However, don't create dialogue for the primary purpose of facilitating such exchanges. Characters who *talk* about conflict are poor vehicles for getting readers to experience conflict's emotions. Unless your characters are arguing with each other or dealing with some other problem at the time, an informational exchange is not likely to lead readers to feel the tension that keeps them turning pages.

> "[W]hat is said is not always what is meant and what is not said is often just as important, if not more so, as what actually is said. . . ."
>
> Brett Jocelyn Epstein , in the magazine of Mensa[47]

You have many ways to keep informational talk from turning deadly dull. See if your scenes are built around opposing agendas. See if your dialogue includes some paraphrase to speed the pace as you work a little data into a scene with borrowed conflict. Be careful not to dilute the tension. Too much data at one time causes (dare I say?) a tension deficit disorder.

Create conflict by putting your characters in situations that produce anxiety. Even if they are friends you can find something for them to argue about. Send them fishing (as I suggest in CLUE #12). Then pump up the pressure. Make your protagonist seasick. Or fall overboard.

If she wants something from her friend, she has to force herself to play nice and not, uh, rock the boat. That effort alone adds a tension dimension. Focusing your characters on different priorities lets you write *bypass dialogue:* two people talking but not communicating.

Transforming allies into temporary combatants adds conflict and builds empathy for your protagonist, whose suspicions are most likely pooh-poohed by everyone she seeks support from. Readers root for the underdog. Moreover, her determination to be proven right—despite disbelievers, especially a doubtful close friend—increases her motivation to go after what she wants. Remember to establish a credible reason for a friend's resistance, impatience, or skepticism.

PARALLEL CONVERGENCE

When a scene lacks the potential for conflict, should you leave it to sputter and die? Noooo. If readers are kept aware of your characters' agendas, you can make the tension from unsatisfied goals felt from one scene to the next. Also, you can borrow tension from an unrelated source, such as a minor character who sets off a short-term conflict. Or invent some other business that offers its own action.

What do I mean by other business? Here's a scene from the Agatha-nominated *Blues in the Night* by Rochelle Krich, the first title in her third mystery series. Molly Blume, reporter, is seeking background about the victim of a mysterious hit-and-run. Among those she interviews are the managers of the building where the victim lived. Because Molly cannot attain her goal if this interaction is adversarial, Krich borrows conflict from a tennis match taking place on TV:

> "We were shocked when her mother told us Lenore died," Marie said, her voice rising to compete with the droning of a former tennis champion turned commentator. . . . "Just shocked. Weren't we, Tom?". . .
>
> "Shocked," he agreed. "She was a nice gal. Pretty." He fixed his eyes on the television screen.
>
> ". . . It's just so sad what happened, isn't it, Tom?"
>
> "Rotten shame."
>
> "How long was she living here?" I asked, sipping the iced tea Marie had insisted on serving me.
>
> "Seven months," Marie said.
>
> "Did you ever meet her ex-husband?"
>
> "Son of a bitch," Tom muttered.
>
> I turned to him. "Why do you say that, Mr. O'Day?"
>
> He looked at me and blinked. "What?"
>
> "Mr. Saunders was a son of a bitch?"
>
> "Was he?" He shrugged. "I wouldn't know. Never met him."
>
> He returned his attention to the screen. "That ball was on the line, you imbecile!" he shouted.   [p. 82]

Tricked by Krich! First, she has Tom respond to his wife's comments about the dead woman. Then the author switches Tom's focus, without warning, and has him respond to the televised event. Where his two scripts converge, Tom's remarks make sense in *both contexts*. Counterpoint.

Molly is fooled, and so are we.

This episode is a superb example of dramatic irony. In addition, it borrows conflict and injects it into an ordinary fact-finding mission. Tom's emotional outbursts continue to punctuate the scene to its end.

BREVITY, PLEASE

Not every development merits its own scene. Instead of inventing a situation solely to create tension for an informational exchange, see if you can pare the data to its essentials and merge those essentials with another scene.

You already know not to echo every *um* and *ah* of actual speech. What you might not realize is how much other garbage collects—from dialogue's too-frequent opening word "Well" to the unnecessary hello-how-are-you chatter. Misguided efforts to simulate realistic conversation serve no useful purpose. So please, please take out the garbage.

To help you grow bolder in your own rubbish removal, I invite you to edit one of dialogue's worst offenders: the phone call. I wrote the following based on an extremely brief phone conversation from Chapter 20 of *Death's Domain,* the sixth Cassidy McCabe mystery by Alex Matthews.

Cass has already questioned a number people associated with the murder victim. Now, while sitting in her car, she thinks of one more person to interview. To learn the man's name and address, she phones her husband at work.

Here's the set-up to the call as Matthews wrote it:

> He'd mentioned the name of his company but the corporate title was unfamiliar to her and had failed to lodge itself in her memory. Zach, however, would have it written down. Fishing her cell phone and a spiral pad out of her tote, she called him.

Next comes my chit-chatty version of the call itself, which begins immediately after the words "she called him." Edit it by drawing a line through every unnecessary word—no rewriting needed.

> "Hi Zach, it's me. How y'doing?"
> "Oh, hi Cass. Not bad. What's up?"
> "Well, I forgot to ask you something. Do you have a minute?"

> "Sure, I just filed today's story."
>
> "Remember that man we wanted to question," she asked, "the one who worked for the company on the other side of town?"
>
> "Yeah, I do," he replied.
>
> "Well, I can't think of the company's name. I figured you wrote it down. Do you have it?" she asked.
>
> "Yeah, I can get it," he said. "Just give me a minute." She sat on hold for a while. Half a minute later Zach was on the line again. "Got a pencil?" he asked.
>
> "Yes," she answered.
>
> "Escovar is the name you're looking for. I've got the address right here on the screen. . . ."

Obviously, my deliberate wordiness ruined the author's actual dialogue, the same way I've seen thousands of writers ruin theirs.

Before you look ahead at the professionally written lines on which I base this little test of your editing savvy, observe that nothing about this phone call involves conflict, drama, or tension. Nor is there any reason it should. Why would the author even include such a call? Perhaps:

- ➽ to show how Cass gets information she didn't know she'd need until after she interviewed someone who might warn the man of her interest (remember: account for who knows what, when, and how)

- ➽ to add one more hurdle to challenge Cass, who wants to question the man before someone else warns him about her.

Two purposes? That adds density.

Since there's no value in turning this utilitarian call into a conflict, Matthews was wise to keep it brief. Hint: go back and take out more words. Go on. See if you can reduce my bloated passage to one paragraph. Then compare your version to the author's.

With apologies to the award-winning Alex Matthews for my parody, here is the phone call as she wrote it, beginning immediately after the words, "she called him."

> "Yeah, I can get it," he said. "Just give me a minute." She sat on hold for a while. "Escovar is the name you're looking for. I've got the address right here on the screen. . . ."   [p. 182]

That's it. No need to hear Cass telling Zach why she's phoning—we learn why before she calls him. Zach's "Yeah, I can get it," occurs immediately. No filler, no gabby chit chat, no transition. Chit chat this far into the story would destroy the pace and serve no purpose. Once dialogue—or any action—serves its purpose, nothing is gained by prolonging it.

Since readers would be well aware by Chapter 20 that Cass's husband is a reporter, the reference to Zach's filing a story is unnecessary, the kind of background an insecure writer repeats for insurance. (More malpractice.)

The information exchange written by Matthews is crisp, compressed, and clear. It moves like an express train. Mine derails—a train wreck. The original reaches its destination in only thirty-two words, no excess baggage. Mine puffs and chugs along with more than four times the freight.

INTERIOR DIALOGUE

Self-talk, monologue, internal dialogue, thought—all these terms refer to a technique we love to read and write but hate to hear when our partners do it aloud: talking to oneself.

The questions I'm asked about this technique always involve the mechanics of how to show thoughts on the page. The conventions are simple: never enclose self-talk in quotation marks, and use one of two font styles:

- *italics*—the traditional type style, or
- roman (non-italics)—the style preferred today by many editors.

Although roman type makes thought look like other text, three factors distinguish it from narrative:

- Placement: put thought on the same line as the viewpoint character's spoken words or on the line immediately following it.
- Content: relate thought to what the viewpoint character just said aloud or heard, adding to it or contradicting it; talking back.
- Tone: make it reveal the character's voice and true attitude, often sardonic or sarcastic.

To begin, here's a scene in third-person that shows a workable solution for two kinds of thought. It's from *Thou Shalt Kill Thy Neighbor,* a novel-in-progress by Michael Salisbury. Ben is bringing a picture to the former owner of his house, now living in an old age home. He tells her:

> ". . . It must have fallen when you were moving out."
>
> "Those movers were worthless! They ruined everything they touched. I barely got half the estimate from the consignment shop. And if I'd known *that* was the picture Ruth Anne called about, I'd have saved myself all this bother." The short tirade winded her. She paused for breath. "Still, you might have thought to frame it for me."
>
> A recollection from an assertiveness training workshop prompted Ben to find something, anything, in what she said that he could agree with. He rehearsed it in his mind: "Yes, I *might* have framed it for you." Right. It would have been the wrong kind of frame, wrong for her and her room, it would have captured fingerprints and smudges, it would have sheltered and nourished germs and contaminants.
>
> "Ruth Anne and Sarah said hello."

Ben's "Yes, I *might* have" is in quotation marks because it's rehearsing what he could say aloud, distinct from his other thoughts, which follow immediately without quotes. Anticipating more fault-finding, Ben overrides his impulse to find agreement and changes the subject instead—always an effective technique for showing evasion and reasserting control.

A few paragraphs later the old woman makes a particularly nasty remark:

> "You know, you practically stole that house from me."
> The old harridan.
> "Do you have any idea how much those realtors take, how much they *steal,* for listing a house? Do you know how much that cost me?"
> Now he knew why Sarah hadn't wanted to accompany him.

The old harridan is direct thought, not filtered through the narrator. It needs no formatting beyond its own line to show Ben's silent response to an insult. The last line returns to the original third-person POV.

Scott Nicholson, who's been likened to Stephen King, writes Appalachian horror novels. He uses italics for Tamara's self-talk in her scenes in *The Harvest,* and for her disk jockey husband, Robert, in his scenes. His self-talk keeps him from mouthing off to his call-in radio listeners:

". . . Might be one of them UFO's I been hearing about."

Why would an intelligent alien species want to land in Windshake? Robert slid a CD into the second player.

"Maybe you ought to videotape it and send it in to 'Unsolved Mysteries,'" he said. "Listen, I've got to go. Bye, now, and thanks for listening to WRNC."

He hung up the phone and flipped the mic switch over at the same time. He drew air down into his abdomen, the way he had learned in college, then belted out in his artificially cheery baritone:

"That was 'Dream Love' by Mariah Carey."

And I hope you were smart enough to turn your radio off before she really got rolling.

"It's fourteen minutes after eleven and forty-one degrees in the High Country under cloudy skies. Bobby Lee here sharing your day with you."

Only because I can't find a better job.   [p. 56]

In *Spurred Ambition* by Twist Phelan, self-talk is limited to the protagonist, attorney Hannah Dain, who enjoys extreme sports. (Because I avoid even mild sports, I am greatly impressed by that author's engaging in every body-punishing activity she has Hannah do in the Pinnacle Peak series.)

Here, Hannah is driving home after being interviewed for a job by the man who'd previously helped her avoid a fall from rock-climbing—and whom she'd impulsively kissed. She imagines how the topic might come up with her lover, Cooper:

> . . . Her guilty conscience wasn't quite yet ready to face Cooper.
>
> *How did the interview go, honey?*
>
> *Great. I'll be working for the guy I made a pass at Sunday night. At least now I know his name.*
>
> Hannah turned down the volume, no longer in the mood for music. *It was a one-time lapse in judgment, not at all like what Elizabeth had done.* She tightened her grip on the steering wheel, unsure whether she was stating a fact or making an argument.   [p. 57]

As shown by *Spurred Ambition,* italics are effective in simulating both sides of an imagined dialogue. They are also effective for distinguishing between a character's thoughts and his imagined dialogue with the voice of his internalized parent or "evil twin." In the thriller *A Thousand Bones* by P. J. Parrish, the killer is deciding whether it's safe to enter a remote cabin:

> Why couldn't he think? Why couldn't he just *sense* if there was someone inside?
> *Talk to me, Mommie. Help me. Be with me now, and tell me what to do.*
> He shut his eyes, the voice a whisper in his head.
> *Just go inside, son.*   [p. 424]

After he enters the cabin, he spies a deer through the kitchen window.

> *Shoot it!*
> The animal seemed to hold Roland's stare.
> *Shoot it! What's the matter with you? Shoot it, you little pansy!*   [p. 425]

In another scene Parrish again uses italics for the killer's thoughts as he stalks Joe Frye, the only female homicide detective in the Miami Police Department. However, most of the scenes in this well-written thriller are dramatized from Joe's third-person viewpoint, and her self-talk is part of the narrative, in roman type. Parrish's technique of reserving italics for the villain's thoughts has the effect of emphasizing his twisted mind's inner demons.

A Thousand Bones is the first novel in P. J. Parrish's second series, spun off from the *New York Times* best-selling Louis Kincaid series.

> To improve your dialogue-writing skills, "Try writing a play and show character entirely through dialogue. It's harder than you think, but excellent practice."
> Reed Farrel Coleman, author of the Moe Praeger series, speaking as a panelist

NON-ITALICIZED THOUGHTS

And now for the non-italicized aside, the back-talk worked into dialogue and identified by its placement, content, and tone of voice. The following extract is from the literary novel *Foul Matter,* one of nearly thirty books by Martha Grimes. It's a send-up of the publishing industry and its ego-driven authors. In it, the fictional Paul Giverney, best-selling author and egotist extraordinaire, hatches a plot that gets him mixed up with a pair of killers-for-hire, Karl and Candy.

In one scene, Karl compliments Giverney on an Oriental-looking chair, addressing him as Mr. G.

> "Mr. G."? Was this to be the sobriquet he was hence to be known by? And after he was dead? He said, "Late Fung dynasty. A good example."
>
> Karl frowned and looked at Paul almost with suspicion, as if Paul were pushing baby powder and calling it cocaine. "I never heard of that period."
>
> I know you idiot; that's because I made it up.   [p. 357]

A few lines later, the hit men bring up the subject of another author, now in the hospital after an "accident."

> Paul cut in. "Yes, I know about that. We have the same agent and the agent called me right away. It's too bad, but I don't think it's life threatening." Like you two are.

Note that "Mr. G." is the only thought in quotation marks, emphasizing that it repeats Karl's spoken words. The line would work as well without quotes, because at no time is there any doubt about which lines are spoken aloud, and which zingers are silently shot off by Paul Giverney.

The technique produces uncluttered dialogue, thought, and characterization with an attitude, all at the same time. That's density. And that's why the non-italicized style keeps gaining popularity among editors.

Whichever style you select, the measure of your writing skill comes from how you choose and use words to develop characterization. The result makes up your voice. May these examples give you much thought.

Now that we've analyzed and exemplified the mechanics and variety of self-talk, I'd like to point out that most phrases introducing thought are redundant and contain redundancies. Such as the next example.

It doesn't matter who wrote it because you won't be hearing from her again, but it should suffice to eradicate this sort of redundancy from your writing forever:

In his mind he knew this was important.

PACING DIALOGUE

It's a fact that dialogue moves faster than narrative. Even the "look" of dialogue, with lots of white space, encourages more rapid reading than solid blocks of text. Lean, snappy lines and bursts of incomplete sentences make it move faster still.

Is there such a thing as a too-rapid tempo? We know that reading a series of high-speed chase scenes can leave us emotionally out of breath, wanting a break before the next action scene qualifies our emotions for a speeding ticket. Yet dialogue can move rapidly without ill effect, provided it is not so abbreviated that the meaning gets muddled.

> "In composing, as a general rule, run your pen through every other word you have written; you have no idea what vigor it will give your style."
>
> Sydney Smith, founder in the early 19th century of *The Edinburgh Review*

However, rapid-fire dialogue that goes on too long does carry the risk of becoming tedious to read.

Once you take out the meaningless chatter and routine steps that clutter your scenes, you'll notice how everything accelerates. If you find a tightly self-edited scene moving faster than you want it to, several techniques can help you restore a slower pace. Do *not* restore the clutter.

To slow the pace of dialogue:

- break it up with exposition;
- turn some of it *into* exposition;
- make sentences and paragraphs a little longer;
- add some description;
- change the setting.

To see how a change in setting can affect pace, imagine a couple sitting and talking on a porch swing in the moonlight. Next, imagine the same couple shouting the identical words over the roar of city traffic while they try to flag a cab. In the rain. At rush hour.

To accelerate the pace of your dialogue, try these methods:

- Determine whether the road from A to B to C is within the experience of most adults, so that leaping from A to C will be understood.

- Eliminate words, sentences, and gestures that are non-essential and offer no conflict, characterization, or plot advancement.
- Compress what's left, except where a good reason justifies spelling out each statement made by each character.
- Favor short, interrupted, asymmetrical lines of dialogue.

Also review the phone call from *Death's Domain* as Alex Matthews wrote it. I'd like you to appreciate how easily dialogue can be understood even when writers make it leap tall buildings in a single bound.

With practice, you, too, can produce Supertalk.

FIND & FIX CLUE #16: DYING DIALOGUE

- Verify that what your characters say and do, and what others say about them, advances the story, reveals their personalities, and fits their agendas.
- See whether your scenes are built around conflicting agendas so that dialogue is as goal-oriented and adversarial as the scene permits.
- Rewrite exchanges that fail to suggest tension, create conflict, engage the reader's emotions, or expand characterization.
- Invigorate dialogue with interruptions, interrogation, misinterpretation, and the unexpected, minimizing symmetry and avoiding signs of agreement.
- Look for opportunities for your characters to answer questions with a question, to anticipate and challenge implied meaning, and to jump ahead of the other speaker.
- Don't prolong dialogue beyond the point at which it serves its purpose.
- Keep informational exchanges extremely brief or splice them into other tension-producing action.
- Say farewell to good-bys, greetings, chit chat, and other filler.

CLUE #17: TREACHEROUS TAGS

The usual method for attributing words to the character who speaks them is by hanging a little *he said/she said* tag from the line of dialogue. At times that tag is like a forgotten price tag hanging from a debutante's gown: awkward, embarrassing, distracting, unnecessary. To prepare for your manuscript's debut, cut superfluous attributions:

> "Tom, you got one helluva nerve!" Dick bellowed angrily.
> "I told you to stay outta my office," Tom retorted.

Start by deleting adverbs. "Angrily" is redundant when the dialogue itself conveys its speaker's feelings—no authorial interpretation needed. Dialogue *shows;* adverbs *tell.* Wordiness weakens your writing, especially the kind of wordiness I call *adverbosity.*

Next, delete tags such as "he bellowed" and "Tom retorted." Verbs that tell how a line is delivered are rarely needed with strong dialogue, because the dialogue itself reveals how its speaker is behaving. Often, a line can stand by itself, without the crutch that a tag furnishes:

> "Tom, you got one helluva nerve!"
> "I told you to stay outta my office."

Attention-getting verbs such as "bellowed" and "retorted" don't add meaning; like adverbs, they add distraction. Sharp dialogue can stand alone, but if the meaning needs strengthening, use action and body language:

- Action anchors spoken lines in their setting, giving readers something to visualize other than talking heads.
- Body language authenticates the dialogue's content, offering a visual counterpart to the speaker's emotions and attitude.
- Whereas adverbs *tell* how a line is delivered, body language *shows.*

TIP: KNOW YOUR TAG HABITS

Examine how you write dialogue tags by using the search feature in your word processing program to find all close quote marks: "

1. Write with the "smart quotes" feature in "Preferences" turned on. If it's off, turn it on, type a quote mark into both the FIND option *and* the REPLACE option, then hit "All." Your computer will substitute the correct open and close quotes throughout your text. Repeat these steps for the apostrophe.

2. To reduce the total number of hits your computer makes, search for only those quote marks that follow dialogue. Here's how:

   a) Copy or cut a "smart" or "curly" *close* quote mark from your text and paste it into the FIND option.

   b) Press FIND to review each occurrence one at a time.

3. This method lets you analyze the tags you now write. Observe their frequency and pattern.

4. Evaluate all verbs other than "said," and decide for each one:

   a) Would "said" be equally appropriate and less obtrusive?

   b) Is the dialogue meaningful enough to need no crutch—that is, no verb, no adverb, no tag?

5. Armed with this insight, strengthen your dialogue and avoid impeding its flow with unnecessary or ineffective tags.

Consider these examples of how lines are delivered:

> "Tom, you got one helluva nerve!" Dick said, bursting in.
> "I told you to stay outta my office," Tom said as he jumped up, knocking over his chair.

Not bad, but instead of adding action to a tag, as in "Tom said as he jumped up," see what happens when you make the action *replace* the tag:

> "Tom, you got one helluva nerve!" Dick slammed the door he'd just burst through.
> "I told you to stay outta my office." Tom jumped up, knocking over his chair.

That's better. Each of these action statements takes the form of a *beat:* a sentence that incorporates its own attribution. Compare:

- ●◆ Tag: "I told you to stay outta my office," Tom said as he jumped up, knocking over his chair.
- ●◆ Beat: "I told you to stay outta my office." Tom jumped up, knocking over his chair.

The same chair hits the floor each time, but the beat is more effective because it stands alone, which emphasizes its action. The beat also replaces the wordy *said as he.* Where dialogue erupts under its own power, get out of the way and let it flow. Do not give every line of dialogue its own beat; the resulting rhythm and pattern will overpower everything else.

When a line of dialogue is triggered by an action, be faithful to the sequence of cause and effect. If action occurs first, put it first:

> Dick burst through the door. "Tom, you got one helluva nerve!" Tom jumped up, knocking over his chair. "I told you to stay outta my office."

Much better. Scrutinize your dialogue, and you'll find all sorts of treacherous tags to exorcise. You'll also spot adverbosity and other redundancies, like those that haunt this line from *The Murder of Roger Ackroyd:*

> "I'm not very sure," I said doubtfully. [48]

Even the great Agatha Christie could have used a little line editing.

YOU DON'T SAY

In fiction, originality is valued in everything but tags. The plain vanilla *said* is preferred over any of the fancy synonyms Mr. Roget tempts you with: alleged, averred, declared, rejoined, retorted, stated—and so on. While *bellowed* is out there calling attention to the writer's efforts, *said* remains nearly invisible. It lets the dialogue flow, which is why it's preferred by experienced writers (and by the ubiquitous nine out of ten doctors—book doctors, that is).

In small doses, *insisted* and *repeated* are useful, as are *asked, answered, echoed, replied, told, observed,* and *pointed out.* Also effective is the occasional *complained, cried, groused, guessed, mumbled, murmured, muttered, screamed, shouted, shrieked, wailed,* and *whispered.* Did I just hear a hiss? Sorry, no character can hiss a line that doesn't have an *s* in it.

"Occasional" is the key word. More than one *thundered* per book is too much. How often do thesaurus-style verbs pop up in your own speech?

> "So I stated to my boss that I wouldn't dream of retorting in such a manner to a customer, and he rejoined, 'That's what Ellen declared to me that she heard you utter.'"

If you wouldn't talk like that, don't write like that. Reaching for unlikely verbs is reaching for rejection.

Put tags in their place by recognizing them as mere mechanics. An invisible tag such as *said* lets readers skim over it on the way to hearing what the dialogue has to say. Dialogue is the series of snapshots or the portrait; tags are the thumbtacks that merely hold it to the wall.

Let's say you're convinced that *said* is a fine tag, but it's so . . . so ordinary. Surely readers get bored with the same old same old?

If *said* strikes you as boring, the problem is not the tag, it's the dialogue. Chances are, the words and actions you're writing do not reflect what your characters feel strongly about. Bring their agendas into the open and show more of their feelings. Dialogue that puts forth a character's needs, desires, opinions, or attitude is sufficient to identify the speaker. No tag needed.

BODY LANGUAGE

If you doubt the value of beats over tags, look at the following passages. The first is from Roberta Rogow's *The Problem of the Evil Editor,* set in the London of Arthur Conan Doyle, Lewis Carroll, and Oscar Wilde:

> "Last night Mr. Basset told me to retype these manuscripts. I have done so. If you please, Mr. Levin, I would like to collect the money that is owed me. My mother is waiting for me at home." Miss Harvey raised her chin in an attempt to gain dignity.   [p. 145]

Rogow presents the typist's body language as a beat separate from the woman's "I" statements, avoiding the awkward *said as she* construction.

Next is an excerpt from a novel-in-progress by Maya Davis in the category of contemporary women's fiction. Notice that all body language is presented in beats, not tags:

"Your eyes lie, Cal." I move forward on the couch. "Were *you* in that tunnel, and was that part of the plan? Did someone kick Pixie thinking she was Mom?"

Angry color darts across his face, lingering on his cheekbones.

I don't back down. Eyebrow raised, jaw clenched, I lean toward him.

The words trembling on his lips fall away into silence. He brushes a hand over his eyes, then down his cheeks. Whiskers rasp, the only sound in the room. He deflates under my pinprick stare.

Finally he responds. "I suppose I deserve that. But, I promise, I did not have anything to do with the attack."

"That strains believability."

He picks up the cooling coffee, simply holding it. "I have no way of proving my guilt or innocence."   [ms p. 291]

The dialogue continues with the occasional beat but nary a tag. Davis's style is cleaner and smoother than if she had written: *"Your eyes lie, Cal," I say as I move forward on the couch.* Tags as simple as *I say,* and *he* or *she says,* are clean as well as unobtrusive—but often unnecessary.

In *Jasmine's Fate,* third in the Ace Edwards private eye series by Texan Randy Rawls, one character—and I do mean character—is attorney Candi Maladay. About Jasmine, the lovely suspect, Candi tells Ace by phone:

". . . Get a phone number and I'll call her. In the meantime, make sure she keeps her mouth sewed shut in the presence of the cops. I'll be in Dallas tomorrow and will make time to see her. Maybe you can be there. This might call for a good PI." She hesitated before adding, "Guess you'll have to do." Her witch's cackle traveled across the airways.   [pp. 4-5]

Ace, the usual object of her barbs, adds, "Insults were part of her charm." Note both tag and beat. A beat is able to identify the speaker and establish a visual anchor. It does not have to relate to the spoken line it accompanies.

Here's a line from *In Her Blood,* a humorous novel-in-progress by Myrna Elliott that features a trio of unorthodox criminals. It demonstrates the flexibility possible with an unrelated beat:

"If Tony Cambria doesn't kill us before we freeze to death, and by some miracle we live through this night, we'll never come to Wisconsin again." The flaps of Dooley's fake fur hat tied under one of his chins gave him the appearance of a squinty-eyed bulldog.

DISSONANT TAGS

Sometimes dialogue uses humor or sarcasm to disguise the meaning behind a character's words. Sometimes characters lie about their feelings to themselves and others. Sometimes they just lie. When you want readers to see a discrepancy between the spoken word and a hidden feeling, don't use an adverb; use a gesture, body language, or other behavior:

> Dick chuckled and wagged a finger at his partner. "Tom, you've got one helluva nerve."

What happens when the writer picks a gesture that fails to convey the intended emotion? The result is vague, its meaning ambiguous:

> Dick shrugged and said, "Tom, you've got one helluva nerve."

Something is out of whack here. A discrepancy between dialogue and body language suggests the writer's need for sharper people-watching skills. Either revise the body language to convey the character's real feelings, whatever those may be, or change the dialogue to reflect what Dick is likely to say after he shrugs.

On the other hand, sometimes you might want to portray an intentional discrepancy between a character's words and body language. In *Thistle and Twigg,* the first title of the second series by Mary Saums, Jane Thistle is concerned about an elderly man being held overnight in jail:

> Detective Waters stood immovable, like a mountain, with a resolute, expressionless face. Once again, his look switched to an instant smile. "Come this way, please."
> ". . . I thought I should come and see about him. I'd like to talk to him, if I may."
> The detective nodded in a friendly, attentive way as I spoke. "No, ma'am. That won't be possible." I was taken aback momentarily, as I'm sure was his intent.   [p. 113]

Another intentional discrepancy can be seen in the Edgar-nominated *Sunrise,* first in the series featuring Leigh Ann Warren, a D.C. cop—though far from the first novel by the prolific, award-winning Chassie West:

> . . . An expert at going for the jugular with a Teflon-coated stiletto, she oohed and aahed over me, patted my cheek and gazed in mock sympathy at Nunna. "Such a shame," she said. Her beady eyes flitted between us like a fly undecided about where to light. "All that money spent on your education and you wind up directin' traffic and writin' tickets. Couldn't pass the lawyer's exam, I reckon?"   [p. 77]

West's portrayal of this chatty, catty neighbor, with her mock sympathy and flitting eyes, reveals the feelings beneath all that oohing, aahing, and superficially innocent remarks. In the larger context of the novel, this episode serves a dual purpose, more important than characterizing a minor player. The neighbor's condescension triggers Leigh Ann's renewed pride in her profession as an officer of the law. That change in attitude signals Leigh Ann's development and takes the plot of *Sunrise* in a new direction.

SELF-IDENTIFYING SPEECH

To keep dialogue moving, a question-and-answer structure is the next best thing to an argument. Alternating lines mirror an adversarial pattern and leave little doubt who is speaking.

With such a pattern, the need for tags becomes minimal or non-existent, as in this dialogue from *There Was a Little Girl* by Ed McBain. Presented as a remembered conversation from the past, McBain omits even the quotation marks, and the dialogue works fine without them:

> . . . It was Warren Chambers, instead, who'd given her the first job she'd had since her nosedive two years earlier.
> Tell me about the job, okay? she'd said.
> First tell me you're clean, Warren had said.
> Why? Do I look like I'm not?
> You look suntanned and healthy. But that doesn't preclude coke.
> I like that word. Preclude. Did you make it up?
> How do you like the other word? Coke?

> I used to like it just fine. I still think of it every now and then.
> But the thought passes. I'm clean, Mr. Chambers.   [pp. 71–72]

After a series of tagless statements it's a good idea to reinforce the identity of the speaker by inserting an occasional attribution—a tag or a beat, or a line of direct address, such as, "I'm clean, Mr. Chambers."

DIRECT ADDRESS

This brings us to the technique in which fictional speakers address each other by name to indicate who's who. Don't overdo this technique or it becomes more conspicuous than the content it supports. In actual conversation, how often do you say the name of the person you're speaking with?

> "Hey, Jerry. The coroner's report just came in."
> "What's it say, Corinne?"
> "Well, Jerry, bad news," she replied, handing it to him.
> Pete looked up from the next desk. "I'm on my way to lunch
> but I'd rather listen in on this. Jerry, what if I have Selma hold
> all calls?"
> Selma's voice called from the reception room, "Okay, Pete."

Awful writing! But surprisingly common. Use your pencil to perform major surgery on this passage. Anything will be an improvement.

Here's one rewrite; many others are possible:

> "Hey, Jerry, the coroner's report just came in." Corinne
> handed the file to her boss. "Bad news."
> Pete decided this wasn't the time to go to lunch. He buzzed
> the receptionist to hold all calls and edged his chair closer to
> his boss.

Compare your rewrite with mine. See if you are using surgical techniques similar to these:

- ◆◇ slicing words that fail to expand characterization or advance the scene ("~~What's it say, Corinne?~~" "~~Well, Jerry. . . .~~");
- ◆◇ splicing wordy lines (~~she replied~~. Corinne handed . . .);
- ◆◇ condensing or eliminating characters and their spoken lines (~~Pete looked up~~ . . . "~~I'm on my way~~ . . ." ~~Selma's voice~~);
- ◆◇ paraphrasing for economy (Pete decided . . . and edged).

Read your dialogue aloud and note awkward and artificial phrasing. Revise, then ask someone to read it to you. If your buddy is agreeable to your tape-recording the reading, replay later and listen for any tripping, stumbling, or misplaced pauses.

BY THE NUMBERS

When you revise, weigh the value of every scene in advancing your plot. Know the specific contribution each character makes in furthering the purpose of each scene. Keep readers aware of the agendas pursued.

Scenes with two characters are stronger than those with more. For a two-person dialogue, use tags with only one of the speakers, none with the other. As the number of roles expands, drama and conflict become diluted and the need for identification grows exponentially. So thin your crowds, especially those in which several characters fill similar functions or share similar agendas.

Ask yourself, does this scene really need separate speaking parts for five police officers? Combine roles where you can. Where you cannot, think about having someone else speak for a character who gets called away from the meeting or gets stuck in traffic and can't make the meeting. Be sure to plant a reason for this absence in advance and keep it plausible.

When a number of characters must be present, control how often each gets to speak. I've seen manuscripts in which lines of dialogue are apportioned in perfect rotation among three or more speakers, as if the writer were dealing a hand of poker. Such "dealings," I suspect, come less from an innate sense of fairness than from sensing the dialogue's blandness and need for action, which the writer attempts to compensate for by adding more characters.

Perversely, rotation increases the need for speaker attribution, and it produces a rhythm that itself is a source of monotony.

If reducing the number of characters doesn't do justice to the different ideas you need to put forth in a given scene, you have other options:

- Focus on only two speakers at a time instead of bouncing back and forth among all of them.
- When a third character speaks, have one of the original two remain silent for a few exchanges so that no more than two speakers are in the spotlight at any time.

❧ Identify the third speaker as soon as her words begin, so they aren't mistakenly heard as coming from one of the first two:

"I wonder," said Carmen, who'd been quietly knitting and listening, "if you two considered that Marco might have. . . ."

❧ Or introduce the new speaker with a beat preceding her lines:

Carmen, who'd been quietly listening, put down her knitting. "I wonder if you two considered. . . ."

❧ Not every comment needs presenting via dialogue. Some comments can be paraphrased and put forth as exposition:

Carmen, who'd been quietly listening, put down her knitting and reminded everyone that Marco might have. . . .

For a "town hall" or crowd scene, limit speaking parts to the fewest named characters. Additional remarks can come from unnamed onlookers. Walk-ons don't need names; epithets will do: *said a woman in red; the teacher announced;* and so on.

Enjoy this exchange among three members of a family. The scene is from *Soul Patch,* the fourth Moe Prager mystery by Reed Farrel Coleman, set in the decaying neighborhood of New York's Coney Island. Ex-cop Moe remembers when it wasn't like that:

My dad used to take Aaron and me to Coney Island on spring Sundays. . . . Dad loved the parachute jump.
"La Tour Eiffel du Brooklyn," he'd say in an accent less French than Flatbush.
"What's that mean, Dad?"
"The Eiffel Tower of Brooklyn, you idiot!" Aaron would snap. "You ask that every time."
"Aaron!" my father would bark.
"Sorry, Dad."
"Don't apologize to me. Apologize to your little brother."
"That's okay."   [p. 19]

Have you any doubt which one of the three characters speaks each of the last three lines? I hope you hear little Moe's voice as clearly as I do. Content makes this possible, with sensitivity, brevity, and complete clarity.

When a scene involves no issues that identify characters by the position each takes, and most lines have to identify their speaker, decide whether the goal-obstacle content is compelling enough to warrant being a scene.

CROWD CONTROL

I'm not advocating a structure as complex as the next example, the interrogation scene from Sandra Brown's *The Alibi.* But I do want you to see the techniques she uses to manage five speaking parts, each with a distinct function. Four of the characters, readers met in the first fifteen chapters. Hammond Cross is secretly smitten with the mysterious Dr. Alex Ladd, the murder suspect. She is about to be questioned by homicide detective Rory Smilow. Observing is Steffi, Hammond's associate in the D.A.'s office. She is suspicious of Alex. The only new character is Perkins:

Asked what editors would be looking for in the future, literary agent Donald Maass replied: "Quality writing, by which I mean beautiful prose and flawless storytelling, regardless of category. The bar is so much higher now than it was ten years ago."

Sisters in Crime-Internet Chapter newsletter, 3rd quarter 2005

Frank Perkins spoke first. "Hammond, this is a complete waste of my client's time."

"Very possibly it is, Frank, but I would like to make that determination for myself. Detective Smilow seems to think that what Dr. Ladd can tell us warrants my hearing it."

The lawyer consulted his client. "Do you mind going through it again, Alex?"

"Not if it means that I can go home sooner rather than later."

"We'll see."

That comment had come from Steffi, and it made Hammond want to slap her. Turning the Q and A over to Smilow, he propped himself against the closed door, where he had an unrestricted view of Alex's profile.

Smilow restarted the tape recorder and added Hammond's name to those present. "Did you know Lute Pettijohn, Dr. Ladd?"

She sighed as though she had already answered that question a thousand times. "No, Detective, I did not."   [pp. 196–97]

Let's analyze Brown's method for handling multiple speakers. The passage begins by naming the newest character, whose role as attorney is made clear by his own words, "my client's time." Other lines of dialogue are identified either by direct address or by the action that precedes them.

One line, "We'll see," is identified after it is spoken, and not as a tag, beat, or anything accompanying the spoken words. It is identified indirectly, as part of Hammond's next line, when he reacts to the "We'll see"— a line so brief that as soon as we start to wonder who spoke those two words, the answer appears: *That comment had come from Steffi.*

The line that begins *Turning the Q and A over to Smilow* re-anchors Hammond and Smilow in the scene and builds a bridge to the interrogation. Once the first question establishes who is asking and who is answering, Brown is able to keep their dialogue going for twelve more paragraphs without a single tag, beat, or other form of address.

Selective content and form make most identifiers unnecessary.

More than one author admits to using another technique for dealing with excess characters once they serve their purpose: kill 'em off.

CONTENT AND FORM

I've listened to writers spend more time discussing how to attribute dialogue than how to write it. Dialogue's content is what a character says that no other is likely to know or say. Content that's purposeful and agenda-specific can stand on its own, needing little support from attributions, adverbs, or adjectives that tell readers who the speaker is and how he feels.

Here is a challenge to help you practice making your dialogue more effective. Up to now I've been suggesting that tags be seen as an option to cut *if* you revise your dialogue to stand alone. Now I'd like you to pretend your year's supply of tags is used up and your dialogue *must* stand on its own. In this way, content becomes the only source of speaker I.D. This belief forces you to strengthen what your characters say.

Unlike content, dialogue's form deals with how speaking parts are presented. When form obeys certain conventions, most readers understand what's meant by the presence of quotation marks, alternating lines, gestures, beats, direct address, and idiosyncrasies of speech.

One convention I want to call your attention to is the punctuation mark that's *not* there: the close quote. Traditionally, this is dropped from the end of a paragraph whenever a speaker's words runneth over to the first line of the next paragraph. Used correctly, quotation marks for uninterrupted speeches should reflect the following pattern:

> "Blah, blah, blah," Windy said. "Blah, blah, and so much
> more blah that I need another paragraph.
> "Furthermore," he continued, "blah, blah, blah."

The open quote mark at the start of the second paragraph, following a missing close quote at the end of the first, is a convention worth noting for more than mechanics. It signals that Mr. Windbag is going on too long.

Only the writer can keep a character from running off at the mouth. To paraphrase the WWII poster, loose lips sink scripts.

People typically speak in short sentences and fragments. They interrupt each other (show with a dash) and *occasionally* let a line trail off (show with an ellipsis). Use those ellipses sparingly. Overuse is one sign of an amateur. Make speeches shorter, sharper, less like oratory. And there are no semicolons in dialogue.

If you have a good reason for a character's lines to continue to a second paragraph, interject another's reaction, even if it's a silent gesture or a line such as: When Dick didn't respond right away, Tom continued.

TIP: USING DOTS & DASHES

For an interruption in dialogue and for an afterthought, use a dash. Known as a 1-em dash (because it's as wide as a letter M), it is simulated in a manuscript by two hyphens--without spaces. If you don't like the way the hyphens separate at the end of a typed line, make the first one a nonbreaking hyphen:

in Windows: Control+Shift+Hyphen;

in Word for the Mac: Command+Shift+Hyphen.

Do not use an ellipsis (three dots) for interruptions; use only for showing dialogue that trails off . . . incomplete. When the trailing off occurs at the end of a sentence, add a fourth dot to represent the period. . . .

Some word processing programs convert three dots in a row into one tightly spaced representation of an ellipsis. Turn off the keyboard shortcut for that feature, because the size and spacing of the dots never match the rest of your punctuation, especially when you have to add the terminal period.

"If a stranger were nearby would she try to eavesdrop on this conversation?" Ask this question when deciding whether to use dialogue or narrative to convey something.
Gary Provost, *Make Your Words Work*, p. 159

I hope you are convinced that the most effective dialogue identifiers come from content: *what* is said that's unique to the character and the situation. Tags and other mechanics are the Wizard's manipulations behind the curtain, seldom needed for dialogue that possesses heart and brains.

Bottom line: any time readers might be uncertain about who says what, dialogue needs attribution. More likely its content needs strengthening.

FIND & FIX CLUE #17: TREACHEROUS TAGS

- Use the search feature of your word processor (or a highlighter on the printout) to get a visual picture of your tag habits and other forms of attribution. (See the TIP on page 182.)

- Evaluate all tags for their contribution to clarity and see how many can be simplified with "said," or eliminated altogether, or replaced by a beat that expands meaning.

- Delete adverbs; instead, show how a speaker feels through action and dialogue.

- Rewrite action and dialogue to make a character's feelings evident, except where the plot requires hidden feelings.

- Reduce the need for tags by writing dialogue so specific to each speaker that most lines of dialogue are able to stand alone.

- Verify that your scenes involve the fewest characters who can achieve the scene's purpose.

- Read dialogue aloud and listen for awkward pauses and breaths, unnatural or difficult phrasing, and long speeches that need repairing, rewriting, or slicing.

D.O.A.

PART VIII: ROGUES GALLERY

Author and syndicated columnist Ellen Goodman says
she is happy rewriting. Her first draft is for getting her ideas
and theme clear. She compares her next pass through
to "cleaning house, getting rid of all the junk, getting
things in the right order, tightening things up." [49]

CLUE #18: MISTAKEN IDENTITY

When you are introduced to a group of strangers at a party, how many names do you remember? Some of us feel lucky to recall *one* name—and that one because we spent a little time getting to know the person. Meeting strangers in a book is similar. Too many new names introduced too soon makes all of them forgettable.

One novel I started to read named twenty characters in the first chapter. If I hadn't been looking forward to reading that author, I would have viewed the family tree on the flyleaf as the omen it was. Still, I stuck with this population explosion through six chapters, until the effort of keeping track of who's who far outweighed the pleasure of reading.

Eventually, my $14.95 purchase went into my donate-to-the-library pile, and my interest in exploring anything else by that author vanished.

Writers of mysteries know that characters who make up a pool of suspects cannot be introduced in the last half of the book. But in any genre, stuffing everyone into the first one or two chapters is a thinly disguised ploy to introduce the cast. First chapters are hooks, and the ultimate hook is to feature one character readers will come to care about. It's hard being intimate with a crowd. So delay bringing folks on stage until you are ready to develop the action that makes each new character memorable.

I came across a novel in a bookstore that mentioned six names in the first *paragraph*. Despite my belief that this naming frenzy would run its course, encountering it in the opening killed my curiosity to find out. That's a book I didn't buy. When I read to relax I don't want it to seem like work.

Editing is different. I expect to take notes about every character when I edit a manuscript. Readers don't take written notes, nor should they have to. A roster of names that keeps rolling, like credits at the end of a film, holds as much interest for readers (especially screener-outers) as it does for the typical moviegoer. What have audiences been conditioned to do on seeing a long list of names roll past? Get up and leave. Don't let your submission make busy screeners want to do the same.

Review your manuscript to see that you bring on only one or two characters at a time, and that each arrives with memorable action or dialogue.

ONE NAME, TWO

Madonna, Cher, and Oprah notwithstanding, real people need two names. Fictional people do not, unless they are main characters. Spenser is an exception—he's been single-namedly solving crimes for more than thirty of Robert B. Parker's novels.

In general, limit first and last names to major characters, because double names are interpreted in the same way an overly detailed description is: a sign of a character's importance. Whether that's true for your story, avoid sending mixed signals. In naming, put clarity ahead of cleverness.

Characters with secondary roles manage quite nicely with a single moniker, especially if it's catchy. Bit players can spend their moment in the limelight identified by function only: the cab driver, the kid on a bike.

Even for major players worthy of two names, both do not need announcing the moment those players appear. Behavior is more meaningful. After Johnnie-One-Name's actions capture and hold our interest, a full I.D. can be added. First, make readers interested enough to care about him.

Kathy Reichs introduces several minor players in the next example. It's from *Death du Jour,* second in the series that became the television series *Bones,* featuring Temperance Brennan, forensic anthropologist.

> I'd worked with Claude Martineau before. The other tech
> was new to me. We introduced ourselves as they set up the
> screen and portable light.
> "It's going to take some time to process this," I said, indicat-
> ing the staked-out square. "I want to locate any teeth that might
> have survived, and stabilize them if necessary. I may also have
> to treat the pubes and rib ends if I find any. Who's going to
> shoot pics?"
> "Halloran is coming," said Sincennes, the second tech. [p. 37]

The first tech's name is mentioned as part of Tempe's statement that she
had worked with him before. The second tech's name comes two paragraphs later, slipped in as part of a one-name tag, Sincennes. A third name,
Halloran, is also a single name, and it is spoken of in advance of his appearance.

Notice Reichs's technique in saying *we* introduced *ourselves* while others set up the equipment.

REPEAT OFFENDERS

Does repeating the same name and pronoun for a character seem monotonous to you? Some writers make such an effort to avoid a he-he-he
effect that they have different characters refer to the same individual by
different names. Detective Robert Smith might sometimes be addressed as
Robert, Rob, Bob, Bobby, Detective, Detective Smith, Smitty, or just plain
Smith.

Okay, I'm exaggerating again, but not by much. I see more bizarre efforts at variety than that, and not solely in unpublished manuscripts.
One best-selling author of legal thrillers applies what I call the Muddle
maneuver: having the narrator use different names to refer to the *same*
individual.

Here's an example, details changed to protect the blameworthy:

> I didn't trust Muddle. I suspected he'd change his story the
> next time the subject came up.
> When the supervisor brought in my mail, I noticed Stuart
> sorting through it, apparently looking for something. What
> is Muddle up to now, I wondered.

Is Muddle the surname of Stuart? Or of the supervisor? The narrator could be referring to two different characters, or three. Or one. Maybe we should keep reading and hope the next paragraph clarifies the confusion. Or we could stop and flip back a few pages to see how this name was originally introduced.

When confusion profusion shows up in the screening process, the busy screener-outer chooses to flip the pages—onto the "no" pile.

Whenever writers cause readers to stop, even for a moment, to wonder who's on first and what's on second, immersion in the fictional world is interrupted. Illusion vanishes. Attention drifts, sometimes not to return.

Don't worry about repeating the same pronoun. Worry about causing confusion. Focus on writing interesting people and action. If you sense a need for variety in how you refer to your protagonist, you might be sensing your own flagging interest in the character. Build interest by dramatizing a well-drawn, empathetic individual facing a tension-filled predicament.

LIMITED CONSISTENCY

Unlike the Stuart Muddle muddle, in which different names for the same character are used by the same person (the narrator), here's a scene with different speakers using different forms of address for the same character. The technique is clear and effective because the key is consistency.

Hurricane Party is Steve Brown's fifth Susan Chase mystery, a tribute to Agatha Christie's locked-room puzzles. Six characters, mostly strangers to each other, are literally and metaphorically weathering a violent storm in a Victorian mansion on the Carolina coast.

You might be overwhelmed by encountering six names in this next example, but readers of *Hurricane Party* will have gotten to know all six by page 92. They are Susan Chase, former lifeguard; Chad, her fiancé; Sarge, a military man employed as a security guard for the "party"; and two other guests, Jeremy and Reynolds. Oh, yes, there's Helen. She's the corpse.

> Sarge shouldered his way past my fiancé, reached down, and put fingers against Helen's throat. He straightened up and nodded. "Dead for sure." Sarge looked at me. "Was it you that done it, Chase?"
> "She was dead when I found her."
> "Or after you killed her," accused Jeremy.

I stepped back, readying myself as I do when confronted with any prick. "Why would I kill Helen?"

"I don't know," Sarge said. "That's for the authorities to find out."

"I agree. Not some rent-a-cop."

"Now, Suze. . ." started Chad as he got to his feet.

"Miss Chase, it doesn't help to call people names."

Reynolds Pearce finally came to life, speaking from the entrance to the living room. "A lifeguard is supposed to trump a security guard? You've got to be kidding."

"I can't believe. . . ." Jeremy stood, then shook his head. "Susan, how could you do something like this?"

"You didn't see anything, Jeremy," said Chad, "so watch your mouth."   [pp. 92–93]

Recall that consistency is the key: *Suze* is a nickname used only by Chad, her fiancé, as a term of endearment and an attempt to appease Susan when she starts acting like . . . well, like Susan.

Those who use her first name include friends and those who pretend to be. *Chase* is what she's called by those who dislike her smart attitude—authority figures and any jerk she has to interact with.

Sarge, the military man, always addresses her courteously as *Miss* or *Miss Chase*—except for one moment in the above scene when he lets down his guard and calls her *Chase*. This subtle change from his usual formality signals a shift in his attitude toward Susan and an attempt to place suspicion on her for the murder. He immediately recovers, saying, "Miss Chase, it doesn't help to call people names," which is understood as his response to Susan's rent-a-cop insult two lines earlier.

The tension inside the mansion escalates along with the noise of the wind outside, and soon a thump on the porch is heard:

"Hey, in the house! Let me in."

I pulled out of Sarge's grasp and put my ear against the door.

"Who is it?" I screamed.

"It's me, babe. Kenny Mashburn."

"You're right," I said, leaving the door. "There's no one out there."   [p. 174]

Kenny is a low-life dope dealer who adds a comic element. His role introduces yet another name for Susan: *babe.* Each form of address is consistent for its speaker. None is ambiguous when read in context.

For your own cast party, note how Steve Brown uses forms of address to communicate his characters' relationships with others. Observe when he uses tags and beats, and when the dialogue lets him omit those aids.

Also notice the absence of adverbs, adjectives, and thesaurus-style verbs. Though one character *accused,* you can be sure that if *howled* or *thundered* appeared it would refer not to a line of speech but to the hurricane.

VARIETY AS RELATIONSHIP

As with any technique, examine your purpose. If different names conceal a character's identity, the technique's purpose is plot-related. If those different names signify different relationships, the technique's purpose is character-related. But if the purpose is variety for its own sake, that's the Muddle maneuver.

> "The essence of writing is rewriting. . . . I consider it a privilege to be able to shape my writing until it's as clean and strong as I can make it."
>
> William Zinsser, *On Writing Well,* p. 223

Return for a moment to our fictional Robert Smith. His captain might call him Smith, his partner, Smitty. His wife might call him Robert or Dear. Strangers would address him as Mr. Smith or Detective, and the written narration might alternate between "the detective" and Smith. Chances are his grandmother still calls him Bobby.

These variations may seem less confusing than they did earlier, because you now see how each name is a consistent expression of the relationship between the detective named Smith and whomever he is talking with.

HURLING EPITHETS

Whenever the same name repeats in sentence after sentence, I imagine some long-ago teacher having made the writer afraid of pronouns. Repeating a name avoids those pesky disagreements between a pronoun and its antecedent, but the result is clumsy and monotonous. Use pronouns. Your critique partner will let you know if they're wrong.

Or use an epithet: a short phrase to stand in for a name, or a nickname (Smitty), or a function (the bag lady). For extremely minor characters whose names would clutter the story and confuse readers, epithets are handy:

TIP: SWAPPING NAMES

Your computer makes swapping words easy; sometimes too easy. Be careful using the global search-and-replace feature to change your characters' names. For example, if you are replacing the nickname "Art" with "Arthur," avoid peculiar results such as "He drew a carthuroon" by choosing "replace whole word." Much safer is the "find next" command that lets you check each occurrence individually before okaying it, thereby avoiding oddities such as "It hung in an arthur gallery."

If you decide to switch the order of your scenes, beware of the naming problem that led to this criticism in a book review in *The Nation:*

> "On more than one occasion, the authors mention someone either just by first or last name whom I had not remembered, causing me to flip back through the pages in a futile search to find what I missed. Then I would move on and find the person introduced pages later. In this and myriad other ways, the authors turned the cut-and-paste function of their word processors into tools of torture."[50]

Although gray as a badger and pushing sixty as hard as he could push, the man was lean and fit with a tennis player's body. Money there, I thought. Big money.

Big Money looked at Jimmy, then at me. . . .

Betty Webb, *Desert Noir,* a Lena Jones Desert mystery, p. 14

Riley nodded. "Guy has a really weird name," he said. "It sounded like 'Evil Eggplant.'"

A chill ran through me. "Do you mean Yves Laplante?". . . .

My first order of business would be to track down an evil eggplant.

. . . As he walked toward me with his big belly hanging over toothpick legs, he really *did* look like an ambulating eggplant.

Kathryn Lilley, *A Killer Workout,* ms pp. 191–203

The taller man examined the ceiling edge. His bottom teeth stuck out farther than his top ones. When he looked up and jutted out his jaw, his upper lip disappeared into his mouth. He stared at a phony security camera that Steven had seen advertised on TV as a way to deter unsuspecting burglars.

Jut-jaw's eyes shot from the camera to the clock. The minute hand snapped to attention and stood in its upright position.

Carol Kenny, "Closing Time," a short-story-in-progress

An effective epithet is often descriptive and clever. The shorter the better. A lengthy phrase, such as "the man who knew too much" or "our partner in crime," is effective one time but becomes strained with repetition.

In *What a Woman's Gotta Do,* Evelyn Coleman's protagonist, Patricia Conley, invents epithets to characterize a couple sitting next to her at the marriage license bureau. Afraid her fiancé is a no show, Patricia tries to distract herself by speculating about the couple—he, tattooed; her, biting her nails:

The engagement ring on her finger made me wonder if Tattoo Man might have a pocket full of bubble gum, since I was reasonably sure the ring didn't pop out on the first try.

By 4:10 P.M. when Kenneth still hadn't shown, I asked Tattoo Man and Biting Nails, "Excuse me. Got any chewing gum?" Despite the tears stinging the corners of my eyes, I almost burst into laughter when he pulled out a handful of colorful balls.

[pp. 11–12]

Since few waiting room encounters include an exchange of names, Coleman's use of epithets is logical. It's also creative: Tattoo Man and Biting Nails are far more imaginative than "the man and the woman."

INTRODUCTIONS

You can keep readers from mistaking someone else for the lead if your protagonist is the first character you introduce. I recall when some romance lines used to specify that hero and heroine had to meet on page 1.

Today, you have considerable leeway in how you introduce your characters. You might state their names directly, as in the first of Rebecca Miller's three stories that make up *Personal Velocity:*

> Greta Herskovitz looked down at her husband's shoes one
> morning and saw with shocking clarity that she was going to
> leave him.   [p. 1]

With an equally provocative, direct first-person statement, here's how
Kathy Krevat opens her work-in-progress, *PTA Meetings Are Murder:*

> My name is Tiffany.
> For that alone I could kill my parents.   [p. 1]

At the other extreme, the first-person narrator of thirty-three of Bill
Pronzini's eighty-some novels never tells his name, and no one addresses
him by name. Book reviewers refer to him as "Nameless" because they
have to refer to him in some way. Even Pronzini's publisher prints the
cover of his books with the words: *A "Nameless Detective" Series.*

A comfortable middle ground exists in *Deep Sea Dead,* fourth in a series of six Pauline Sokol novels by Lori Avocato, romance and mystery
author. The first form of address for the protagonist occurs in paragraph 7:

> "Don't call me doll. Ever." I sat straighter in my seat across
> from his mold-covered desk. Okay, maybe mold-covered was a
> bit strong, but I was guessing there had to be something
> growing beneath the used paper plates, coffee cups, piles of
> ashes and files. He had my folder in his hand.
> "Okay, newbie—"
> "Pauline, Ms. Sokol or Investigator Sokol will do. . . ."

As late as paragraph 9 we learn Pauline's name and her job title: investigator. In the meantime we also learn that the man who prompts her out-
burst by calling her "doll" is her boss, and we witness their attitudes toward
each other, their personalities, and their fractious relationship. All this and
more makes for a dense, multi-purposed introduction.

However, what I want to call attention to is the indirect way the subject
of Pauline's name comes up. It's a correction in the midst of a conflict. The
inciting incident is Pauline's objection to being assigned to investigate medical insurance fraud as an undercover nurse on a cruise ship. That information comes up indirectly, too, in later paragraphs.

Okay, time to go back and look at how this novel opens:

"What? A boat? I mean a *ship?* I could fall overboard and drown! It could sink! Look at what happened to the Titanic!"

Here are some techniques I'd like to see writers make greater use of:

- ➤ Open with conflict over a change that your protagonist resists.
- ➤ Keep the conflict going, keep it dominant, and keep up the pace.
- ➤ Splice bits of background information—including the character's name—into the action indirectly, keeping all background subordinated to the conflict.

UNIQUE INTRODUCTIONS

If you fail to use the techniques illustrated by the next three examples, they will not cause your submission to be rejected. I include them to inspire your imagination and encourage originality—both in shorter supply these days than you might realize.

Liz Zelvin, a therapist and addiction counselor, writes witty fiction about a pair of literate ex-drunks and one raging codependent. In her first novel, *Death Will Get You Sober,* her lead character is spending Christmas Day in detox. Here's the interesting way she introduces a character's name while also poking fun at her narrator:

> . . . a small, pale female hand stuck a paper cup of juice under my nose. A sweet, cool voice commanded, "Drink!"
>
> To my roommate, she said, "Put that out, sir! You know better. And offer one to the new man."
>
> Looming above us, she bored into him with a gimlet eye until he stubbed out his smoke on a plastic pill bottle and offered me the pack. I thought I was hallucinating because she seemed to be dressed like a nun. But I never said no to a cigarette.
>
> "Thanks, bro," I said, taking two. "And thank you, sister. You're an angel."
>
> "It's for later," she snapped. "Smoking room only."
>
> Ichabod laughed until his dentures popped. When the nun trotted off to get him some water, he said, "Your first time here, huh? That's Sister Angel." [p. 2]

The Case of the Greedy Lawyers is one of five novels set in Minnesota by Carl Brookins . He has fun with both his subject, a gentle send-up of the detective genre, and his series character, a 5-foot-2, quick-witted P. I. named Sean Sean. This doubled name gives Sean an advantage. It confuses people, gets them to laugh, and makes them hesitate while deciding how to address him. They start thinking about something other than how to hurt him.

In other words, Sean's name is not merely tacked on for fun. His name is a running gag that affects the plot.

A third technique shows up in Deb Baker's two mystery series. Gertie Johnson is a self-defined detective and a Yooper—someone from the U. P. or Upper Peninsula of Michigan. She is the comic lead in *Murder Passes the Buck, Murder Grins and Bears It,* and *Murder Talks Turkey.*

Gertie also plays a minor role, by telephone, in Baker's Dolled Up to Die series, in which she offers outrageous ideas for solving crimes to her niece, Gretchen Birch, a doll repairer / amateur sleuth in Phoenix, Arizona.

That Gertie communicates with her niece at all irritates Gretchen's other unorthodox aunt, Nina. Whenever the Yooper's name comes up, Nina points out that she's not related to that other, odd side of the family.

Baker's use of the same character in two different series fulfills several functions. Because Gertie has a negative effect on Nina, who plays an important role in the Dolled Up to Die series (but none in the Yooper series), the technique brings out a side of Nina that expands her character and adds to the humor. And because Gertie's wacky advice influences Gretchen's actions, Gertie does affect the plot. Further, having a character's name cross over from one series to another raises interest in an author's other series.

The term I coin for this technique is *cross-addressing.*

SOUNDS LIKE?

A sure way to confuse readers is to assign names that begin with the same letter, look similar in print, or have sounds in common, like Barton and Baxter, or Megan, Marilyn, and Margaret. Three that I kept tripping over in one best-seller were Jackie, Richie, and Teddy.

Use only one of a sound-alike set per novel and save the others until each can have a book of one's own. (Apologies to Virginia Woolf.) Also avoid hard-to-pronounce names. Or do as Shelly Reuben does in *Weeping,* her first Fritillary Quilter mystery: limit the unusual name to an attention-grabbing introduction, and thereafter use a simple form of it: Tilly.

In some manuscripts, names sound alike because they call up images that look alike. I'm referring to the novels in which every character bears an Anglo-Saxon name. Editors value diversity. A steady diet of white bread could suggest that the writer's world view and experience are a tad narrow.

Let's distinguish between two kinds of ethnic naming in American fiction. One is based on the write-what-you-know axiom; the other, on the melting pot phenomenon.

When you write what you know, your characterizations are authentic, and the names you assign represent individuals whose cultural heritage permeates their values, actions, and interactions.

An example of ethnic authenticity can be seen in Lydia Chin, one of S.J. Rozan's two alternating series characters. Rozan's portrayal of Lydia's family and community goes deeper than the mother's addressing her daughter by her Chinese name, Ling Wan-ju. The following passage is from *A Bitter Feast,* fifth in Rozan's award-winning series:

> [U]ntil I was 20 or so, all the characters I invented had WASP names—like Mitch Mitchell, Robert Robertson, Elizabeth Anderson, Bob Briggs. . . . None of the kids I grew up with had such names. They were all Weinbergers and Hamburgers and Blotniks and Briskins and Friskins. There were even some Singhs and Tsongs. . . . The Mitchells in my high school class could be counted on the digits of one severely frostbitten foot. . . . But they were in all my stories.
>
> Erica Jong, "The Artist as Housewife"[51]

> "Yang Hao-Bing thought I was a very well brought up young lady," I said, following her and the food.
>
> "He did?" She sniffed, but I could see she'd felt the compliment. Emptying the grocery bag, she said, "Perhaps, as wise as he is, he can see the great effort even when the results are poor."
>
> I suddenly realized how I could make a gold mine out of this.
>
> "What he wanted, Ma," I said while I dumped the tofu into the brine-filled container we keep for it in the fridge, "was to tell me he's been following my career. He wanted to express his satisfaction at how well I'm doing. He's very pleased at the fact that my work keeps me in Chinatown."

> Her eyes widened involuntarily; otherwise, she kept her
> attention on the bok choy as she peeled off its outer leaves. "If
> Yang Hao-Bing has been following your activities, Ling Wan-
> ju, you have drawn too much attention to yourself."
> "He said Chinatown's future was in young people like me.
> Also like Lee Bi-Da." I thought I'd haul Peter in under H. B.
> Yang's umbrella while I could. "Young people who stay here,
> who put our talents into helping the community. The way we
> would if this were our village in China."
> "If this were our village in China your future would be with
> the husband from the next village I would have found for you
> by now. . . ."   [pp. 98–99]

Rozan does her homework. She reads widely, has many Chinese friends, and spends much time in lower Manhattan's Chinatown.[52] Her award-winning books are populated with interesting, credible, three-dimensional characters. Some, like Lydia, reflect the outlook of the ABC generation: American-born Chinese. Others, like Lydia's mother, are infused with old world values.

If either your heritage or your research does not equal or exceed Rozan's level of authenticity, don't fake it. Editors and other readers know stereotypes when we see them. However, lacking specialized knowledge of another culture does not mean you have to purge all traces of diversity from your manuscript. That's where the second type of ethnic naming comes in. It is based on a reality that touches the daily lives of all but the most reclusive writers.

RAINBOW COALITION

The reality of America's melting pot is that people of color and folks with ethnic surnames fill nearly every role in society. This means you could name secondary characters Felipe Ricardo and Lucia Campanello just as easily as naming them Phil Richards and Lucy Bell.

Because minor characters are not fully developed major players, their cultural heritage is not expected to affect the story.

Tokenism? Yes. Superficial? Absolutely. Seeding your manuscript with an ethnic-sounding name or two is admittedly a form of tokenism. But think about the alternative. Considering America's multicultural history, the *absence* of ethnic surnames from a contemporary novel is unrealistic. So is a monochromatic cast of characters.

Please don't misunderstand; token name-dropping is *not* acceptable for primary characters. Someone whose life is unaffected by his or her upbringing and cultural values is ill-suited for the role of a well-rounded major character.

Minor roles, on the other hand, can be filled by almost anyone, just as in real life. You won't need to adjust the role to "fit" the name, either, provided you don't go beyond writing what you know—or what you can accurately research and have verified by someone knowledgeable.

A computer search-and-replace that substitutes "Anatole Smolansky" for "Nate Smith" won't convince anyone you're a sensitive soul. But substitution will add a little diversity to a WASP monopoly that itself misrepresents the realism for which the aware, observant writer strives, and which today's editor is open to seeing.

FIND & FIX CLUE #18: MISTAKEN IDENTITY

- Review your character list to see who does not need both a first and last name—or doesn't need both right away.
- Introduce characters one at a time, always as part of some action, letting readers become acquainted with each before bringing others out on stage.
- Prevent confusion; avoid names with similar letter combinations or sounds.
- Consider using a few distinctive nicknames and catchy epithets.
- See if your characters are consistent in how they address each other, and that variations occur for a reason, such as a special relationship or a changing attitude.
- Evaluate the ways your manuscript reflects the ethnic and racial diversity of the story's universe.

D.O.A.

CLUE #19: STRANGLED SPEECH

Profiles you write help you keep your characters from looking alike. When it comes to keeping them from sounding alike, most profiles are silent. Whatever variations in speech do make it to the page are predictable and stereotyped. Yet there's a heap more to writin' dialect than allowin' spellin' and 'postrophes to take over ev'ry *i-n-g* endin'.

The majority of submissions are populated with folks who reflect the same syntax, grammar, idioms, phrasing, vocabulary, regional expressions (or lack of), and level of formality or informality.

As a result, they sound like each other. I've no doubt they sound purty near like their author, too.

While editing one manuscript, I sensed the same three-word expression occurring a little too often: "Why don't you—." I proved my hunch with a computer search and found the identical expression coming from the mouths of three different characters.

A minor point? It's a sign of careless characterization and automated speech.

> "Technique is the ability to reproduce what your ear wants to hear."
>
> Barry Weinberg, music teacher, performing in Pearl River, NY, stating a variation on a theme of Leon Fleisher

How many of us are conscious of our own speaking habits? It's hard enough to express *what* we mean without thinking about the *how*. But writers of fiction must do both—though not necessarily at the same time. That's what revision is for. So read your dialogue aloud and listen for the voices your future readers will hear.

Individualized speaking styles contribute to characterization by reflecting education, place of origin, and other background influences. They add interest, at times furnish comic relief, and satisfy the ears of your readers—especially your first reader, the busy screener-outer.

SUBTLETY IN SPEECH

Ideally, every character should manifest a slightly different speaking style. In reality, you're on safe ground if the noticeably distinctive voices are limited to minor characters who make a single appearance or a few brief appearances. As for your protagonist, use "normal" speech, because readers identify more easily with a character who sounds "like them"— meaning the way we think others hear us. (It's a fact that we don't hear our own regional accents.)

"Normal" speech is especially agreeable for the main character and the narrator in a full-length novel. For a short story, the narrator's voice can be unique, as in the following examples of authentic, credible dialogue.

"One Too Many" is a short story by Southern writer Betty Beamguard in which a grown woman finds herself sandwiched between caring for her mother and her mother-in-law at the same time:

> And I swanee, if Phil's mama didn't fall out the back door
> and break her arm two days later, I'm not settin' here. And did
> she call 911? She did not. She called us and we had to leave
> Mama all by herself at eight o'clock at night to carry Alma to
> the emergency room.
> I asked her, "What in the Sam Hill were you doing outside
> after dark?"

In addition to language and expression, Beamguard captures subtle speech characteristics: variation in sentence length, inflection, and the woman's answering her own rhetorical question. Her attitude reveals an assumption of the right to control her mother-in-law's actions.

Dottie Boatwright, also a Southern writer of short stories, presents "By Gawd, We Ain't Like That." See if you can identify the advantages of writing this situation from the close third-person viewpoint of a young girl:

> Georgiann didn't know if it was another one of them bad
> nightmares she had or if her Pa really had done shot that gun
> over their heads last night. All she could remember was waking
> up to him on the warpath again a-yelling and a-swearing.
> Mama'd done told them not to listen when he cussed like a
> sailor thataway. Said to just let it go on by. . . .   [pp. 27–28]

By writing in Georgiann's voice and viewpoint, Boatwright avoids dramatizing the violence. It's an effective technique for understating events as experienced by a youngster, one who'd been trained by her mother to run and hide, thereby only hearing the ruckus and seeing only its aftermath.

MODERATION

Beware of presenting too many idiosyncrasies at a time, making them too noticeable, or repeating them too often. A little flavoring goes a long way.

Also be wary of putting more than one character with a unique speech habit in the same scene—unless their habits are

> "What sense is it we use for writing? It's hearing. Writing is listening, and reading is listening, too."
>
> Margaret Edson, Pulitzer prize-winning playwright, at The Spoken Word, Atlanta 2001

sufficiently different. Perhaps one individual could be a source of rich, colorful expressions; the other, a poster child for a starved vocabulary.

The reason such roles should be brief and kept to a minimum is that a small amount of conspicuousness is . . . er, conspicuous.

When we talk with someone face to face, all kinds of stimuli compete for our attention, so we tend not to listen closely. We're distracted by background activity. We're thinking of what we want to say next.

We're also watching the speaker's gestures and facial expressions and silently forming opinions about her touched-up hair, turned-in toes, turned-up nose, or turned-down hose.

When we *read* dialogue, though, especially when it's effectively written, our concentration is focused. Eccentricities on the page become magnified. Bizarre speech habits applied with a heavy hand become absurd; at best, they distract from the reading instead of adding to it.

A speech characteristic repeated once or twice comes through loud and clear—no need to pound it home, unless you are writing comedy.

DIALECT

In the late nineteenth century, Bret Harte and Mark Twain popularized the trend toward local color and regional dialect, but these literary giants went too far. Today it's a chore to read the authors of a century ago who tried to reproduce what the ear seemed to hear. That's because written dialect, though intended for the ear, is seen first with the eyes, which perceive strange spellings and prolific apostrophes as obstacles to reading.

Inexperienced writers who represent dialect phonetically always overdo it. Use restraint with pronunciation—great restraint. To simulate a character's habit of dropping the final letter of *i-n-g* words, do so once to give readers the general idea without burdening them with a faithful rendering. Then, use about a dozen correct endings before dropping another.

More effective than efforts to replicate pronunciation are the colorful idioms and expressions that perceptive writers put in the mouths of their characters. Here's the unique New Orleans speech captured by John Kennedy Toole in his mainstream novel, *A Confederacy of Dunces:*

> "Oh, Miss Inez," Mrs. Reilly called in that accent that occurs south of New Jersey only in New Orleans, that Hoboken near the Gulf of Mexico. "Over here, babe."
>
> "Hey, how you making?" Miss Inez asked. "How you feeling, darling?"
>
> "Not so hot," Mrs. Reilly answered truthfully.
>
> "Ain't that a shame." Miss Inez leaned over the glass case and forgot about her cakes. "I don't feel so hot myself. It's my feet."
>
> "Lord, I wisht I was that lucky. I got arthuritis in my elbow."
>
> "Aw, no!" Miss Inez said with genuine sympathy. "My poor old poppa's got that. We make him go set himself in a hot tub fulla berling water."   [p. 16]

Toole's distinctive spellings are few. Instead, his novel is flavored with the unique expressions of his New Orleans characters.

Equally distinctive is the Scottish burr heard in the historical mysteries of Charles Todd. Hamish is the voice of conscience that invades the mind of Scotland Yard Inspector Ian Rutledge, home from the hell of World War I.

John Kennedy Toole killed himself at age 32 in despair over constant rejection of his novel. For the next ten years his mother continued to circulate his manuscript. After it was eventually published in 1980, it won a Pulitzer.[53]

The words of the dead soldier, whom Rutledge had been required to shoot for disobeying an order, provide a continual source of conflict for the inspector, beginning with *A Test of Wills,* the first of eleven novels so far:

> "Ye'll no' triumph over me!" Hamish said. "I'm a scar on your
> bluidy soul."   [p. 328]

Because readers experience Hamish entirely through his speech, his voice
has to be distinctive. It is.

Margaret Maron's Judge Deborah Knott series, set in a fictional North
Carolina county, occasionally includes the Southern expression "might
could" in dialogue—as in the following line from *Bootlegger's Daughter,*
the first novel to win the "big four" in mystery awards: the Edgar, Agatha,
Anthony, and Macavity:

> "Your brothers: both free to come and go without punching time
> cards or anybody keeping tabs on them. They alibied each other
> for Wednesday, which we might could question. . . ."   [p. 62]

To the non-Southerner, the "might could" construction is so unexpected
that a New York editor would be remiss in not querying whether the usage
is intentional or accidental. Intentional it is, because Maron excels in characterization, and because New Yorkers (that would include me) have much
to learn about Southern dialect.

Tamar Myers uses the same idiom in *The Ming and I,* the third mystery
in her Den of Antiquity series. She also has her narrator, South Carolina
antiques dealer Abigail Timberlake, comment on that distinctive usage:

> "Well, Gloria, you certainly have a point. But we might could
> squeeze a little extra out of petty cash, if we tried really hard."
> Please don't misunderstand. "Might could" is a perfectly proper
> speech construct in Rock Hill.   [p. 47]

For your own characters, your comfort level might lie somewhere between the rare *a-yelling* and *might coulds,* and the more vigorous *arthuritis*
and *I swanee.* Whichever style works for you, representing believable voices
takes astute listening, judicious selecting, and restrained writing. And of
course, scrupulous self-editing.

GRAMMAR

Depending on how you use it, ungrammatical language can make a character sound like an average Joe or an unqualified jerk. In *Final Jeopardy,* a
Macavity award nominee, Linda Fairstein uses grammar to characterize

the good-looking stud who'd been sleeping with the now-deceased Isabella. This novel is first in the series featuring Alexandra Cooper, sex crimes prosecutor for the Manhattan D.A.'s office.

> "So did Iz talk about me a lot?"
>
> "She told me a lot about you, yes."
>
> "Good things, mostly?" he said jokingly. "We had some kinda good times together, her and me."
>
> The English major in me winced. He may have been great in bed, but his syntax was as atrocious as his manners. He was shoving the bread in his mouth each time he came up for air, rinsing it down with the vodka.
>
> "Did Isabella tell you how we met and everything? We was a hot ticket for a while."
>
> Enough about me, now talk about what Iz thought about me. This was going to be a long evening.   [p. 229]

Fairstein develops our impression of this murder suspect by letting us hear the egotism in his words and see his vulgar table manners—a technique that parallels a strong visual image with a powerful verbal image.

PURPOSE

As with every technique you use, select speech differences for a purpose: to expand characterization, furnish variety or comedy, simulate authenticity for a time or place, or present a glimpse of today's culture through one specific slice of life.

Janis Holm's "Shopping with Winona" is a work of flash fiction, a literary form of extreme brevity also called microfiction. As we hear the narrator fantasize about going on a shopping spree with Winona Ryder (who was once caught shoplifting), what do the run-on sentences, diction, and content tell you about the speaker and her values?

> . . . we're whispering and telling secrets, popping pills and making fun of the salesladies, it's a blast. We try on everything we see and pretend we're someone else, a high-society snot or a supermodel, Britney or Christina. And in the dressing room we fill our bags, our purses, we hide the thongs in our bras, we say we are so hot, they should pay us to wear their stupid clothes.

The speaker's age is suggested by her behavior, attitude, and vocabulary, her economic status and perhaps working class background are hinted at in her attitude toward the prices of the clothes she takes: "they should pay us."

Both her rebellion and need to prove that she feels good about herself are indicated by her overstated bravado in the closing line, added as they walk out with all their "stuff":

> . . . and we're high, we're cool, we know who we are, we're
> the best ever to walk the planet.

Another type of distinctive, contemporary speech can be seen in *Bad Luck,* Suzanne Proulx's second mystery featuring Victoria Lucci. The name of the series character is pronounced "Lucky"—something Victoria is not. A hospital risk manager, she has just taken the risk of offering a ride to the talkative street urchin whose cat she accidentally hit with a borrowed SUV.

The girl tells Victoria she's a witch.

> Right. "I guess you're psychic, too."
> "Only a little bit, sometimes, yeah. I mean, like, I can't
> tell you what the Lotto numbers are gonna be."
> More's the pity. "So that's how you knew I was a lawyer?" I
> glance at her as I say this. She looks puzzled.
> "Well, no, you know, like, I thought you told me that."
> "I don't think so."
> "One way or another," she says, "you told me. So, like, yeah,
> I'm psychic, I know I am, some other things have happened.
> Like. . . ."   [p. 14]

Humor seems the only purpose of this exchange, yet the scene introduces characters and a situation that become plot-related. In addition, the protagonist's straight role in relation to the girl's kookiness expands Victoria's characterization and showcases her sardonic style.

Be cautious in using slang and other contemporary expressions because they could date your writing. Although "I mean, like" could be safe to use. After all, it's been around for at least fifteen years and might continue for, like, the next fifteen. More's the pity.

TIME AND PLACE

The purpose of using distinctive speech is to add authenticity, especially when reflecting a specific place or a time in the past. Having researched public records from the seventeenth and eighteenth centuries for the first book I wrote, I doubt that official documents ever reflect the vernacular of their time. Fortunately for my early readers, I wrote no dialogue.

Writers who specialize in the cultures and periods of the far distant past have almost no written material to guide them. To my knowledge, no explorer has yet unearthed a narrated Dead Sea CD.

Judith Geary, who sets her young adult novel, *Getorix,* in ancient Rome, tells me that writers of historical fiction frequently debate the question of how to create the illusion of authentic dialogue. Considerable research involves learning not only when words came into use but also when the concepts we now associate with those words came into use.

Some science fiction writers invent their own language, but if you write historical fiction—whether Regency romance or fifteenth century fantasy—I'm honestly impressed by the extent of research you do to represent convincing settings, dress, conventions, and dialogue.

Listen to a scene by Maine author Lea Wait from *Seaward Born*, a historical novel for ages eight to twelve. Time and place: summer 1805 on the docks of Charleston, South Carolina. Michael, a thirteen-year-old slave, is working alongside an older slave, who's been looking out for the boy:

> "How far would a man have to go?" Michael couldn't help asking. "How far to be free?"
>
> "Farther north you get to, the better. Farthest in these United States would be District of Maine. It be the north part of Massachusetts, before the north seas and Canada."
>
> "I knows Maine!" Michael smiled at the memory. "Mistress had a fancy dinner party and Sam brung a whole barrel full of big green lobsters from the wharves. They was packed all around in sawdust. And ice. From Maine!" [p. 16]

When Michael's benevolent ownership changes, he has to decide between remaining a slave or taking the risk of escaping to the north.

Another young adult title, this one set in the 1820s, tackles a long-standing feud that began in South Carolina's upcountry and lasted well beyond the

Revolutionary War battles in the region. *Abbeyville Farewell: A Novel of Early Atlanta and North Georgia* by Estelle Ford-Williamson introduces the fictional Joseph John. In the following passage, the teenager encounters a man who knew his grandfather:

> "Tell me more. Was Joseph a hero? Did he whup the Tories?"
> The old man's eyes saddened. His voice lowered. His slightly reddened lower eyelids were suddenly wet.
> "Son, they's eighteen hundred widows and orphans throughout all of Ninety-Six when it was all over, my wife Obedeime and my two sons Charles and Andrew died with 'em—all because of that war among the neighbors."   [p. 33]

EAVESDROP

Review your character profiles and specify how you want each individual's speech to reflect place of birth, social class, education, job-related jargon, and so on. Instead of telling background, show its influence through your characters' dialogue. Fit grammar to education, fit idioms and slang to age and lifestyle. A few instances are sufficient to suggest a larger picture. Research by eavesdropping in unfamiliar places.

Grab a notebook and sit next to families in the waiting rooms of the Social Security office and the hospital emergency room. Listen for regional expressions, idioms, and everyday colloquialisms. Tune in to call-in radio. Hang around the exit of Kmart. Stand in line at the symphony and the Stop & Shop—or should I say *on* line?

Depends where you grew up. South Boston doesn't sound like South Dakota or South L.A., and no place on earth sounds like the South Bronx or South Mwaukee.

Cindy Daniel keeps her Hannah Fogarty mysteries lively with expressions from the fictional denizens of Destiny, Texas. In *Death Warmed Over,* the first book of the series, Hannah says of her sister:

> . . . and before you could blink an eye Ruth was in deeper than a rancher's boot in a full pasture.   [p. 1]

The idea is not to scatter expressions throughout your story like wildflower seeds, but to select specimen plants for deliberate effect in choice locations. Here's a bit from *Hog Wild,* Cathy Pickens' third novel:

"Hate I missed you at the plant rescue," I said.
"Wadn't there."   [p. 109]

In *Signs in the Blood,* the first Elizabeth Goodweather mystery by Appalachian author Vicki Lane, a character who brings a food donation says:

"It ain't but Colonel Sanders but I reckon someone kin worry
it down."   [p. 1]

Here are two voices I happened to come across, though I had not been looking or listening for them. The first was said by a North Carolina cable television provider in a newspaper interview:

"Programming kept going up every year and it put a hurtin'
on us."

I overheard the following in a fast-food restaurant in Tennessee:

"We useta could."

You won't use all your field research, and you won't use it verbatim, but eavesdropping will help you hear voices in your head other than your own.

DESCRIBE IT

Instead of attempting to echo a speech characteristic, you can briefly describe it. Here's an example of such a description from *Offer of Proof* by Robert Heilbrun:

"Why, all of a sudden, the dinner date?" she wanted to know,
when we were seated in our booth. "What's up?"
She pronounced "up" as if it had two syllables.   [p. 312]

Here's another, from Terry Hoover's first mystery, *Double Dead,* a finalist in the St. Martin's Press/Malice Domestic contest:

"We used to work together down at the dairy. I was in
bookkeeping; she was secretary to Mr. Hollings." She pronounced it sec-a-tary.   [p. 70]

In *The Other Side of Silence* by Joseph L. S. Terrell, the Depression causes a boy and his family to spend one Asheville summer living with kinfolk. All are seated at the supper table when they hear the voice of the neighbor's son outside:

> Hubert stood by the kitchen window calling Uncle Roy. "Mr. Britton! Mr. Britton!" His voice had the thin mountaineer twang to it so that he stretched out the first syllable of the name twice as long as most people would say it. [p. 43]

In *Done Gone Wrong,* Cathy Pickens' first novel, she offers this colorful description of the speech of a South Carolina attorney:

> . . . Jake sat behind a desk roughly the size of Charleston harbor, drawling every sentence in an accent as thick and sticky as marsh mud. "What can Blaine Demarcos do for us?" His words had no r's, just a soft rise and fall like tide on a sand flat. [p. 7]

Another way of describing speech is to comment on a character's usage. In *Death of an Obnoxious Tourist* by Marie Hudgins, a group of Americans and an Englishman are touring Italy and setting their next day's departure:

> "If we leave here by cab about thirty minutes before, we should be in plenty of time," I said.
> "See you half-nine, then," Geoffrey said, as he turned toward the elevator.
> Half-nine. Funny, the way the English say things. Half-nine. Nine-thirty. [p. 137]

FOR REALISM

Whatever your purpose, individualized speech offers a sense of realism and contributes greatly to characterization and setting. Sometimes you write it simply for fun—which is my own reason for including the following as the final selection in my crusade against strangled speech. It's from *Glitz* by that master of dialogue, Elmore Leonard. His protagonist hails a cab in Atlantic City, New Jersey. (The absence of quotation marks is Leonard's.)

> Yeah, rain helped business, the cab driver told Vincent. Rainy night, wind blowing. But otherwise, say you want to go a few blocks on Pacific you hop a jitney, six bits. You want a broad? They're on the corner. Look, there's one—got everything but a

> sign on her. Or you call an escort service. You *walk* to the
> casinos, the ones up at this end.   [p. 106]

When you revise, use your growing awareness of speaking styles—in moderation—to differentiate your characters. Naturally, all dialogue should sound . . . well, natural. If this seems like a lot of work, it is. You are attempting to simulate human-like beings who don't sound like clones of you. That's almost as difficult to do on paper as in a petri dish.

Sometimes, despite your efforts, the dialogue you write comes across as weak and ineffectual, and no technique that you experiment with manages to distinguish one character from another. The problem might not lie in their speaking styles but in the characters themselves. Be sure to see them as fully materialized individuals, each with his or her own agenda.

It takes a while to reach the state that authors describe as their characters taking over and speaking for themselves. Face it, some characters never do. They need more than a good talking to; they need rubbing out.

FIND & FIX CLUE #19: STRANGLED SPEECH

- Review the character profiles you create for each character to "hear" how you want each one to sound to reflect that individual's background in his or her speech.
- Use the barest minimum of phonetic spellings, *if any,* to merely suggest a character's pronunciation, and avoid unusual punctuation and almost all dropped letters.
- Have someone read snatches of your dialogue aloud to you in random order, without any identifying tags, to see if you can tell your characters apart by the tone, grammar, vocabulary, sentence structure, and expressions you give them.
- Cultivate your ear for speech patterns and regional expressions by eavesdropping and picking up the different ways that ordinary people speak.
- Use contractions that simulate a natural conversational style.

CLUE #20: KILLED BY CLICHÉ

Dull as dishwater. That's both a cliché and a style of writing that litters manuscripts with expressions that haven't been fresh and original since Moses was a pup. Yup, that's a cliché, too. In a majority of manuscripts, the protagonist is always waiting for minutes that seem an hour, or for hours that seem an eternity. One character is sure to be described as having hooded eyelids. And at least once per book, a frown creases someone's brow.

Unfortunately, trite, overused expressions are not limited to the work of neophytes. One evening when I relaxed with a much-acclaimed medical thriller, I came across a description of an autopsy room as a *beehive of activity* and the new widow as wearing *a ton of makeup.* The investigating officer managed to *fan* his partner's anxiety *to a fevered pitch,* and another character felt that her *fears had come to pass.*

The clichés continued, each drawing part of my attention away from the story. Determined to discover why this clumsy, verbose author was so popular, I forced myself to spend two hours slogging through his best-seller before giving up. Each hour seemed an eternity.

The popularity of this author and others like him should not make you complacent about your own forms of expression. One hackneyed figure of speech on the opening pages of your submission is enough for a busy screener to condemn it to the "no" pile, brow firmly creased.

INTENTIONAL TRITENESS

When you self-edit your manuscript, make an extra pass to catch all your outworn, overworked expressions. Change them or get rid of them—with a few exceptions. One exception is where clichés in dialogue reveal a character's reliance on old saws. That's what Terry Hoover does in her first novel, *Double Dead,* by having a character say, "since Moses was a pup."

CLICHÉ AS CHARACTERIZATION

Although you want to avoid writing dialogue that is itself trite, you can include a few clichés *in* dialogue to reveal a character's impoverished vocabulary. The technique helps expand your characterization—provided you show your awareness of doing so. Demonstrate your intention by limiting the idiosyncrasy to one character.

However, two characters throw hackneyed sayings at one another in *Framework for Death,* the second Tory Travers/David Alvarez mystery by Aileen Schumacher. The result is effective. Not only are these duets brief and confined to only two of many scenes in which the rival law enforcement agents interact with each other, but their dialogue has each character acknowledging the triteness of his expressions.

Excerpts from those scenes follow. One speaker is the series character, Detective Alvarez, a Texan. The outsider is a federal drug enforcement agent from the Midwest. The bilingual Alvarez speaks first:

> "I hate to rain on your New Year's parade, but I think you're barking up the wrong tree. There's more weird shit to this case than a three-dollar bill, but I don't think your guy did his wife."
> There was a pause. "Do you always talk like that?"
> "Only when I speak English. My partner taught me all the clichés I know."   [p. 149]

Five chapters later the federal agent resumes their verbal contest:

> "But there's no point sitting here crying over spilt milk, while Boyce is out there making hay. See, I've been working on some midwestern clichés for you."
> "Before we move on to greener pastures, so to speak, one last thing. . . ."   [p. 217]

Again, Alvarez gets the last word. Schumacher's technique functions on multiple levels. First, on the literal level the dialogue continues the men's discussion of the case. Second, their verbal banter expands their rivalry into the arena of repartee. Third, their quick-wittedness adds to characterization by showing the pair of crime-fighters equally matched.

Fourth, as entertainment, Schumacher's parody is a tour de force proving the richness of her writing style.

CLICHÉ AS SELF-PARODY

To show that using an old saying is intentional, the narrator can label it, as Gayle Wigglesworth does in her short story "I Love a Parade!" The narrator, a recently retired woman, says:

> Every time I thought about one of the projects my former business was managing I reminded myself it was no longer my business or my worry. Life and problems escalated for me until finally, being a witness to a brutal murder had been the proverbial straw that broke this camel's back.   [pp. 74–75]

Betty Gordon, in her short story "Dead by Breakfast," writes:

> She and Mama taught me everything important in life and their lessons just keep making me toe that proverbial line."   [p. 6]

Brenda Wallace's *Mind Trip,* a novel-in-progress, shows Lauren receiving an eerie letter from an anonymous sender who knows what no one still alive could know. It had arrived when she'd been open to a diversion:

> . . .Unwanted, the cliché hooked itself inside her brain, repeating like an obnoxious advertising jingle. *Be careful what you wish for.*   [ms p. 53]

Have fun with this technique, as Heidi Anna Johnson does in her first-person novel-in-progress, *Flash Memory:*

> I hesitated. Knowing what I knew, I didn't relish the idea of being alone with him. But if I refused to let him in, he would know that I knew what I knew. It would tip my hand, let the cat out of the bag, spill the beans before I had gathered enough for a pot big enough to serve in court.
> I'd run out of clichés. I let him in.

Similarly owning up to the use of old saws is Rabbi Aviva Cohen, the protagonist of Ilene Schneider's mystery series. In *Chanukah Guilt,* the rabbi learns that a young woman she'd tried to counsel is dead:

> Clichés exist because they're true. My heart leaped into my throat. I couldn't breathe. The room was spinning. My vision dimmed.   [p. 35]

Aviva later interrupts an uncomfortable silence with this adage:

> "That which doesn't kill us makes us stronger." They turned
> and stared at me now. "Sorry, I figured it was time for a
> cliché."   [p. 95]

By poking fun at those who use unoriginal phrases, writers leave no doubt that their methods are deliberate. Failing that, their lapses catch the attention of screener-outers, who have seen every cliché imaginable.

Donna Andrews, winner of numerous mystery-writing awards, says in an email: "I think it's unrealistic *never* to use clichés, though I also think it's reasonable for a self-aware person to acknowledge when s/he uses them." Exactly!

> Published authors get skewered in public: columnist Stanley Fish criticizes "pleasantly plump"in an opening line, an unneeded phrase that he says "dumps you on a cliché, which might be all right if the author gave any sign of knowing that it was one. This guy is going to hit false notes for 300 pages, but I won't be listening."
>
> "Murder, I Read," Op-Ed in *New York Times,* March 28, 2007

TWIST THE TRITE

Another clever way to use gray-haired sayings is to give them an unexpected twist. Earlier I criticized the overuse of *he ran a hand through his* [x-color] *hair.* Chuck Hogan, whose short story "One Good One" in *Ellery Queen Mystery Magazine,* offers a twist on that phrase:

> He ran his hand through his hair and it came back wet with
> scalp sweat.   [p. 192]

Yech. But it *is* original. So is this twist on the oft-used *hour that seemed an eternity* in the first novel by Edgar winner John Hart, *The King of Lies:*

> I sat there for what my watch said was only fifty-five minutes.
> The watch lied. It was a lifetime.   [p. 244]

In *Death and the Hubcap,* fourth in the Trudy Roundtree series, author Linda Berry spins an overworked metaphor as part of the dialogue of a small-town chief of police, Henry Huckabee. Her technique adds to the book's humor and expands the folksy characterization of Huckabee. If that weren't enough, Berry also uses the cliché to clarify a plot point:

"You young'uns have perched me right up on the horns of a wigglin' dilemma and it is not a comfortable place for me to be. On the one horn, there's the fact that you have broken a number of laws and are up to your collarbones in something serious. The car you—Rusty—were drivin' made nice clear photogenic tracks all over a man. I can't just shake my finger at you and say, 'Naughty naughty, don't do it again.' On the other horn, there is the fact that I know you are not hardened criminals and I don't want to give you the electric chair, even if I could. . . ."

. . . "Any questions?"

There may have been any number of questions, including what kind of an animal a dilemma might be, but nobody raised them.   [pp. 180–81]

CLICHÉ AS PLOT

Unlike clichéd expressions, a clichéd plot seldom causes the quick demise of a submission. Screeners spot other, more immediate clues to average writing well before reading far enough to experience the plot's triteness.

Still, to round out this topic, I'd like to expose a few overused situations. "The butler did it" may not apply to your story, either because your fiction has no butler in it or because you want to avoid the jokes about this oft-disparaged domestic servant. Other overdone, stereotyped situations include these:

- the wrongly accused who's saved by the arrival of a long-lost twin;
- the virgin whose middle-of-the-night nightmare makes her scream, which brings the cop asleep on the couch running to check on her safety, and when they realize they are nearly naked—;
- the prostitute who plans to quit the profession as soon as she earns enough to be a real mom to the baby she gave up years ago;
- the phone caller who has urgent information, but for some never-explained reason can't talk about it on the phone, and whose corpse the protagonist is surprised to stumble over upon arriving for their clandestine meeting only one hour later;
- the sole witness who walks her dog the night before she testifies and is not seen again, though Buster turns up in a dumpster;

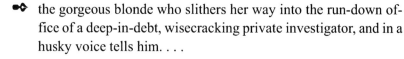

- the hero, tied up and about to be killed, who tricks his captor into bragging about how he really "did it"—which no one would otherwise know—and is rescued at the very moment the killer conveniently supplies the final proof of his guilt;

- the gorgeous blonde who slithers her way into the run-down office of a deep-in-debt, wisecracking private investigator, and in a husky voice tells him. . . .

You've been here before, often, so I'm sure you can think of many more stale examples. The clichéd plot situation, like the clichéd expression, is good for one thing—parody.

J. L. Abramo spoofs a medley of classic P. I. stereotypes in his Jake Diamond series, achieving both humor and mystery. Here is the opening to his *Catching Water in a Net,* a Shamus award-winner for best first private eye novel:

> The phone on my desk rang so unexpectedly that I nearly spilled the Mylanta onto my only unstained necktie.
>
> It was my trusty assistant calling from her sentry post out front. . . .
>
> "There's a woman here to see you."
>
> I'd figured we had a guest. The place was small. Usually when Darlene wanted me she just hollered.
>
> "Count to twenty, Darlene, and send her in," I said, determining that we were on a secure line.
>
> "Is that one, two or one Mississippi, two Mississippi?"
>
> I quickly assessed the condition of the desk.
>
> "Make it one Montgomery, Alabama, two Montgomery, Alabama."

You've been here before, too, but without being as entertained, perhaps, as in the cramped office of Diamond Investigation.

Jake asks his new client how he can help her. She replies:

> "It's my husband."
>
> If I had ten cents for every time I've heard that phrase I could have all three ties dry-cleaned.
>
> "I can't find him," she added.

"I assure you, Mrs. Harding, he's not here."

"What?"

"It's a joke I use to relax new clients."

"It doesn't work."

"I can see that. How long has your husband been missing, Evelyn?"

"Since Saturday evening."

"That would be four days."

"I can see now why you came so highly recommended."

Evelyn Harding was as personable as an Office Depot catalog.   [pp. 3–5]

SELF-APPRAISING PHRASING

The time to root out the wretched expressions from your writing is not when they fly from your fingertips as you romance the keyboard. Words that come easily to your mind serve as surrogates for ideas that might vanish if you stop to self-edit. Clichés can be shorthand placeholders to help you get your first draft committed to paper or pixels. So keep on writing; revising comes later. That's when you dump the dull-as-dishwater expressions and replace them with fresh.

Writers who are not as sensitive to worn-out phrasing as they could be might be similarly oblivious to what editors call a *howler:* the comical result of using an expression with a figurative meaning in a context that unexpectedly brings out its literal meaning. For example:

> A writer of science fiction whose skill in storytelling exceeded his craft emailed me to say that his first editing experience taught him techniques he'd never been aware of. He added: "An avid reader does not necessarily make for a knowledgeable writer."

Whenever the boss's son walked in, Waldo was deep in thought, eyes closed. The young man would always say, "Stop daydreaming and get to work, Pops. You act like you got Alzheimer's."

Waldo had half a mind to prove the kid wrong.

Detecting your own howlers and killer clichés is not easy. The computer program has yet to be designed that can redline gray-haired expressions.

If you lack graydar, the next best way to detect outdated expressions is with a thorough line edit of your manuscript.

To get the most value from a professional edit—whether or not you choose to apply every recommendation to your current work-in-progress—keep a running list of all editorial comments, including every expression identified as a cliché. Keep adding to that list over time and refer to it whenever you self-edit future manuscripts.

DEADER THAN A DOORNAIL

Mark my words: expressions as old as the hills are the kiss of death. First and foremost, they cast a pall over your writing and yank the rug out from under your labor of love in the blink of an eye. Needless to say, they offer proof positive that the writer is wet behind the ears. If you've heard it once you've heard it a million times: one rotten apple can spoil the barrel.

Unless you are bending over backwards to tickle your reader's fancy, you're skating on thin ice with those tried and true sayings. A word to the wise: don't shoot yourself in the foot. Forewarned is forearmed.

Last but not least is this hard and fast rule of thumb: avoid clichés like the plague.

FIND & FIX CLUE #20: KILLED BY CLICHÉ

- Eliminate as many trite expressions in your writing as you can find and get help in finding the rest of them.
- If a cliché benefits your story in some way, acknowledge it as a cliché or a proverb so your use of it doesn't seem like an oversight.
- Verify that any clichés used in dialogue are consistent with that character's speech pattern and the personality you want to project.
- Treat clichés in dialogue as you would any distinctive speech habit: sparingly—which requires your being aware, during self-editing, of every word you've written.

D.O.A.

CLUE #21: GESTURED TO DEATH

Gestures are handy little devices that anchor characters in their settings and furnish quickie images for readers to visualize. The carefully designed, purposeful gesture, mannerism, or display of body language is a versatile do-more-with-less telephoto lens that adds depth and meaning to actions and dialogue. It reveals what a character is feeling or doing at the moment he or she speaks—whether that feeling or behavior is in or out of sync with the speaker's words.

The well-crafted mannerism snaps a picture worth a thousand adverbs.

Regrettably, most submissions suffer from what I call *gesturitis,* a glut of pointless, stereotyped tics and fidgets. One character pauses and takes a deep breath, another wipes away a tear. He ran a hand through his hair. A frown creased her brow. He nodded and turned. She shrugged and shook her head. They sighed. He sat down. She laughed and stood up. He smiled and looked around. She looked at him. He looked out the window. I yawned.

The same predictable busyness fills manuscript after manuscript, none of it adding insight. Differences between characters fade under the burden of perpetually meaningless perpetual motion.

Identical images make the majority of submissions seem written in the same average voice. Screeners get a sense of *déjà* view—the feeling they are viewing many submissions from the same writer whose efforts they'd previously consigned to the "no" pile.

VALUE ADDED

When revising your manuscript, take a good look at the gestures and mannerisms you assign. Know why you select one over another.

- Do they add value to the story by deepening your characterization?
- Or do they merely add an assortment of tics and fidgets?

Analyze the function you want each gesture to serve. Know what attitude or change in attitude you want your characters to reveal. The next excerpt, by June Willson Read, shows a young woman in the early 1900s starting a job at a hotel restaurant in Calgary, far from her Dakota home:

> On her first day in the dining room, Pearl, the head waitress, began Marie's training by asking her, "Ever wait tables before, Dearie?"
>
> "No, but I've eaten at nice restaurants, so I know what good service is."
>
> "Now don't take me wrong, honey. We get a lot of pretty faces coming through that can't take the guff these guys hand out."
>
> "I can handle myself." Marie lifted her chin defiantly. Then she lowered it. "I appreciate your help, though."   [p. 6]

This glimpse of a change in demeanor reflects the author's dedication to portraying the many sides of Marie Fisher Law, in the creative nonfiction biography *Frontier Madam: The Life of Dell Burke, Lady of Lusk*. Using the name Dell Burke, Marie went on to operate one of the most famous brothels in the West. Yet she closed on Sundays, believing her customers should be in church, and she used her earnings to help the town of Lusk, Wyoming, avoid insolvency during the Depression.

SHOWING, NOT TELLING

Although gestures make effective beats or tags to accompany dialogue, they are not mere substitutes for *he said/she said*. An effective mannerism or glimpse of body language can signal tension, show contradictions between spoken words and unspoken feelings, and hint at emotions and attitudes that a character keeps hidden or is unaware of.

Little behaviors add meaning to what is said—and imply what isn't.

Too Close to Evil by Beth Terrell shows P. I. Jared McKean interviewing the coworker of a murdered woman. While the stylish younger woman mentions that the victim had dressed as if she'd been self-conscious about her weight, the coworker's own mannerisms reveal a similar concern:

> Unconsciously, she sucked in her stomach, slipped a thumb into the waistband of her skirt and tugged.   [p. 79]

Twist Phelan dramatizes a scene in *Spurred Ambition* in which the series character, Hannah Dain, learns how her sister views their father's attitude toward his two daughters. Hannah always believed her father
disapproved of her while favoring her sister, Shelby, who says:

> ". . . Daddy's treated you differently since the moment you
> were born. He always said you were cut from a different cloth."
> Hannah sucked in a breath. "Did he say anything else? About
> the cloth, I mean."
> Shelby frowned in annoyance. "What are you talking about?
> It's just an expression."
> "Right." Hannah plucked at a loose thread on the bedspread.
> Shelby studied her with narrowed eyes.
> "Is there something you expected him to say?" she asked.
> Hannah's hand tightened into a fist, crushing the jelly bean in
> her palm. She had forgotten how keen her sister's radar could
> be, especially when it came to detecting secrets.   [p. 11]

Mannerisms and what they reveal can also be used to furnish a little
social commentary. In Roberta Rogow's *The Problem of the Evil Editor,*
set in 1888 London, a grin offers the opportunity for such an observation:

> "Right-ho, guv!" The youth grinned, displaying teeth that
> would never see a dentist.   [p. 196]

The importance of small mannerisms is also highlighted in a psycho-
logical thriller by Deborah and Joel Shlian, *Wednesday's Child.* Here, Leigh
plays back a terse message on her answering machine from her mother:

> "Your letter arrived. I'm disappointed."
> Her mother, Leigh thought bitterly, a true economizer of
> words, able to convey meaning with a raised eyebrow or curled
> lip, simple phrase or pointed question.   [p. 28]

In another novel by the Shlians, *Rabbit in the Moon,* the attitude of the
pampered son of a wealthy Korean businessman offers a look at two levels
of social class. David's elitism shows in his annoyance over the habits and
mannerisms that broadcast the lower status of another businessman:

"Speak Chinese!" David snapped, annoyed not only by the man's lateness, but by the way his padded cotton jacket and baggy blue trousers contrasted with his own impeccable cashmere coat and Pierre Cardin suit. Lee Tong hadn't even bothered to shave. Hard to believe such a man owned his own factory. "Anyone hearing Korean will assume we're spies and I don't think even your *hou-tai*," he said, referring to Tong's Party connections via his father, "will protect you."

"Sorry." Tong nervously checked the crowd before lighting an unfiltered Camel. . . .

David winced as Tong grasped his cigarette between thumb and forefinger. Vulgar, he thought. Like some low-class coolie.

[p. 13]

SUGGEST EMOTION

Go for the gestures that convey emotion, because it's through a character's feelings—about others, the world in general, a situation, or oneself—that readers relate to a character and experience the same emotion:

This is how it feels when you realize your child is missing. The pit of your stomach freezes, while your legs go to jelly.

Jodi Picoult, *The Tenth Circle* [p. 1]

Bitsy picked a fallen twig up off the deck and began to strip the bark from it. "I think he's graduated up to some of those other things. . . ." Kathryn R. Wall, *In for a Penny* [p. 136]

Bitsy is reacting to questions about her son's possible steroid use. Does her body language tell you she is worried, distracted, wrapped in thought? Trying to dissociate from painful reality or working hard to control her emotions? All of the above? Does the emotion have to be named? No.

The value of showing a behavior instead of telling about it is that interpretation is unnecessary. Wall captures a mannerism so familiar that we recognize having stripped a few twigs ourselves. Certain experiences are universal, their associated emotions buried in our memories.

The amateur writer who attempts to dramatize a similar situation either tells us what the emotion is or inserts a vague, ubiquitous *pause,* which could mean anything or nothing.

In this next excerpt, the main character is being let into the apartment of two murdered strippers by the building manager, whose words suggest her feelings. But it's her hand actions, *shoved* and *threw*—plus a brief comparison—that reveal the weight of those feelings. She says:

> ". . . these places like the Tip Top"—she shoved the key into the lock like she was mad at it—"they got no sense of purpose." She threw open the door with the same disdain. "And these poor little girls, they got no purpose either."
>
> Phillip DePoy, *Easy* [p. 91]

Effective body language allows readers to draw their own conclusions about a character's feelings. Here are two passages from *Deadly Appraisal* by Jane Cleland, a series featuring antiques appraiser Josie Prescott:

> "Oh, look! There's Britt!" Maisy flitted away in Britt's direction. Britt Epps, the honorary chair of the Gala and the most influential lawyer in town, was looking downright dapper, his bulk well disguised in a custom-made tuxedo. I watched as they air-kissed.   [p. 3]
>
> Detective Rowcliff began to tap his pencil, startling me out of my reverie. . . . He was chewing gum as if he wanted to kill it while watching me through uncaring eyes.   [p. 3]

Only a few hints are needed—an air kiss, a catch of breath, a swallow—to let us experience our own emotions in a character's body language:

> Lifting my reading glasses, I looked down and caught my breath, captured again by that smile. This time the young woman looked up at me from the pool, chin resting on her arms.
> *Oh dear! Oh my!*
> "It's Eve, isn't it?" her deep voice asked.
> I swallowed. I'd forgotten how pleasant her voice was because then, like now, I'd been looking at her engaging smile, trying not to stare at the rest of her.
>
> Barbara Bristol, "Eve's Holiday," in *Tales of Travelrotica for Lesbians* [p. 57]

If you cannot easily show a mannerism that communicates what you want it to, show what you can and tell what it looks like:

> ". . . What a bunch of suckers we were back then, right?" Karl skidded the heel of his palm off his temple in some larking "Oy" gesture.　　　　　　　　Martha Grimes, *Foul Matter* [p. 99]

> Dalton tossed a leg over the visitor's chair and pulled it in under him.　　　　　　Lonnie Cruse, *Married in Metropolis* [p. 201]

> Felicity fidgeted with her pen, then slowly twirled it between her fingers. Her coral nails were so long that she had to use the pen to dial her touch-tone phone.
> 　　　　　　　　　　　　Beth Terrell, *Too Close to Evil* [p. 79]

> I had met my hero. He smoked his cigarette cupped backward in his hand. I first noticed him sitting on the back of a park bench. Leaning forward, elbows on his knees, black Wellingtons on the seat, smoking a cigarette.
> 　　　　　　　　　　　Jeanne Ainslee, *A Country Girl* [p. 31]

> "I actually did fill one out," Tanisha said about the Vatigrim application, her eggplant-colored nails tapping through a dish of mixed nuts and olives.
> 　　　　Kristin Thiel, "Pilgrim for Hire," in *VoiceCatcher2* [p. 29]

> Lettie stood up and shook out her pants legs. I could tell she was anxious to leave.
> 　　　　　Maria Hudgins, *Death of an Obnoxious Tourist* [p. 195]

When I see awkward, ineffective gestures and body language, I believe they come from the writer's lack of awareness of what readers need for experiencing the scene. To some extent, awkwardness comes from an attempt to communicate feelings that the writer wants to show but doesn't know how to. For example:

> The detective looked at me like he didn't believe me.

Expressions like this one, which tells, suggest that the writer either has a limited imagination or doesn't understand the difference between telling and showing. What does *not believing* look like? Catherine Coulter effectively combines showing and telling in the following passage from *The Edge,* fourth in her FBI series featuring Ford MacDougal:

> Detective Castanga didn't believe me. He turned to Laura, a dark eyebrow cocked up a good inch. [p. 148]

If for whatever reason you cannot show the appropriate body language, come up with a creative representation of it—which is how Coulter handles another of Mac's observations:

> Detective Castanga slowly straightened. He was surprised, I could see it in the sudden twitch in his cheek, the slight hitch in his breathing. [p. 147]

Metaphors and similes offer unlimited opportunities for bringing creativity to your gestures:

> He looked blanched and worn for a minute, like laundry that had been out on the line too long.
>
> Walter Sorrells, *Will to Murder* [p. 31]

> He stops in mid sentence, calms down and looks at me. "I am assuming," he says, "that the witness is a male?" He stands there, a big-eyed question mark.
> I offer him the social intercourse of a chimney brick.
>
> Steve Martini, *Prime Witness* [pp. 277–78]

CUMULATIVE EFFECT

Here is a scene from Elizabeth George's fifth novel in the Thomas Lynley and Barbara Havers series, *For the Sake of Elena.* Subtle behaviors show how the two New Scotland Yard detectives feel about an elusive suspect. Inspector Lynley says to Havers:

> ". . . So if he did kill her, I imagine he'd have set himself up with an iron-clad alibi, don't you?"
> "No, I don't." She waved her teacake at him. One of its raisins dropped with a plop into her coffee. She ignored it and continued. "I think he's clever enough to know we'd be having a conversation just like this." [p. 124]

Havers' ignoring a consequence of her hand gesture subtly reveals the distance between her social class and Lynley's. It also suggests how focused Havers becomes about a case. Moments later, Lynley:

> . . . shoved his coffee cup to one side. "What we need is a
> witness, Havers."
>   "To the killing?"
>   "To something. To anything." He stood. "Let's look up this
> woman who found the body."   [pp. 124–25]

Consider the gesture *he shoved his coffee cup*. Why not *moved, placed, shifted?* Because a shove captures Lynley's determination to find the guilty party—no adverb or further description needed.

He stood suggests his resolve to get on with the investigation. Ordinarily, *stood* would have little meaning. Here, however, it follows from a forceful *shove* and the clipped reply, "To something. To anything."

Taken together, these small movements work in concert to strengthen our insight into the inspector's feelings. At the same time, his body language is minimal enough to support his dialogue without overpowering it.

MOTION OR MEANING?

Not every movement has to be meaningful. However, a glut of position-shifting that serves primarily to stave off rigor mortis is not action. It's not even activity. It's fidgeting. It's letting average writing habits take control, as if the creative process were set to automatic pilot.

For the screener, such a manuscript isn't worth the tree it's printed on.

The typical manuscript is filled with characters who keep sitting down and standing up. To see if you rely on meaningless movements, use your word processor to search for the word *stood,* as well as its assorted forms, *stand* and *standing*. Then search for *window,* as in *walked to* and *looked out of.* Evaluate all this moving about to see if it adds to either character portrayal or tension.

If you have difficulty finding precisely the right gesture, reexamine each character's script and the agenda that propels it, and act out the script.

> Satirical novelist Chuck Palahniuk, author of *Fight Club*, writes in public so he can look up and study people whenever he needs to see what someone is doing with a hand or foot.
>
> Jordan E. Rosenfeld, *Writer's Digest*, October 2007, p. 49

Consider exposing more of each buried agenda through dialogue or body language. Reduce or eliminate empty gestures and the emptier chit chat they attempt to animate. Replace with dialogue that carries its own meaning. (Take another look at CLUES #15 and #16.)

And come up with original observations.

THE PAUSE THAT REGRESSES

Take the pause. Take it out in the alley and shoot it, I beg you. As a dialogue breaker-upper it can make a character seem hesitant when you want her to come across as pensive. An excess of pausing—including its first cousins *stopped to think for a moment* and *became silent for a bit*—makes the writing sound immature.

Whenever I cross out pauses in a manuscript, the pace stops dragging and the writing becomes stronger.

One useful function for a pause (there aren't many) is to signal that a character is reversing himself or changing the subject:

> "I didn't go to her house that night." He paused. "Well, I sort of did. I drove by, but I didn't go inside."

A pause is not the only way to indicate a change or correction. Here's a slightly more imaginative alternative:

> "I didn't go to her house that night." He studied a hangnail.
> "Well, I sort of did. I drove by, but I didn't go inside."

If your scene is already busy with many little mannerisms like the above, a single pause in the right place might be a relief. A series of *unrelated* mannerisms produces a choppy effect, but see what happens when you develop a theme that multiplies and unifies their effect:

> He studied a hangnail.
> "Well, I sort of did. I drove by, but I didn't go inside." His studies advanced to using one fingernail to clean under the nails of his other hand. "I saw the Honda parked in the driveway again. I wanted to, uh, you know, see what they were, ah, doing, but. . . . "
> With all ten digits accounted for, he graduated to picking at a scab on his wrist.

Here's a welcome alternative to the overworked pause from Betty Webb. In *Desert Noir,* Lena asks her friend if he'd like to meet her for a drink:

> The man had enough silences left in him to make a 1910
> movie.   [p. 224]

As for hesitation, analyze these scenes, rich with detail and nuance:

> . . . So what's this really important thing you wanted to talk to me about?"
> She leaned against the table, arms crossed in front of her like a shield. She shifted from one foot to the other, uncrossed her arms, pulled her ponytail to the front and twisted a section of hair between her fingers. I knew it would find its way into her mouth before long.
> "You're moving to Australia," I guessed. "You've been asked to go on the next space shuttle mission to take pictures of space aliens. You've signed up for a sex change operation."
> "I'm pregnant," she said.
>
> Beth Terrell, *Too Close to Evil* [p. 136]

> . . . He dropped into a chair and stuffed a doughnut into his mouth. "No time for breakfas'—need my honey fix," he mumbled through the doughnut. Honey glistened at the corner of his lip. "Chief called seven o'clock, wanna—"
> "It'd better be good news. Don't tell me if it isn't."
> "Well, not bad news anyway. Not exactly good, either, but encouraging—"
> "Say it then."
> "I'm trying, Ruthie, gimme a chance to swallow."
> She waited. He swallowed. Finally it came. . . .
> . . . He traced a tiny cross in the sugar the doughnuts had dropped on the table. "She just disappeared. They stopped all the cars going out, alerted the whole town. Nothing. It's like she flew into thin air. Houdini-like." He snapped his fingers and crumbs sprayed her cheek.
>
> Nancy Means Wright, *Mad Cow Nightmare* [pp. 208–209]

A master at reticence is Elizabeth George's creation of Terrence Cuff, head of Elena's college in *For the Sake of Elena*. In this scene he is being interviewed by Inspector Lynley:

> "There were troubles?"
> Cuff took a moment to tap the ash from his cigarette into a porcelain ashtray. . . .   [p. 58]

When Lynley challenges one of Cuff's responses, it sets off a series of evasive actions:

> Cuff got up from his chair and went to the fireplace, where he lit the coals that formed a small mound in a metal basket. The room was growing cold, and while the action was reasonable, it also bore the appearance of temporizing. Once the fire was lit, Cuff remained standing near it. He sank his hands into his trouser pockets and studied the tops of his shoes.   [p. 60]

Twice more the head of the college is shown rearranging the coals before answering a question. One time he is said to shrug. This is not an indiscriminate physical gesture, nor the redundant "he shrugged his shoulders." George uses the verb in its figurative sense to clarify that:

> Cuff shrugged off both question and implication.   [p. 61]

In eight pages of stalling behaviors by the reticent Mr. Cuff, not one of them is a pause.

LIKE THINGS DETRACT

Avoid mannerisms that can be interchanged with any of a dozen others without affecting the story. Moreover, if gestures do no more than mirror the words they accompany, they are redundant.

> "That's very puzzling." He frowned and scratched his head.
> "It sure is," she said, nodding in agreement.

Almost every manuscript submitted by a first-time writer contains at least one *nodding in agreement,* further reinforcing the "yes" effect of nonconfrontational, symmetrical dialogue (CLUE #16). Other redundancies I come across include *He shook his head negatively* and *She shook her head back and forth.* All that head-wagging hurts my eyebrows.

Some gestures are so common they've become clichés. Worse, writers using them aren't thinking: *shrugged her shoulders; reached his hand; nodded her head; thought to himself; hesitated a moment.* Redundant, all.

Repetitive, meaningless, empty gestures weaken your writing. Weak writing is uninteresting, and uninteresting writing remains unpublished.

Watch those eyes. *Winked an eye* and *blinked his eyes* are also redundant. Don't send anyone's eyes to unlikely places in improbable ways, such as *she threw a glance out the window; he cut his eyes to the knife on the counter; he cast his eyes out to sea.* Congratulate yourself if you also recognize the last three as howlers. My appreciation to science fiction writer Vonda McIntyre for this one: *His eyes fell to the floor. (Boing! Boing!)*

One editor grew so fed up with the expression *she tossed her head* that she took to writing "to whom?" in the margin of manuscripts.[54] My own method of raising awareness is not as amusing, but you can apply it to your writing by running a computer search for certain overused gestures.

What follows is the product of a word search I performed on a single fiction manuscript of 83,000 words. Each numeral represents all forms of a word—that is, *sitting* also represents *sat, sit, seated,* and *took a seat.*

This list totals 1,440 separate gestures, and I've probably missed a few:

5	guffawing	38	shrugging
5	gawking	43	breathing (as in took a deep
9	pausing		breath, *not* under his breath)
9	moaning	52	staring
14	gasping	63	standing
22	grimacing	80	nodding
22	shaking head	81	grinning
23	showing nervous-	83	turning (to, toward, away,
	ness		around)
25	snickering	88	glaring
25	chuckling	94	sighing
27	bolting (from seat,	98	sitting
	bed)	105	smiling
33	smirking	144	laughing
37	frowning	215	looking

With each verb needing at least one pronoun and another helper word, I can conservatively triple this figure and say that 4,300 words out of a count of 83,000 portray mostly empty, repetitive fidgets, twitches, and tics.

An electronic search of the same manuscript also turned up fifty-one mentions of the word "cigarette." I made no attempt to computer-count the many related actions, such as "struck a match," "lit," "took a drag," "smoked," or "tapped the ash." Of approximately 300 words that went up in smoke, only one reference was plot-related.

Aside from revealing a weak style of writing, all this tobacco use seems to have caused no other harm: my computer counted only four coughs.

Computer-search your own draft using the list on page 240. It might indicate more repetition of empty gesturing than you suspect. Remedies:

- ●◆ Sharpen your people-watching skills.
- ●◆ Create more compelling action.
- ●◆ Craft more purposeful dialogue.

TIP: REVIEW YOUR GESTURES

Here's how to computer-count the most common gestures that you write, using the list of verbs on the opposite page.

1. Copy all your chapters into one backup file to facilitate a global search.

2. Instead of searching for whole words, determine the root letters common to all forms of a verb. For instance, the letters *paus* are common to *pause, paused, pauses,* and *pausing.*

3. In your search-and-replace feature, type the same letters in both fields. If you search for *paus,* replace it with *paus.* This ensures that when you click "replace all," you replace every occurrence with itself. Your manuscript is unchanged, but your word processor shows you the total number of occurrences.

4. Diagnose the way you present your characters' body language and correct as needed. Add other verbs to this list that you use often.

ALSO:

Try www.wordcounter.com, a free (at the time of this writing) Internet tool into which you paste a chapter or so of text, and have it count your most frequently repeated words.

BE OBSERVANT

A yawn, blink, scowl, or shrug is occasionally effective in the right situation, but original phrasing and fresh observations are preferred. Avoid sprinkling mannerisms like salt on popcorn. Instead, treat each one as you would herb seasoning to bring out the flavor of the main dish.

> "That's great," Waters said, leaping to his feet and pumping my arm like he was trying to bring up water.
>
> Katy Munger, *Legwork* [p. 123]

> Mrs. Bradford was beating muffin batter, her arm slapping against the side of her chest.
>
> Deborah Adams, *All the Great Pretenders* [p. 186]

When you're ready to revise your writing for its gestures, assemble all your characters in a big circle. Ask them to do nothing for one full minute but nod, sigh, blink, yawn, scowl, grimace, and shrug. Visualizing this epidemic of tics and fidgets might be enough to help you replace an unconscious habit with selective body language that speaks with originality.

FIND & FIX CLUE #21: GESTURED TO DEATH

- Make every gesture serve a purpose, just as you do with all the other details you select.
- Know what each of your characters' pauses is meant to show, and show it in a less vague, more interesting way.
- Revise body language so it expands characterization, communicates attitude, or contributes a fresh observation, thereby adding value.
- Analyze the specific ways you have your characters' body language offer clues to their emotions.
- Use your computer's search feature to see how often you repeat certain gestures, especially those used most often by most unpublished writers.

D.O.A.

PART IX: LOOSE ENDS

David Morrell, author of 30 books—including *First Blood*, which became the movie *Rambo*—says he emphasizes at least two senses in every scene other than sight, which he uses minimally. This technique makes readers think his fairly lean descriptions are fuller, and they add the details they imagine.

David Morrell, *Lessons from a Lifetime of Writing* [p. 138]

CLUE #22: SNITCH VERSUS SPY

Old-time gangster films offer a useful contrast between two techniques that I think of as the Snitch and the Spy. One is a stool pigeon, a sniveling tattletale who explains everything, as if readers couldn't size up your characters by watching their behavior.

The other is a professional spy, a trained observer who lets audiences see characters in action and draw their own conclusions. The Spy's success depends on capturing actions with a tiny camera and state-of-the-art sound system hidden in his pinky ring, then knowing how to edit the film and play it back.

Which caricature does the audience cheer?

The triumph of Spy over Snitch demonstrates a basic principle in fiction: *show, don't tell.* Review your writing to make sure you take advantage of the Spy's talent for observing behavior and recreating it.

Three little words are handwritten across more manuscripts than the "I love you" on Valentines. Those three little words are *show, don't tell.* Showing has to be the most misunderstood principle of fiction writing. Often, it's easier to let the Snitch take over. Snitches love story*telling.* Where's the story*showing?* Make sure your own narrative doesn't resemble another well-known saying: long time, no see.

SHOWING VS. TELLING

Novels and short stories contain a substantial amount of narrative, so this must mean narrative and exposition are to blame. These forms tell, don't they? Not necessarily. See for yourself in this narrative passage from *Pious Deception* by Susan Dunlap, author of some twenty novels:

> . . . He saw himself climbing aboard the Greyhound cruiser
> and heading east, sitting by the window, listening to the crackle
> of wax paper from the seats behind him, inhaling the spicy
> aroma of fried chicken, the garlicky smell of roast beef sand-
> wiches. He could feel the scratchy wool of a sweater wadded
> between the window and his neck as he let his eyes close and
> the rumble of the bus lured him to sleep. The dark safety of the
> bus, broken by pinpoints of light here and there. Then the bus
> would jolt, and he would shift in his seat, open his eyes, and
> suddenly outside would be the gray of dawn.   [p. 64]

Without a doubt, this writing *shows,* and most effectively. Dunlap's passage is loaded with sensory details of sound, smell, taste, touch, and sight, which evoke the same rich sensory experiences in her readers.

Need another example to prove that narrative, per se, isn't the problem? Here's a passage from Erin Hart's *Lake of Sorrows,* second in her series featuring pathologist Nora Gavin. Its rich sensory detail shows, not tells.

> She sat for a moment longer, listening to the strange music of
> the wind as it whistled through the furze bushes along the road,
> watching the bog cotton's tiny white flags spell out a cryptic
> message in semaphore. Bits of organic debris danced overhead,
> caught in the updraft, and the strangely dry air contained some-
> thing new, a mineral taste she could not readily name.   [p. 10]

Even a small amount of sense data used here and there in a scene enriches the reader's experience:

> . . . the beach lay empty, silent except for the sibilant *sshussh* of
> the breakers and the occasional *plop* as the brisk breeze sent a
> pine cone toppling on to the sand.
> > Kathryn R. Wall, *Resurrection Road* [p. 261]

> . . . he whispered, his voice like sand.
> > Sallie Bissell, *A Darker Justice* [p. 144]

All these examples are expository, yet they show. Telling comes from
exposition that presents interpretations and conclusions, based on no evidence that would convince any jury: *he was worried, she looked sad, they
felt angry.* Conclusions are expressed by writers on automatic pilot, who
don't work at creating the behavioral details that reflect such emotions.

Telling is easy; showing takes observation, thought, and creative effort.

Don't tell us that an attractive man is being kind, or friendly, or respect-
ful—all of which are interpretations of behavior. Instead, show us the man's
actions and let us draw our own conclusions—which is exactly what Lois
Patton does effectively in "The Empty Chair," a story that won second
place in a regional short story contest:

> Looking out the window, she could see that Tom had stayed
> back, letting others board before him. . . . He had a quick smile
> for the older gentleman who needed a hand getting on the bus.

Similarly, instead of telling us that a retired judge is a cantankerous old
codger, Patricia Sprinkle shows him interacting with others. This passage
is from the second of her Sheila Travis series, *Murder in the Charleston
Manner.* Judge Black and his wife, Annie, have just been offered a drink:

> "Pour it quick, before my old woman objects. She's always
> going on and on about saving my heart. At eighty-nine, who the
> hell does she think I'm saving it for?" He cackled at his own
> wit.   [pp. 10–11]

The conversation soon turns to the host's resident nurse:

"She ain't full-time nursing." Judge Black chuckled. "Meeting Heyward under the magnolias in the dark. Probably takes him in the house, too, when you ain't looking."

"There's no such word as 'ain't,'" Annie burst out. "And why a man with your education and experience—"

"Woman, when a man has my education and experience, he can say any damn word he pleases. And what's got you so riled up ain't my language. It's the thought of what them young 'uns might be up to. . . ."

"I could kill him," Annie muttered. "Sometimes I could just kill him."   [pp. 11–12]

The judge's own words substantiate his temperament and let us experience his nature up close and personal. If this scene were told to us instead of shown, the richness of the judge's persona would be filtered through the narrator. Any intermediary puts distance between readers and characters.

SHOWING EMOTION

Fear, love, passion, anger, hurt—it's one thing to show emotion on the page, another to create it in the reader. Once readers care about a character and come to identify with her, we begin to experience the emotions she does, provided the writer is doing an effective job of portraying it.

In her first mystery novel, *Calculated Risk,* Denise Tiller shows the reaction of California actuary Liz Matthews to hearing from her mother after thirty years. She is in the middle of making a salad for dinner when the phone rings:

. . . "Elizabeth, this is your mother."

My cheeks burned as if she'd slapped my face. "I don't have a mother!"

I slammed the receiver down and pressed my hands against my ears to block the echoes of playground taunts. "We know what happened. . . . Your mother left because she didn't love you."

I squeezed harder. "It's not true. She's not my mother."

"Lizzie! Who was that?"

I jumped and dropped my hands when I saw Jack peering into my face. "Wrong number. I didn't hear you come back."

> I pulled a long knife from the block and dismembered a weak
> cucumber with savage chops.
>   Jack sucked in air. "Who's not whose mother?" He leaned
> against the refrigerator with his arms folded, waiting for an
> answer. Meanwhile I attacked a ripe tomato. Red juice and
> seeds sprayed across the counter.
>   "Thought you said your mother was dead."
>   "She is as far as I'm concerned," I muttered as I hacked. "She
> abandoned Dad and me when I was a baby. I haven't heard from
> her in almost thirty years." I waved the knife, dripping with
> juice, in his face. "And if that woman thinks. . . .
>   The phone rang and I slammed the blade into the cutting
> board. It stuck straight upright. . . .   [pp. 26–27]

Tiller helps us experience Liz's emotions through her senses (feeling her cheeks burn, hearing the taunts of her childhood) and through her actions (slamming the receiver down, attacking defenseless veggies). Reinforcing Liz's murderous impulses are Tiller's vibrant details: the juice of a ripe tomato spraying across the counter . . . a long, dripping knife waving in Jack's face . . . the blade slammed into the cutting board.

Notice that the backstory is brief and presented through dialogue, where it neither weakens the scene nor slows its pace.

THE UNSHOWABLE

Now that our friend, the Spy, has shown what narrative and dramatization can achieve, let's further expose the nefarious work of the Snitch:

> Mr. Nabor, the man next door, appeared upset and agitated as
> he described what he had seen.

First, *upset* and *agitated* are conclusions. (You knew that.) They offer no specific images of Nabor's eyes, mouth, voice, body, or hands—any of which would let us see his emotions for ourselves. Second, *appeared* (as well as *seemed* and *looked like*) hint at a second meaning, especially in paranormal and sci-fi, where things are not as they appear.

As readers, we store any suggestion of reality vs. illusion in our short-term memory banks and anticipate the writer's settling the account. When there's no payoff, readers lose interest.

If you want readers to know that a character looks uncomfortable, show something to back that up. Maybe the poor fellow squirms in his seat, runs a finger around the inside of his collar, or dabs at his forehead with a grimy handkerchief. Emotions that are not easily mirrored are more challenging. Here's another Snitch kind of statement:

> Naomi sat there with a vindictive expression on her face. She said, "I guess so."

What does a vindictive expression look like? I can't picture how Naomi communicates this meaning, can you? And the dialogue is of no help.

Not every emotion can be rendered through body language alone. Some need the context of the character's words or thoughts. Some need a little telling, too, with the telling and the showing complementing—not contradicting—each other.

To support a hard-to-justify conclusion, combine show-and-tell. Add a line of dialogue. Use a simile or a metaphor:

> Judging from Raab's expression, this interview wasn't
> starting well. The look he gave me could've deboned chicken.
>
> Cathy Pickens, *Done Gone Wrong* [p. 180]

> Glancing at her as if she were something he'd scraped off
> the bottom of his shoe, the boy selected the biggest stone from
> his pile and threw it as hard as he could.
>
> Denise Swanson, *Murder of a Small-Town Honey* [p. 51]

> Mr. Sheriff gazed at me as if my pilot light had gone out.
>
> Chassie West, *Sunrise* [p. 61]

> "Your husband's taste in clothes is. . ." It wasn't clear
> whether Nuri's inadequacy in English produced that struggle
> to find the right word—or tact.
> "Dull," I offered. . . .
> "No, Tracy." Nuri tossed his hand in a throwaway gesture,
> which struck me as very Old World in nature, though I'd never
> seen its like from Tony. It was a gesture that conveyed the
> complex thought: We will never speak of this, though we both
> know it's true.   Kris Neri, *Revenge of the Gypsy Queen* [p. 124]

> Like a child caught with her hand in the cookie jar, a startled,
> frightening look crossed Mary's face. "Huh, no. No. Of course
> not. How could I possibly have known her?" She wet her lips
> and looked away.   L. C. Hayden, *Who's Susan?* [p. 46]

Show and tell support each other in these examples, and dialogue and action provide corroboration. Symbiosis. However, beware of overstatement—saying the same thing in several different ways:

> Jed felt relieved. "I'm glad you're not pressing charges," he
> said, smiling and leaning back in his chair. Joan saw his
> shoulders relax and the creases in his forehead fade.

Do you recognize that *Jed felt relieved* is a conclusion? It's also redundant, along with any three of the four images that make the identical point.

OVERSHOWING

Because I point to instances of telling versus showing throughout this book, my CLUE #22 is brief. The only passage I want to revisit appears way back in CLUE #1, where I turn a compact, effective hook of only seventeen words into an amateurish example of excess at three times the length:

> I was lazily watching my tall, tanned bodyguard mowing
> the lush green lawn in her bright pink bikini when I heard the
> loud, insistent buzz of a small private airplane flying overhead.
> When I looked up I saw the very scary sight of a man's limp
> body falling from the cloudless blue sky.

Here's the hook to *Dead Over Heels* as Charlaine Harris wrote it:

> My bodyguard was mowing the yard wearing her pink bikini
> when the man fell from the sky.

Harris's brief original shows action, whereas my parody smothers the action and bludgeons readers with an epidemic of adverbosity and adjectivitis. Watch for signs of these disorders when you revise your own writing. For each modifier you find, question your reason for using it.

Modifiers (like *scary*) tell us what to think, instead of showing us what to imagine. I've read scenes that tell me a poorly lit street is also very dark, deeply shadowed, inky, and dim—all on the same page. Footsteps don't merely echo, they echo loudly, repeatedly, and ominously. Better to show how the character experiences these sights and sounds by using sensory impressions to let us feel what provokes the character's reactions and arouses her emotional responses.

Modifier overkill suggests performance anxiety in writers who don't trust their words to evoke the desired reader response, and who don't trust their readers to interpret behavior when it's dramatized.

> **"Real Writers Submit"**
>
> Slogan of the Wisconsin
> Regional Writers Association

If you write *what a frightening moment Harvey faced,* that's telling. You are drawing a conclusion and stating your emotional interpretation of the scene, not Harvey's. The Snitch that lurks within you feels pretty smug about putting something over on you. Don't let him get away with it.

FIND & FIX CLUE #22: SNITCH VERSUS SPY

- ☛ Look for examples in your manuscript of interpretations, conclusions, and summaries that tell readers what to think.
- ☛ Avoid generalizing; show behavior that readers can interpret for themselves.
- ☛ Double-check that you portray your characters through their dialogue, actions, body language, and thoughts.
- ☛ Review your expository passages to see whether they include impressions from the five senses to evoke rich, vivid imagery that shows, not tells.
- ☛ Beware of redundancy when you supplement what's shown with what's told.
- ☛ Show your characters' feelings, not your own.

D.O.A.

CLUE #23: NOISY VOICE

By now, your self-editing is moving right along. Your hook is so well sustained that readers wouldn't think of getting away. There's no perilous prologue or toxic transcript to sidetrack your plot's progression. Bloody backstory and fatal flashbacks are (ahem) things of the past.

You dumped those dastardly descriptions, jettisoned the juvenile gestures, and ousted every ounce of overwriting. All accidental alliteration has been axed and clichés clobbered—though the effort of doing so caused many a frown to crease your brow.

Actions and emotions are shown, not told, and conflicting agendas keep tension idling on every page. Your settings demonstrate a keen sense of place, and your point of view shifts only when you want it to.

Congratulations. You cleared much of the static that obscures your voice.

Still, you wonder what other weaknesses you might have overlooked. So you devour three books on characterization and three more on plot, conflict, and suspense. You know your manuscript is good, but is it good enough? Does it have density? Style? Pizzazz?

WHAT'S PIZZAZZ, ANYWAY?

Editors used to talk about talent, a quality inherent in the writer, not the manuscript. Today, it's risky to mention talent; writers might interpret rejection as implying they haven't any. Rejection is hard enough to deal with.

Pizzazz, on the other hand, is mysterious and indefinable, therefore safer to throw around. Besides, the word seems to apply to the submission, not to a deficiency in the writer. One dictionary defines *pizzazz* as "glamour, vitality," but most resources, including a popular online dictionary, don't even list the word. It's indefinable, all right.

I maintain that everyone has a voice, but it cannot be heard over the noise of amateur writing habits. At least ninety percent of manuscripts are rejected instantly because the writer's voice is merely average. An average voice is like a weak radio signal drowned out by static, which makes every station sound alike.

> "Editors can spot a good voice in a few paragraphs. . . . How? They read first for *mistakes!* They spot lack of craft in the first few paragraphs. . . . Unique voice sells the story. Lack of one begets rejection. Voice has substance. It is something you, the writer, can shape."
>
> Doris Booth, founder of Authorlink.com, speaking at the 2002 Harriette Austin Writers Conference

It's uncanny how the same ineffective techniques and identical writing habits make the majority of submissions sound alike. Despite differences in character and story, most manuscripts sound as if the same person wrote them. To an editor, the voices all shout *amateur*.

As you are discovering, the first step in voice rehabilitation is finding the evidence and getting rid of it. That alone will set your writing apart from other submissions. Your underlying voice may still be weak, but it's yours, and you can learn to strengthen it. Most writers need time and practice before their unique voice develops.

READING WIDELY

An essential step is to read widely. Pay special attention to the authors who stir excitement in your heart, who make your fingers itch to grab a pencil and get back to your own writing. They have style; perchance pizzazz. Absorb the sound of their voice, even if you cannot analyze it.

I'm not convinced that deliberate voice development is the way to go, because the result could sound pretentious and overly literary—which some call "writerly." So I'm passing along the next idea if you want to try it.

A few writing coaches advocate parroting the style of authors you admire. Not their content, mind you. Write your *own* story. But write it as if an author whose style you like were writing it. The idea is to echo the voice of one author at a time until you feel comfortable with the style of each.

Then combine the best of your efforts. Through exercise and practice, the theory is that you eventually develop a voice to call your own.

Skeptical? Prefer that I talk about talent? I wonder if you'd really believe me if I said: *while it is impossible to make a competent writer out of a bad writer, and equally impossible to make a great writer out of a good one, it is possible, with lots of hard work, dedication, and timely help, to make a good writer out of a merely competent one.*[55]

You might not believe my telling you this, but I think you'd believe Stephen King if you knew those insightful words were his. They are.

He and I attended the University of Maine at the same time, then taught writing there at the same time—but on different campuses, so I never met him. Not until his autobiographical *On Writing* came out in 2000 did I encounter the passage quoted above. Yet, for thirty years before that I'd based my life's work as a teacher and editor on the very same belief— though King expresses it more effectively than I'd ever thought to do.

I remain convinced of its truth because I keep seeing the results.

FIGURATIVE LANGUAGE

The rest of this CLUE reviews figurative language, parallel structure, symbolism, and other techniques that enrich your writing by taking it beyond a single layer of meaning. I'm not suggesting that depth and richness are matters of technique alone. Style cannot be stuck onto a story like bows on a gift box. Still, effective writing can be cultivated.

You are already familiar with many types of figurative language. You met its forms in junior high. Try them in your own writing—in moderation—to bring a fresh, original quality to your voice.

Work with a technique until the effect is just right. But don't force it. Struggling to devise a clever remark can make the result seem clumsy or clunky.

> "Smart writers. . .create a crisp style and produce tight, polished manuscripts that pull ahead of the pack. . . . If style makes the difference, why don't all writers improve their style and succeed in any way they define success? Simple. Few people have the capacity to evaluate their own writing."
>
> Bobbie Christmas, *Write In Style,* p. 7

Over time, a variety of linguistic and structural techniques may become a natural part of your style. However—and this is important—their absence from your writing indicates no error on your part. Neither does their inclusion ensure success.

Used effectively, they can make your writing more exact, interesting, colorful, textured, expressive. They can help you develop your voice.

Expressive writing differentiates your voice from the hundreds of thousands of identical sounds that live for a desperate moment trying to catch the eye and ear of a busy screener-outer.

If nothing else, figurative language is fun to play with—a process that reveals new ways for writers to multiply levels of meaning.

SIMILE

A simile is the easiest type of figurative expression to write and to recognize:

> "Alexandria Vilkas," he cried. His joy charged me like a mug
> of steaming tea.   Silvia Foti, *The Diva's Fool* [p. 9]

> She stared at Jeff and refused to move, like a plant growing
> roots.   L. C. Hayden, *Who's Susan?* [pp. 67–68]

> [I] headed for the front door, my car, and fresh air. I needed to
> slough off the sleazy feeling that covered me like morning film
> on teeth.   Sue Ann Jaffarian, *The Curse of the Holy Pail* [p. 92]

In general, keep similes simple and straightforward. Let them make their comparison quickly and move on, eliciting a figurative nod from the reader or an appreciative smile. Use one here or there, usually not more than one per page, so you don't draw too much attention to your own cleverness.

The next two, from *Soul Patch* by Reed Farrel Coleman, do occur on the same page—one at the top, the other at the bottom. But they work well in proximity because both are concrete images that represent intangibles, and intangibles benefit the most from the well-done comparison:

> . . . We had hit the inevitable impasse, that stage in marriage
> when each day is like a long drive through Nebraska.

> . . . I thought Katy had stumbled upon the secret, the one her
> father and I kept wedged between us like a bottle of liquid
> nitroglycerin.   [p. 1]

As for similes in a character description, save the most attention-getting for the minor characters, because those descriptions should be brief anyway and highlight only one or two principal features:

Detective Zarrabi and I shook hands. . . . His moustache and eyebrows were both bushy, like three black caterpillars marching parallel across his face.

> Sue Ann Jaffarian, *The Curse of the Holy Pail* [p. 36]

She wore a psychedelic muumuu that covered her three-hundred-pound frame. . . . Claire sank into the easy chair draped in a colorful crocheted blanket, maneuvering herself like an ocean liner into a crowded harbor.

> Silvia Foti, *The Diva's Fool* [pp. 96, 109]

Often, the description is less physical, more behavioral:

Belle's elder by ten years, Miriam was like a no-nonsense sister who reminds you that your boyfriend eats with his mouth open even though he owns a BMW and has shares in Microsoft.

> Lou Allin, *Memories Are Murder* [p. 1]

Sheriff Wood raised his hand and smiled at the others like a candidate acknowledging a group of voters.

> Joanne Clarey, *Skinned* [p. 25]

"It was no trouble at all . . . uhh . . . Sterling," I said, trying on his first name like a pair of narrow shoes.

> Sue Ann Jaffarian, *The Curse of the Holy Pail* [p. 17]

Beware the overdone, the outrageous, the gross—like this winner of a "Worst Beginning Sentence" contest:

He was in love with her, loved her like he loved lasagna, not just any lasagna, especially not the vegetarian kind, but the meaty juicy savory kind with extra cheese, and he could tell by the way her face flushed like steaming marinara sauce underneath a thick layer of melted ricotta that she must feel the same way; he only hoped that their love didn't end like his love with lasagna always ended. . . . [Ed. note: ending cut for length]

> Julie Wright, first place in romance category
> of the *Deseret (UT) Morning News* contest

As if you couldn't tell, I collect interesting similes and metaphors. Lucky you that I still have a few more to share:

> The white working-class neighborhood of Yorkville had fallen prey to developers who put in high-rises with Sheetrock walls as thin as a corned beef on rye in a greasy spoon.
>
> Elizabeth Zelvin, "Death Will Clean Your Closet,"
in Murder New York Style [p. 49]

> "Well, I guess if there's no more custard left, I'll have to try one of those." Courtney took a raspberry paczki, but was still eyeing my custard, even as I bit into it. "I just don't see why every year they send us so many of the other types when everybody's favorite is custard. It just doesn't make any sense!" Courtney was a number cruncher in accounting, and I sometimes thought the numbers got to her one day and made her the way she was: as thick as two short planks.
>
> Therese Szymanski, Another One Bites the Dust,
novella in It's all Smoke and Mirrors [p. 114]

> She rose from her seat and pulled her black rolling suitcase upright. Filled with clothes for eight weeks, it bulged like a fat woman in Spandex.
>
> Kathleen Whelan, Cocktail Cove, novel-in-progress [p. 1]

> The small city lay in a grid, most of its streets straight and long, except for the unexpected park plopped down willy-nilly, as if some mighty being had sneezed without a handkerchief.
>
> Pari Noskin Taichert, The Clovis Incident [p. 17]

> Believe me, I've been around here a long time, and I know exactly how these men think. I could read Harvel's mind like his forehead was made out of Cling Wrap.
>
> Mary Saums, Thistle & Twigg [p. 11]

METAPHOR

Creating a fresh, effective metaphor is a challenge. Select a tangible image to stand in for the inexpressible, and evoke an emotion relevant to your purpose. Unlike a simile, comparisons are implied rather than stated:

In the enigmatic Eastern Arctic there was an other-worldliness about the people, an ancientness to their culture. Here, the Twentieth Century was a stranger just passing through.

> Debra Tillery, *Myth Maker,* novel-in-progress [ms p. 165]

The casino stretched out endlessly, row after row of slot machines . . . many of the gamblers seemed to be plugged in, a cord growing from chest to machine as if for intravenous feeding or some electronic life support.

> Vicki Lane, *Old Wounds* [p. 326]

You don't argue with a woman like Ruby. At least *I* try not to. She's got a race car engine inside a Rolls Royce body.

> Joyce and Jim Lavene, *Swapping Paint* [p. 1]

His hat made him sweat. A shapeless yarn catastrophe pulled down to his eyebrows. . . .

> Chris Antenen, *"Brown,"* short-story-in-progress

Clichés are metaphors repeated too often. So be original. And don't let a figurative expression become so powerful that it competes with the main idea. In some manuscripts the number and complexity of metaphors and similes is excessive. Some are overworked and overstretched to a point at which the writer loses the objectivity to evaluate them.

Critique groups can give helpful feedback. If none exist in your area, start one or join an organization whose members form online critique groups (see Exhibit C of the POST-MORTEM).

> "The overuse of metaphors tells me a writer can't get his or her thought out. I keep wanting to say 'okay, I got it the first time.'"
>
> Elaine Flinn, author of *Deadly Vintage,* fourth in the Molly Doyle mystery series
> (email used by permission)

Extended metaphors are great fun, like Nancy Bartholomew's "smelly egg" (page 93)—especially when well done. The metaphor, not the egg.

ALLUSION

A reference to a book, its well-known characters, an artist, or some other creative source adds texture or resonance to fiction by evoking associations that readers bring to a story from their own experience. For example,

in *Death of an Obnoxious Tourist* by Maria Hudgins, Dotsy Lamb is famil-
iarizing herself with the first names in a family she's traveling with:

> Beth and Meg, as I well knew, were Amy's sisters. Like
> everyone else in the world I had already asked Lettie if they
> had another sister named Jo, and Lettie had informed me that,
> of course, they didn't. They had a brother named Joe.   [p. 14]

Readers who don't recognize an allusion ignore it and move on. Readers who do recognize it feel rewarded, as if the author winked and slipped
them a piece of chocolate. Allusions, like any figure of speech, add texture
and density to writing, both compressing and expanding meaning.

In *Stark Knight,* J. R. Turner's first novel of suspense, Sara recalls:

> How long had she tried to convince herself having a family
> didn't matter? . . . When colonel Bruce Knight, liaison to the
> Department of Defense, had plucked her from juvie at the age
> of twelve, it had been like a fairytale. Daddy Warbucks rescues
> Annie.   [pp. 9–10]

In Laura Lippman's *Baltimore Blues,* the series character, P. I. Tess
Monaghan, seeks information at an upscale gym. To gain access, she feigns
interest in joining and fills in a false name on the application form:

> . . . She had a sudden vision of nightly calls and entreaties from
> Dale, begging her to try the Sweat Shop for three months, two
> months, one month.
> *Tess Duberville,* she wrote carefully, adding the phone
> number for the local weather service. Let Thomas Hardy and
> the forecasters deal with the sales pitch.   [p. 33]

My final example of allusion is from the science fiction novel *The Key*
by Pauline Baird Jones. An Air Force pilot on an inter-galactic mission is
shot down, lands on an inhospitable planet, and takes refuge in a cave. She
realizes she is not alone:

> He blinked, just the once, the green of his eyes disappearing,
> then slowly reappearing. It was very Cheshire Cat—one
> channeling Tim Burton.   [p. 11]

SECOND REFERENCE

Fundamental to both the art and the craft of writing is the ability to find relationships between unrelated ideas and create new meaning from them. Think of puns. Okay, don't think of puns—not everyone's fondest word play, though I can't imagine why. Here is another delightful technique at work: making a second reference to something mentioned earlier in an entirely different context.

When readers encounter the same object or idea at a later time, the change in context adds a fresh twist.

> Voice is what distinguishes fine fiction from a telephone directory. Both contain words, but fine fiction speaks with a unique and compelling voice.
>
> Carol Kenny, author of *Closing Time*
> (email used by permission)

One thing a second reference needs is a first one. To demonstrate, in Kate Flora's *Death in Paradise,* one of seven Thea Kozak mysteries, Thea attends a business convention in Hawaii. Twice, Maui chips are mentioned along with other snacks. Both times, the item appears as a minor, insignificant detail.

So it's enjoyable to come across a scene near the end of the book in which Thea is attacked. Uh-oh, I don't mean the threat of bodily harm to the series character is satisfying. I'd better let the action speak for itself:

> I grabbed the hand that had the knife, shouted for Raoul, and slammed my forehead into her face as hard as I could. The resounding crunch was more satisfying than Maui potato chips.
>
> [p. 327]

Encountering this familiar detail in its new context, very different from the previous ones, creates a rewarding moment for the observant reader.

The less remarkable an object's introduction, the more heightened the effect when readers come upon it later in an unrelated situation. We realize that the author cleverly set it up to entertain us. How pleasurable is the unexpected discovery.

The technique has style, and most certainly density.

Here's another use of the technique in the first mystery of the Carlotta Carlyle series by Linda Barnes, *A Trouble of Fools.* An elderly client has hidden money in a trunk in her attic and hires Carlotta to find it.

> The door opened into shadow, not darkness, therefore the
> attic had a light source somewhere, one sadly insufficient for a
> search. I dipped into my shoulder bag—which weighs about a
> ton because I keep it crammed with picklocks, my trusty Swiss
> army knife, MBTA tokens, and stray lipsticks—in hopes of
> locating a flashlight. My first find [of] the right shape turned
> out to be a can of that old-style lacquery hairspray, which,
> believe me, is just as off-putting to muggers as a can of Mace,
> much cheaper, and you don't need a license for it. I never use
> hairspray for anything else.   [p. 80]

If nothing from this paragraph were mentioned again, the stuff Carlotta carries in her shoulder bag would serve the single purpose of adding humor and expanding characterization.

Yet one item among all these others *is* mentioned again, in a different, unexpected context in the next chapter. It opens with Carlotta feeling nervous about carrying the money she is moving from her client's trunk to a safer hiding place:

> My favorite part of those Gothic suspense novels, aside
> from the climactic moment when our heroine gets a message
> from our hero and waltzes off to meet him at midnight in the
> old abandoned warehouse, is where the heroine goes outside
> carrying thousands of bucks belonging to some secret
> organization, armed only with a can of hairspray.   [p. 85]

The hairspray itself is of no importance; Carlotta doesn't use it for defense. Its value is as a rhetorical device, a second reference that sneaks up on readers and makes us appreciate the author's rich writing style.

PARALLEL ACTION

A more complex technique is parallel action, which combines separate, unrelated events in the same scene. Say your protagonist stops to review what's taken place so far. She thinks, analyzes, theorizes, plans. While all this mental work goes on, what visual images do you offer your readers?

Choose some simple, familiar activity to engage your character that makes no demands on your readers' intellect and lets them stay focused on the workings of your protagonist's keen mind.

In Beth Groundwater's first novel, the Agatha-nominated *A Real Basket Case,* Claire assembles items for a customer's gift basket while she reviews the puzzling events that got her husband arrested for murder:

> Trying to construct a pleasing, ordered arrangement out of a random pile of gift items often helped Claire organize her thoughts. . . . As she stacked and restacked gifts, attempting to make a coherent whole out of the pieces, she tried to fit together a story of [the] murder that made sense.   [pp. 85–86]

Pairing a cerebral process with an unrelated, physical activity establishes a symbiotic relationship between them: neither is compelling enough to support a scene of its own, yet each brings interest and depth to the other.

Observe the technique at work in Lisa Scottoline's second mystery novel, *Final Appeal,* an Edgar Award winner. Attorney Grace Rossi is thinking through the puzzling death of her lover, Judge Armen Gregorian, while she is photocopying his schedule:

> READY TO COPY, the photocopier says. I open the heavy lid, slap the paper onto the glass, and hit the button. The light from the machine rolls calcium white across my face.
>
> Suicide? I don't understand. They were going to file for divorce, if what Armen said was true. I feel a pang of doubt. . . .
>
> READY TO COPY. I hit the button. You don't kill yourself just because you're Armenian. Armen was a survivor. And he hated guns, was against keeping them in the house. Where did he get the gun?
>
> READY TO COPY, says the machine again, but I'm not ready to copy. So much has happened. We found and lost each other in one night. I stare at the glass over the shadowy innards of the machine; all I see is my own confused reflection.
>
> [pp. 51–52]

That final paragraph continues the parallel threads of action and thought —but goes further. It intertwines them. The "ready to copy" light, the reflective glass, and the "shadowy innards" take on symbolic qualities that suggest the depth of Grace's state of mind. Tension grows, and the multiple meanings create density.

COUNTERPOINT

Actions that converge and inform each other with added layers of meaning approach a higher calling: counterpoint. Whereas parallel actions maintain their identities as separate themes, counterpoint does that and more by creating a relationship between unrelated themes.

The new relationship has no existence of its own until the writer recognizes it and gives it expression.

Observe this outstanding example of counterpoint from Michael Allen Dymmoch's *The Man Who Understood Cats,* winner of the St. Martin's Press/Malice Domestic award for best first mystery novel. Dymmoch's series features two professionals, John Thinnes, an overstressed Chicago detective, and Jack Caleb, a psychiatrist and gay man.

Caleb wants to learn who murdered one of his patients, and Thinnes wants to learn if Caleb is the murderer. These personal agendas make it logical for the detective to offer—and the psychiatrist to accept—an invitation to ride along one evening as the police investigate an unrelated case. (Crowne is a junior detective. The single mention of Karsch, who does not appear in this scene, refers to a police consultant who's a psychologist.)

They flagged an old Buick down on Division Street and followed it into an alley, letting it pull several car-lengths ahead. Thinnes and Caleb stayed in the car. Thinnes filled Caleb in on the case, while Crowne got out and walked up to lean against the Buick and talk to the driver, a former gang member in his twenties, who sometimes gave them useful information. As they watched, Thinnes asked Caleb, "What does a psychiatrist actually do?"

"If he's successful," Caleb said, "he helps people solve their personal problems."

A Karsch kind of answer, if ever there was one, Thinnes thought. "Yeah, but how? What exactly do you do?"

"There's nothing exact about it. When a client asks me to help, I have him describe the problem. I listen to what he says. I study his body language for discrepancies. I try to notice what he doesn't say."

He paused as they watched Crowne take out a cigarette and

then hand the pack to his informant. Crowne lit up with a green plastic lighter, which he also handed over. The informant took a cigarette, lit it, and put both pack and lighter in his pocket.

Thinnes could read neither approval nor disapproval on Caleb's face as he continued. "If there's any suggestion of organic impairment, I send him to his physician for a thorough physical, and I test him myself for drugs and anything I think his doctor may have missed."

Down the alley, Crowne walked around the informant's car and got in the front seat. His gestures became mildly threatening, and he leaned toward the informant as the man spoke.

Caleb waited, perhaps for Thinnes to comment, then went on. "If I don't find drugs or any physical cause for the problem, I dig into his family history and try to determine what purpose the problem serves, either for the client or for significant others in his life."

In the informant's car, Crowne shook his head vigorously, almost as if disagreeing with Caleb. He listened to the informant for a moment, then shrugged.

"Motive, opportunity, and method," Thinnes said. "Basic detective work, huh?"

"That, and a bit more. A detective's finished when he's discovered who did it and presented his evidence. At that point in the investigation, a therapist still has to determine if his subject really wants to change, and if he's serious, how to help him do it."

"Sort of a one-man criminal justice system."

"That's one way to put it, although it's more frequently described by critics as playing God."

Crowne got out of the Buick and started back toward them, poker-faced, but Thinnes could tell he'd struck out. Thinnes kept his eyes on Caleb and said, "What do you think, Doctor. Did he score?"

"I doubt it."

Then Crowne opened the door and threw himself into the passenger seat with a resounding "Damn!"   [pp. 84–85]

A great deal is going on in this well-crafted scene. For parallel action, two unrelated events are unfolding side by side. The dominant event is a technical explanation of the process of psychiatric observation—an abstraction. The subordinate event, starring a minor character, Crowne, provides the necessary action to add the visual interest lacking in the abstraction.

Dramatic irony grows as Thinnes watches Caleb in an attempt to read the psychiatrist's body language, while the psychiatrist explains the psychoanalytical method of trying to read the body language of a client.

Each man, it soon becomes clear, is engaged in a form of detective work. The similarity between the men's professions develops, and we realize that Dymmoch is presenting parallel *themes* in addition to parallel actions.

The irony deepens when the themes cross over:

> In the informant's car, Crowne shook his head vigorously, almost as if disagreeing with Caleb.

In less skillful hands than Dymmoch's, a technical presentation of the psychoanalytic process might come off as a lecture. What Dymmoch does so effectively is to introduce parallel themes, carry them out through parallel actions, interweave them, add strains of dramatic irony, and produce a well-orchestrated whole greater than the sum of its already substantial parts.

As in music, counterpoint entwines separate themes that enrich each other and create another entity that multiplies the effect of the whole. What density. What *style!*

SYMBOLISM

My final example of a rich rhetorical device has much in common with parallel themes and counterpoint, but it adds many layers of meaning through the power of symbols. The following scene comes from *Sad Water,* the third novel in the Gale Grayson series by Teri Holbrook, winner of numerous awards. One of the story's main characters is Chalice, a sculptor, who is unable to speak because of an injury to her tongue.

> . . . she sat in the workroom of Markham Studio and examined the clay mask she was fashioning. Kitschy, and not at all her style, but the masks kept her employed. This one's working title was "The Yeller," because of the taut gape of the mouth.
>
> [p. 40]

The symbolism of the gaping mouth seems to suggest the feelings of the mute sculptor. Chalice's hands continue to reshape the mouth as she listens to the conversation between Totty, her sister, and Olivia, her employer at the studio. They are talking about the search for a body:

> Olivia laughed. "That's generally how I feel about the police. They certainly can't come in here without leaving their slobber about."
> Chalice placed her fingers inside the mask's mouth and gently pulled. The clay gave and the lower jaw extended a fraction of an inch.   [p. 41]

Because Totty appreciates Olivia's having employed her mute sister, she often avoids telling the owner of the studio what she thinks. However:

> Chalice knew what her sister was thinking: *Not bloody likely.* But Totty would never say that to Olivia. Totty was too grateful. Beneath Chalice's fingers the lips on the mask cracked. She quickly dipped her fingers in water and ran them over the clay.
>   [p. 43]

The symbolism intensifies as complex meanings continue to develop. Not the least of these is the irony of Totty's ability to speak but choosing not to, compounded by Chalice's knowing what Totty is thinking and why she chooses to hold her tongue, figuratively.

Additional meanings become apparent as we probe the question of whose lips are cracking, those of Totty? Chalice? Or Olivia—an opportunist who uses her power of speech to hurt others?

Perhaps all three, each in her own limited way. The more one contemplates a symbol's possible interpretations, the more meanings swirl and ripple from it.

Symbols are so rich, so multifaceted, words alone cannot mine their depth.

After I critiqued a first chapter for Mike D'Alto, he sent this note (used with permission): "I imagined . . . you would be bowled over by it, drop everything to work on it. In my wildest dreams you wrote and said 'don't change a word!' However, I have learned that the imaginary part of writing is only 50%, if not less."

DENSITY

Experiment with different techniques. You'll discover relationships among ideas that you hadn't realized were there. Truthfully, they are *not* there. Through your unique writer's vision, you discern the potential connections between dissimilar concepts. Your insight won't let you rest until you find a way to explore the possibilities, bring them into existence, and give them expression through your unique writer's voice.

Don't rush to put the revision process behind you. Your heightened awareness of the techniques available to you will help you approach each pass through your manuscript from a fresh perspective.

As they say in *Star Wars*, "Metaphors be with you."

> "In my opinion, 'voice' is the most important ingredient in a successful book. The plot may be clever, but if the voice doesn't engage us, how can we care?
>
> Margaret Maron

FIND & FIX CLUE #23: NOISY VOICE

- ◆ Once you eliminate the writing habits that drown out your voice, experiment to see how you might enrich your writing with the judicious use of similes, metaphors, extended metaphors, allusion, and second references—but subtly and in moderation, lest they, too, call excessive attention to themselves.

- ◆ Look for potential parallels that create visual interest for cerebral content that lacks its own imagery.

- ◆ Continue working with parallel actions to see what multi-layered relationships you can develop among different themes.

- ◆ Explore the possibilities offered by counterpoint and symbolism to deepen your meaning.

- ◆ Read many authors in different genres and study the techniques, style, and voice of each writer you admire—and a little of those you dislike.

- ◆ Write, rewrite, and rewrite again.

D.O.A.

CLUE #24: WORDS & MISDEMEANORS

For big-time help with small-time search and destroy missions, there's nothing like a word processor's search and replace feature. It lets you quickly find and fix the culprits that lurk in your writing—as they do in mine. Therefore, my search command and I are *likethis*.

If, as Samuel Butler said, "Words are the clothes that thoughts wear," most submissions reveal ill-fitting garments with thin texture and unflattering style.

The misdemeanors I discuss in this CLUE are not likely to doom an otherwise excellent submission—if they are not overused. Plenty of untidy writing gets published, as we know. And when a rough spot causes confusion, some readers think it's *them*.

But first readers recognize the clues. They've learned that early evidence of confusion-causing writing guarantees more of the same ahead. So busy screener-outers watch for the earliest reason to lower their piles of never-ending submissions.

"SUDDENLY"

One "suddenly" per book, please. More frequent use signals amateur techniques used by a writer who doesn't know how to structure a scene for maximum effect. To create surprise in readers means catching them off guard, a technique that has no need for the "s" word.

Senior editor Michael Seidman recommends setting up the paragraph *before* the surprise. This makes readers leap to an assumption that's different from your intended outcome.[56]

What assumptions do you form as you read the following extract from *Authorized Personnel Only,* by Barbara D'Amato? It's late afternoon in Chicago, and police officer Suze Figueroa and her partner are taking a break at a neighborhood bar:

"Be right back," Figueroa said. She went to the women's rest room, way down the hall from the men's. It was less convenient, and although she had never been in the men's room, she heard their room was bigger.

She figured a bathroom break right now would be a good idea because she and Norm were going to go back out and spend several hours hiding in the alley. It would also be a good idea to call home. She had told them she'd be back by midnight, which was stupid of her. She should have realized it could take longer.

Yeah, take longer and maybe achieve nothing, she thought.

Still, with Maria in charge and Kath as backup, and Robert getting home by twelve, there shouldn't be a problem.

She'd call anyhow.

She washed her hands, dried them on one of the brown paper towels from the dispenser, and grabbed one of the prepackaged towelettes that had appeared in a dispenser in the washroom a year or so ago.

She gave her face a good, brisk wiping off. Nice lemon fragrance.

Lemon fragrance? Oh, my god!   [pp. 299–300]

You can sense that the last line makes an impact, even though I don't want to give anything away by explaining its meaning. Instead, let's analyze D'Amato's method of building the scene for maximum effect.

Every detail works as a diversion to set us up for the surprise in the last line. Beginning with the image of "way down the hall," our expectations are misdirected. What reader would not become alert to a possible attack on a woman as she enters a long, deserted corridor?

With Suze's mind wandering to the disparity between the men's and the women's facilities, then to the long night's stakeout ahead, the pace slows and our apprehension grows. Suze, *be careful!*

When her walk down the hall proves uneventful, our expectations turn to what might happen when she opens the door to the women's room. Will a dead body fall from a stall? A live one leap from behind the door? Suze, pay attention, *puh-leeze.* But our fears, once again, prove unfounded.

Suze's thinking of home and family continues to slow the pace, and our tightly coiled springs begin to loosen. Five sentences of whether she should phone home force us to concentrate on her decision-making. Add the minutiae of hand washing and drying, and our antennae relax even more. We are lulled into accepting the scene as an ordinary visit to a restroom.

Wham! Wrong again. There *is* a surprise, and it's not at all what D'Amato's techniques led our imaginations to expect. The suddenness of this development gains power from the author's having set us up for it.

And she does this with nary a "suddenly."

Manuscript screeners see the word so often and in ways so unnecessary that we bristle at the sight of it. We suspect the writer also uses "ly" adverbs to bolster action too feeble to provide its own effect.

When you're tempted to use this overworked word, see if *abruptly, at that moment,* and *just then* might work instead.

Here's how insidious the "s" word is. In a recently published novel, this line appears: "Suddenly the phone rang." When, I ask you, does that infernal instrument *not* ring suddenly? Unlike dogs, telephones don't growl a low warning before attacking.

The author may have meant to show that her character was startled by the ring of her phone. If so, compare how Cathy Pickens handles the same circumstance in this passage from *Done Gone Wrong:*

> As I stepped through the opening in the hedge . . . my cell
> phone buzzed. I always jump, startled, when that happens,
> especially when I've wandered off deep in thought. [pp. 34–35]

This reaction expands our insight into Pickens' series character.

An even more colorful image is shared with us by Nancy Pickard in *The Virgin of Small Plains,* an Edgar finalist and Agatha winner. Mitch is creeping quietly down the stairs from his girlfriend's bedroom, barefoot, her unsuspecting parents asleep in their bedroom nearby:

> When the phone rang like a tornado siren going off, he jumped
> as if a doctor had poked a needle in his ass. [p. 27]

Honestly, isn't this comparison more effective than "suddenly"?

Search your own manuscript for the "s" word and see what happens when you delete it. If its absence reduces the power of the surprise, you will have learned an important lesson: it's the *scene* that needs work.

DIES LAUGHING

An easy way to show relationships is to portray characters joking with each other and laughing. Clowning around also lightens a scene's gloom and doom—if that's what it needs. Some writers, perhaps thinking to increase the comedic effect of a scene, go beyond showing these actions to telling us that a line of dialogue was *laughed.*

Words can be said with a laugh or while laughing, but words cannot *be* laughed. Neither can they be smiled, chuckled, snorted, grinned, grimaced, or guffawed. If you use one of these verbs, write it into a beat, not a tag. Tags tell us how the speaker sounds; beats help us see or hear what the speaker is doing. To use a beat, begin a new sentence immediately before or after a line of dialogue that's funny. Whenever I see the dialogue tag *he laughed,* I "hear" the character's words sounding like a horse's whinny. As for *snorted* and *guffawed,* I won't even go there.

When your intention is to have your audience share in the merriment, don't show your characters cracking up; show what is causing them to do so. In this way you let readers react to whatever strikes *them* as funny.

If, however, your purpose is to show up a character for laughing at her own joke, understate the reaction of another character—as in the next example. It's from Sandra Balzo's *Uncommon Grounds.* The protagonist, Maggie Thorsen, is talking with her tax preparer:

> ". . . I suppose I'm going to get killed on taxes," I ventured.
> "Well, we'll see. You know what they say, Uncle Sam wants you—and everything you've got." She was still laughing, freshly buoyed by accountant humor, as I left.   [p. 43]

Balzo reinforces this humor by underplaying Maggie's response to it. In belittling the joke, then leaving, Maggie projects a cool, above-it-all attitude. That understatement gives us room for our own reaction.

When you do portray laughter, make it add value. Here's a line from *Legwork,* the first Casey Jones mystery by Katy Munger:

> Slim Jim began to laugh and I listened as his merriment gave way to the sound of his truck motor fading. . . .   [p. 219]

In the next scene from *Pharmacology is Murder* by Dirk Wyle, the value of laughter lies in what it adds to the portrayal of both the protagonist, Ben

Candidi, a candidate for admission to a doctoral program, and Dr. Taylor, the professor who interviews him. Each man tries to outdo the other with his erudition and wit:

> "Yes, I see," he said flipping back to my transcript. "You also received an 'A' in philosophy. Say, tell me, Mr. *Candidi,* what philosophy did they teach you in that course? That it is the Best of All Possible Worlds!" His laugh rattled the file cabinets.
>
> A flash of inspiration furnished a reply. "Yes, that's exactly what they did teach. The prof's name was *Dr. Pangloss."* Dr. Taylor smiled at my snide answer, so I upped the ante. "At this point could I ask *you* how well am I standing up to the *Grand Inquisitor of Lisbon?"*
>
> This brought out another booming laugh. His chest heaved, and he literally bounced in his chair.   [pp. 47–48]

Readers unfamiliar with Voltaire's *Candide* who miss the allusions central to the characters' repartee are nonetheless entertained by Wyle's imagery. The passage is able to appeal to readers on several levels.

I can't tell you how to write humor. I wish I could. What I *can* tell you are two general principles for the effective presentation of any emotion:

- Underplay the responses of your characters.
- Select details that create the emotion *in* your reader.

Observe what you find amusing when you read. Analyze the techniques of the authors who make you laugh. If you want readers to laugh out loud, write scenes that are inherently funny. Humor that grows from a situation is organic humor. The same process applies to creating any emotion.

Comedian Bob Newhart said that scriptwriters don't write as well when they have canned laughter. It acts like a crutch. [57]

I suspect that writers who prop up their dialogue with *he laughed* use the tag as their crutch, similar to propping up weak action with adverbs, adjectives, and empty gestures. After all, if writers *tell* what others are feeling, they don't have to work at creating dialogue and action to show it.

The same applies to *smiled,* except that frequent smiling has the added disadvantage of making characters look like fools and the writing adolescent. Note the punctuation in the next example, a type of construction to avoid: *"That's a lively dog," Pam smiled.* Less awkward tags are *she said with a smile* and *she said, smiling.* Or turn the tag into a separate beat:

> "That's a lively dog." Pam smiled.
> Damon returned his neighbor's smile. "Yes, I agree."

Sappy writing, but you get the idea. Even better, instead of echoing the dialogue, use a beat to raise the action to another level:

> "That's, uh, a lively dog you've got there." Pam smiled and quickly sidestepped the horny Poodle anticipating an intimate encounter with her leg.

Look to your purpose. Consider whether the reason for including a smile or a laugh is to clarify the true feelings of a character whose lines of dialogue are ambiguous. If so, what needs clarifying is the dialogue, as well as the action and the characterization.

Work on those problems first.

THE POINT IS?

Like the word *suddenly*, the exclamation point can be overdone. Here's advice from the respected *Chicago Manual of Style:*

> An exclamation point is used to mark an outcry or an emphatic or ironic comment. To avoid detracting from its effectiveness, however, the author should use this punctuation sparingly. [58]

This overused mark of punctuation is appropriate for true exclamations, such as "Oh!" "Gosh!" "Ouch!" "Help!" and "Watch out!" If a computer search of your manuscript shows a frequent or indiscriminate use of the exclamation point, experiment with different words and word arrangements until the emphasis you want doesn't come from punctuation but from placement.

That is, place the key words or phrases you want to emphasize at the ends of sentences, and where possible, place key sentences at the ends of paragraphs. Endings vibrate power.

Gary Provost advised writers to arrange sentences with tension in mind.[59]

> *"This may seem like a fine point, but fine points can draw blood."*
> Theodore M. Bernstein

For an example of a power arrangement, examine this ending to Chapter 22 from Sandra Parshall's *The Heat of the Moon,* winner of the Agatha Award for best first novel:

> In the closed alcohol-reeking ambulance, with the keening siren deafening me to all other sound, I forced myself to turn my head and look at the stretcher next to mine.
>
> The medic bent over her, blocking her upper body from my sight. As I watched, he sat back, shoulders slumping. He remained that way for a moment with his head bowed. Then he shifted and I caught a glimpse of her pale cheek before he drew the blood-soaked sheet over her face.   [p. 212]

Compare Parshall's phrasing with this weak rewrite of mine, in which I change only the word order within each sentence:

> I forced myself to turn my head and look at the stretcher next to mine in the closed alcohol-reeking ambulance, with the keening siren deafening me to all other sound.
>
> The medic blocked her upper body from my sight by bending over her. He sat back, shoulders slumping, as I watched. He remained with his head bowed that way for a moment. Before he drew the blood-soaked sheet up over her face, I caught a glimpse of her pale cheek when he shifted.

See how my word order ends each sentence on a weak note? My version would lose even more strength if I reordered the sentences so the blood-soaked sheet were drawn over the woman's face at the beginning.

Think how much more infantile my version would read if I ended it with an exclamation point. Exclamatory punctuation in *abundance* produces the *same* effect as *too much italicizing.* After a *while*, readers *wonder* if the *writer* thinks *readers* are *deaf!* Or *dense!!*

Literary critic B. R. Myers says that unnecessary emphasis is the classic sign of a writer who lacks confidence.[60]

Evidently, many writers lack confidence in their ability to get their point across! Maybe they doubt their audience's ability to read!! A few seem to turn almost every line into an exclamation, which produces a most unusual effect!! *Stop it!!!*

RANGES

For superlatives—biggest, smallest, most, least, and so on—only one exists. That *one* cannot also be a range. Do not write:

- ⊷ The victim was at least seventy-five or eighty years old.
- ⊷ When he reached the scene, as many as twenty or thirty bystanders had gathered.
- ⊷ The child holding the gun couldn't have been more than ten or twelve.

Stop hedging and fudging. Pick a number, already. Say: the victim was at least seventy-five years old, there were as many as thirty bystanders, and the child couldn't have been more than twelve. The words *at least, as many as,* and *couldn't have been more than* provide enough weaseling to protect you from being sued for libel by your characters.

Want more fudge? Keep the range but drop the superlatives:

- ⊷ He guessed that the victim was seventy-five or eighty years old.
- ⊷ When he got to the scene, twenty to thirty bystanders had gathered.
- ⊷ The child holding the gun was ten or twelve.

If you do use a range, *about, around,* and *approximately* are redundant.

DOUBLED PREPOSITIONS

A special redundancy is the doubled preposition: sits *down on* the couch, stands *out in* the hall, leans *out over* the railing. Characters constantly go *over to,* walk *over toward,* glance *over at,* drive *over across.* At times, triplets sprout like weeds, as in look *down below at* the street and come *on over to* the house. Whether twosies or threesies: cut one word from each.

The most common excesses are *up* and *back:* he piled *up* his plate, closed the fingerprint kit *up,* reached *up over* his head, pulled *up into* the driveway, and climbed *up onto* the roof. She went *back* inside, stifled *back* a cry, sat *back* down, headed *back out* the door, went *back up* the stairs, and looked *back up* at him.

An occasional pair of twins might be allowed to take up residence in your manuscript if doing so improves the effect of certain dialogue. The redundancy must be intentional, though, not accidental. Learn to recognize your uninvited guests. You are their host, so you can set your own ground rules to keep them from spreading their stuff out over and around about everything. If any of these excesses resemble your usual manner of speech, no need to fear for your literary career—as long as your speaking habits don't infiltrate your writing habits and sabotage your story. When a multi-prepositional manuscript turns up in the submission pile, the busy screener is likely to set it over onto the "no" pile.

MORE TRASH

Every interviewer asks me to name the most common error I see. Now that you've read 275 pages of misuse and 230 effective alternatives, you know that *all* errors are common. Here in each category are the winners— er, losers. These affect at ninety percent or more of all submissions:

COMMON MISUSAGE

Most frequent misspelling: *loose* when you mean *lose*.
Correct: *Don't lose reader interest by playing fast and loose with grammar.*

2nd most frequent misspelling: *blonde* when you mean the color *blond* *(adjective)*; also *blond* when you mean the woman, a *blonde (noun)*.
Correct: *The blond hair on his jacket implicated the blonde who just left.*

Most frequent punctuation error: *its* when you mean the contraction for *it is*, and *it's* when you mean the pronoun *its*.
Correct: *It's raining on her Volvo, but its wax job keeps its shine.*

2nd most frequent punctuation error: *missing comma* from a compound sentence, needed between complete subject-verb sentences joined by a conjunction, as in:

> The crazed killer shot her and her entire family decided to have the body cremated.

Correct: *The crazed killer shot her, and her entire family decided to have the body cremated.*

Most awkward verb tense: *conditional*, as in:

> He would have liked to have gone home.
> I would have imagined that he would have been unable to have gone home.
> [I did not make these up!]

Better: Either *He would have liked* [then] *to go home* [then].
Or *He would like* [now] *to have gone home* [then].
And *I imagine* [now] *that he would have been unable* [then] *to go home* [then].

2nd most awkward verb tense: *past perfect*, as in:

> Paula announced that she had found the murder weapon. This morning she had gone for coffee as usual and had noticed. . . . *(see discussion pp. 276–77)*

Weakest verbs:	*is* *there is* *are* *there are* *to be* *am*
	was *there was* *were* *there were* *being* *been*

Dull:	There was a note tacked to my front door. *(passive)*
Better:	*A note was tacked to my front door.*
Better still:	*A note tacked to my front door warned me of _____*

Weakest construct:	passive ("note was..."), which produces passive voice:
	Sue was pinched by Mr. J.

Better:	*Mr. J pinched Sue.*
Better still:	*Sue felt Mr. J's pinch and quickly stomped his foot.*
	Use active construction to emphasize the actor; use passive when the action is more important than the actor, as in: *The affair was made known all over town.*

Laziest construct:	*"As"* to link two events and make them seem to occur simultaneously:
	I heard a single gunshot as I went down the stairs and got in my car.

Better:	*The moment I reached the bottom step I heard ____ .*

Most unnecessary words (most of the time):	*just only really rather sort of a bit now even very actually quite kind of that "Well" and then* (often, either *and* or *then* is stronger)

Falsest belief:	that it's wrong to split an infinitive (it's not) and to end a sentence with a preposition (also untrue).

© 2008 by Chris Roerden, *Don't Sabotage Your Submission*

Let me just add, don't even think that you can actually ignore really poor writing habits and just assume that a screener-outer will just skip over those very small mistakes without noticing them even a little bit.

To restate: Don't think you can ignore poor writing habits and assume professional readers will skip small mistakes without noticing them.

TENSING UP

Writers tell me they aren't sure what verb tense to use when introducing material from the past, given that story time already uses the past tense.

> Paula *announced* (past tense) that she *had* found (past perfect tense) the murder weapon.

This sequence of past tense followed by past perfect is appropriate for the first step back in time. However, when the past perfect continues, as

I've seen numerous writers do in their manuscripts, the result—though grammatically correct—is cumbersome. For example:

> Paula announced that she *had found* the murder weapon. This morning she *had gone* for coffee as usual and *had noticed. . . .*

Steer clear of cumbersome. Here's the same example, equally correct, which uses "had" only once, and only to introduce the episode. From then on, the simple past tense prevails:

> Paula announced that she *had found* the murder weapon. This morning she *went* for coffee as usual and *noticed. . . .*

The one-time use of the past perfect tense is usually sufficient to signal a transition to the more distant past, especially when another time clue is furnished, such as *this morning.* After that, the simple past tense is fine. It makes the long-ago action more immediate and less wordy.

To end a sequence and signal a return to story time, you can reintroduce "had" one last time, if necessary. Notice how John Sandford handles the following brief flashback in *Rules of Prey,* his first thriller.

The series character, Lucas Davenport, is flying from Minnesota's Twin Cities to Cedar Rapids, Iowa. The woman in the next seat notices his death grip on the armrests. She volunteers a series of unwelcome platitudes, then adds:

> "Well, don't worry, we'll be there in an hour."
>
> Lucas cranked his head toward her. He felt as though his spine had rusted. "An hour? We've been up pretty long now."
>
> "Only ten minutes," she said cheerfully.
>
> "Oh, God."
>
> The police psychologist had told him that he feared the loss of control.
>
> "You can't deal with the idea that your life is in somebody else's hands, no matter how competent they are. What you have to remember is, your life is always in somebody else's hands. You could step into the street and get mowed down by a drunk in a Cadillac. Much more chance of that than a plane wreck."
>
> [p. 200]

Sandford signals the switch to the remembered past with the line, "The police psychologist had told him"—a one-time use of the past perfect. From that point on, the flashback stays in the past tense:

> "I know that," Lucas said. "I want to know what to do about it."
>
> The shrink shook his head. "Well, there's hypnotism. And there are some books that are supposed to help. But if I were you, I'd just have a couple of drinks. And try not to fly."
>
> "How about chemicals?"
>
> "You could try some downers, but they'll mess up your head. I wouldn't do it if you have to be sharp when you get where you're going."
>
> The flight to Cedar Rapids didn't offer alcohol. He didn't have pills. . . .   [p. 201]

Sandford does not change the verb tense in bringing us back to story time. Instead, he re-anchors us in the current setting: "The flight to Cedar Rapids." He further links the past to the present by repeating, briefly, the psychologist's reference to alcohol and pills. Smoothly done.

If you use similar time shifts in your fiction, stay in current story time with the simple past tense as much as possible. Minimize your use of the past perfect "had" and always avoid cumbersome constructions.

"FINALLY"

This final tip might strike you as more nitpicky than my other observations, but picking nits is part of what editors do.

> "Nit: the egg of a parasitic insect, esp. of a louse."
> Webster's Encyclopedic Unabridged Dictionary

Take the word "finally"—one of the nits that can louse up any action. It belongs at the end of a series of events, not in the middle. Yet the word keeps popping up whenever a character overcomes any intermediate hurdle in a chain of events. Two manuscripts I edited used "finally" on page 1. Here's a condensed version of the typical misusage:

> Yvonne struggled to undo the rusty lock on the outside cellar doors. Finally she got it open. Slowly, cautiously, she made her

way down the rickety ladder to the cellar, listening for any sound. When she finally felt the dirt floor beneath her feet, she stumbled around until her foot hit wood and her groping confirmed a handrail.

She climbed the stairs to the first floor. After quietly checking out each room and finding them unoccupied, she finally came across the doctor's home office. In the light from a streetlamp, she saw three filing cabinets of four drawers each. Just as she thought—her search was first beginning.

For a beginning action or a continuing action, *finally* sends a contradictory message. Readers have as much faith in the action's credibility as in a "Final Clearance" banner across a store window month after month.

"Finally" implies a hurdle overcome, a challenge met, anticipation satisfied. The implication triggers a temporary lessening of tension. You want to increase tension, not lower it.

Consider the use of the more accurate "eventually" or "gradually." Possibly "at last." Or eliminate all adverbs and show the character's feelings. Make readers experience the same emotion the character feels at each step in the sequence: frustration, anger, a momentary sense of relief for contrast, then growing anxiety and fear.

Note that I said to *show* these feelings, not tell.

When should "finally" (or "ultimately") be used? Save it for the end of a series of challenges when you want tension to drop. Its overuse echoes the voice of an amateur.

Of all the words in this clue—admittedly misdemeanors, not major offenses—could any one of them succeed in sabotaging your submission? Probably not, if seen one time only. But habits run in packs, like wolves. Editors know if they see one ineffective technique, one passive construction, more will follow. Why would a busy first reader wait for this prophecy to fulfill itself?

"Creativity is the best revenge. Let's finish our books."

Stone Altman, author

Since only ten percent of millions of submissions rise above the average level of craft, quick rejection is the first reader's proven method of saving time.

Taken together, misdemeanors in craft lead to the Hallmarkian conclusion that the writer didn't care enough to send the very best.

However, you now possess the techniques to kill the static and let your voice sound clearly above the crowd. This greatly improves the odds of your manuscript's being *read.* Many steps lie ahead, but only submissions that pass this first tough screening get the chance to move up the decision-making ladder toward the goal of *finally* getting published.

FIND & FIX CLUE #24: WORDS & MISDEMEANORS

- Use your computer's search feature to discover how often "suddenly" pops up in your writing, and see if you can more effectively surprise your readers by making them anticipate a different outcome.

- Type the letters *laugh* into your search feature and analyze each occurrence, asking yourself why you are depending on some form of the word to tell about any emotion that your dialogue and action could be doing a better job of showing. (For a simple search method, review the TIP on page 241.)

- Repeat the above search using the letters *smil.*

- Review the ways you create emotional reactions in your reader, and verify that you underplay those reactions in the character.

- Search and destroy exclamation points, and rearrange sentences and word order until the emphasis you want comes from the sequence and organization of words, sentences, and paragraphs.

- To cure an excess of exclamation points, look on your keyboard for the period. Use it.

- Search your writing for occurrences of the "common misusage" shown on pages 275–76, and note your personal word habits on the list you are compiling for future manuscripts.

- Finally, search for the word "finally" and make sure it isn't over-used, misused, or mindlessly reused. Reserve it for when you want readers to feel a sense of finality.

If you found this book helpful, please ask the
public and college libraries in your community
to add it to their permanent collections.

To see when Chris's workshops for writers are
coming to your area, look for her itinerary
on www.snurl.com/editorspeaks
or www.bellarosabooks.com

And to learn how your library, college, or
writing group can arrange for Chris to
bring an interactive workshop to your area,
email Pat Meller at patmeller@aol.com

Chris will answer your questions about writing
and getting published on her blog. For time and
place, please email chrisroerden@aol.com and
put "Writing Blog" in the subject line.

For information about group discounts for
Don't Sabotage Your Submission
or
Don't Murder Your Mystery
contact the publisher at
sales@bellarosabooks.com

www.bellarosabooks.com

PART X: POST-MORTEM

SUPPORTING TESTIMONY: ENDNOTES

PART I: DEAD ON ARRIVAL

1. "First thanks go to my first reader," in *Greensboro News & Record,* 4-10-04, p. A9.
2. "Slush," essay in *Editors on Editing,* Gerald Gross, ed., Harper & Row 1985, p. 120.
3. For romance subgenres, see the contest guidelines posted on www.rwanational.org.
4. On 7-15-00 I presented this parable on the "Crisis!" panel, Harriette Austin Writers Conference, U-GA. Later versions by others sometimes credit its original source.
5. "Talking with Justin Kaplan," by Lisa Burrell, in *Copy Editor,* 14:6, p. 3.
6. Exception: writing well is less important once sales get into the millions.
7. Based on letters from agents that writers have graciously shared with me.
8. *The First Five Pages,* Fireside, 2000, p. 13.
9. Kathie Fong Yoneda, *The Script-Selling Game,* p. 2.
10. *Book Business,* New York: W.W. Norton, 2002, p. 43.
11. Interview in *Publishers Weekly,* Feb 14, 1999.
12. Barbara Gislason, agent, speaking at MWA's "Of Dark and Stormy Nights."
13. Quoted by Jennifer King, F&W Publications, in the newsletter of Mid-America Publishers Association, July 1996, p. 1.

PART II: EVIDENCE COLLECTION

14. "The Plot Quickens," by Sandra Wales, in *SPAN Connection,* VII:11, Nov 2002, p. 5. (Wales writes fiction under the name Haley Elizabeth Garwood.)
15. This is from the blog of Joe Konrath, known as "A Newbie's Guide to Publishing," www.jakonrath.blogspot.com.

PART III: FIRST OFFENDERS

16. From a presentation by Elizabeth Daniels Squire at the North Carolina Writer's Network Conference, Asheville, Fall 1999.
17. Foster-Harris, University of Oklahoma Press, 1960, p. 80.
18. Since 1982 the English Dept. at San Jose State University has sponsored the Bulwer-Lytton Fiction Contest to write the worst opening sentence to a novel. The contest was begun by Prof. Scott Rice, who unearthed the source of the line "It was a dark and stormy night." www.bulwer-lytton.com.
19. Research conducted on the DorothyL listserv.
20 Interview with Jessica Faust, Bookends, May 17, 2002, via email.
21. Email from Jim Huang dated Jan 22, 2004.
22. Carolyn Wheat, *How to Write Killer Fiction,* compares mystery and thriller.
23. *How to Grow a Novel,* p. 229.
24. *The 38 Most Common Fiction Writing Mistakes,* pp. 11–12.
25. *Technique in Fiction,* New York: Harper & Row, 1955, p. 21.

PART IV: KILLING TIME

26. Sol Stein, *Stein on Writing,* New York: St. Martin's Griffin, 2000, p. 144.
27. "Good Writing is Good Editing," in *AMWA Journal,* 17:1, p. 28.
28. *The Fiction Writer's Toolkit,* e-reads publication, 1999, p. 48.

PART V: THE LINEUP

29. Lawrence Block, MWA 2003 Mid-Atlantic Conference, reported by Peter Abresch.
30. Speaking at the MWA Skill-Build, Aug 16, 2003, Columbia, SC.
31. "Bruce Holland Rogers," in *Wisconsin Regional Writer,* 52:4, Winter 2004, p. 2.
32. "Newsmakers," interview in *Newsweek,* Dec 23, 2002, p. 75.
33. *The 38 Most Common Fiction Writing Mistakes,* p. 11.
34. "Standing in the Line of Fire," interview in *Newsweek,* July 5, 2004, p. 56.

PART VI: CHANGE OF VENUE

35. Posted on "10 Mistakes List," www.holtuncensored.com.
36. *Writing Crime Fiction,* London: Teach Yourself, 2003, p. 10.
37. Quoted in "The Spooky Art," *Newsweek,* Jan 27, 2003, p. 64.

PART VII: THE USUAL SUSPECTS

38. "Fred Chappell," by Maria C. Johnson, in *Greensboro News & Record,* 1-19-03, D2.
39. *The 38 Most Common Fiction Writing Mistakes,* p. 31.
40. Patricia Highsmith, *Plotting and Writing Suspense Thrillers,* p. 65.
41. Isabel Zuber, "Mining the Memory," in *N.C. Writers' Network News,* 11-12-02, p. 20.
42. *From Pen to Print.* New York: Henry Holt, 1990, p. 32.
43. "The Sport of Fiction" in *Writer's Digest,* Oct 1992, p. 32.
44. This reference is to "The Pit and the Pendulum" by Edgar Allen Poe.
45. "Suspense," in *Mystery Writer's Handbook,* MWA, New York: Harper, 1956, p. 105.
46. No need to write to tell me that pornography and erotica are not the same. I took some license here for the sake of a little humor. Very little, I agree.
47. "Fiction," in *Mensa Bulletin* #461, Jan 2003, p. 14.
48. In Chapter 18; p. 186 of the Pocket Books edition, 1939.

PART VIII: ROGUES GALLERY

49. Donald Murray, *Write to Learn,* Harcourt Brace College 6th ed., 1998, p. 217.
50. Carl T. Bogus, "Guns in the Courtroom," in *The Nation,* Mar 31, 2003, p. 40.
51. Erica Jong, "The Artist as Housewife," in *Ms. Magazine,* I:6 (Dec 1972), p. 66.
52. Interview by Qui Xiaolong on www.mysteryreaders.org/athome.html.
53. Original publisher, Univ. of Louisiana Press. Reprinted 1987 by Grove Weidenfeld.
54. Renni Browne & Dave King, *Self-Editing for Fiction Writers.*

PART IX: LOOSE ENDS

55. Stephen King, *On Writing,* p. 136.
56. *Editing Your Fiction,* Cincinnati: Writer's Digest Books, 2001, p. 128.
57. "Bob Newhart," by Tim Williams in *TV Guide,* July 17, 2005, p. 15.
58. 14th ed., Univ. of Chicago Press, §5.17. The 15th ed., §6.76, adds: "should be used sparingly to be effective."
59. *Make Your Words Work,* p. 245.
60. B. R. Myers, "A Reader's Manifesto," in *Atlantic Monthly,* 288:1, 104.

EXHIBIT A: STANDARD MANUSCRIPT FORMAT

Times or Courier—that question sets off some of the lengthiest discussions about formatting. Here's what you need to know: The submission preferences stated by each recipient always take precedence over anything else you've been told. If none are stated, use the standards below.

Font: `Monospaced, as a typewriter,` unless Times is stated. This is 12 pt Times New Roman (it's proportionally spaced). `This is 12 pt Courier (it's monospaced; letters are the same width).` Times is preferred by editors who want a quick read; Courier is preferred by most hands-on manuscript editors. Unless instructed otherwise, use Courier. To mimic typesetting is to look like an amateur. If you use a typewriter, "pitch" refers to characters per inch: `elite = 12 pitch or 10 points;` `pica = 10 pitch or 12 points.`

Title page: Same size font as the text; never larger. Capitalizing is optional.

Serif font: Courier and Times have little "feet" that make them easier to read, so never use a sans serif font (like this one) for manuscripts. *Go easy on the italics;* AVOID ALL CAPS and *all decorative or display type.*

Double-spaced typed text: This does NOT mean one-and-a-half lines of space. It means that for 12 point type, make spacing or leading exactly 24 points. For footnotes and quotations use the same 12-point double-spaced type.

Margins: Minimum 1" top and bottom, 1.25" sides. Large margins make it easier for an editor to write notes and for the author to read them.

Headers: Top left: last name, one word from the title. Top right: page number.

Alignment: Flush left, also known as ragged right. Never justify.

Paragraphs: Don't skip lines between. To separate scenes within a chapter, hit "return" once and type # # # or * * * (with spaces) in the center of the line.

Paragraph indents: One tab or 5 spaces.

Tabs: Use only for indents, never for columns, tables, or centering. Instead, use the word processor's features meant for those functions.

Underscore: This tells copyeditors and traditional typesetters to set words in italics, a separate font that is not always the same as your keyboard shortcut. Use for most foreign words and to refer to titles of books, plays, movies, and TV series. (Use quotation marks for titles of articles, chapters, acts and scenes, short stories, and TV episodes in a series.) To show that italicized text should not be italicized, underscore the text and write rom (for roman) in the margin.

Bold face: May be used for headings and subheadings, never in text. If emphasis is required, underscore to represent italics.

Dash: Type as a double hyphen--without spaces--so its length is unmistakable. Don't type a 1-em dash because a change in font can alter its appearance.

Ellipsis: Show with 3 periods, with or without spaces; 4 periods when trailing off occurs at the end of a sentence. (Please see the TIP on page 193.) Turn off the keystroke feature that creates 3 condensed dots.

Hyphenation: Off.

Page numbers: Must be in sequence start to end, including front matter—no pages missing, repeated, or out of order. (Use the auto-numbering feature of your word processor's header and footer options). If necessary, hand-write page numbers on the printout; never type them on individual pages in a word processing program; they get scrambled when revisions are made.

Chapters: Start each on a new page and drop the first line half a page. (Not necessary when submitting to your personal manuscript editor.)

Footnotes (for nonfiction): If the work is being submitted for editing, use your word processor's footnote or endnote feature and set all notes and biblio-graphic material to print the same as all the other text: 12 pt Courier double-spaced. Or type the actual note directly into the text where you want it referenced, and enclose it in brackets without numbering.

Graphics: Avoid embedding charts, tables, figures, etc., in the main text. Number each graphic, and show where it belongs by typing a corresponding number in the text, adding the words: "Insert figure __ here."

Paper: Standard white 8-1/2" by 11"; no pin-feed tear-offs or hole punching. Avoid erasable bond, which smudges. Avoid heavy bond; the added weight increases shipping costs and makes editors judge the length as excessive.

Printing: One side of the paper only; one column of text.

Black ink: Use a laser or ink cartridge that produces clear, sharp text. If submitting a photocopy, it should be a first generation copy. Handwritten text must be typed. If accepted for publication, text must be available electroni-cally, so use a computer. Scanning is not recommended.

Binding: None. Loose pages only, not stapled, not clipped, not bound in a looseleaf or any kind of binder. Punched holes get in the way of an editor's marginal notations. Use a big rubber band.

Never fold manuscript pages when mailing for editing.

Never send photos or drawings without permission or your only copy of anything.

END: Type this word at the end of your manuscript. It lets the editor and typesetter know they received the entire manuscript.

EXHIBIT B: RECOMMENDED NONFICTION

FICTION CRAFT AND REVISION

Bickham, Jack M. *The 38 Most Common Fiction Writing Mistakes (And How To Avoid Them).* 1992.

Browne, Renni, & Dave King. *Self-Editing for Fiction Writers.* 2005.

Christmas, Bobbie. *Write in Style: Using Your Word Processor and Other Techniques to Improve Your Writing.* 2004.

Lukeman, Noah. *The First Five Pages.* 2000.

Obstfeld, Raymond. *Fiction First Aid.* 2001.

Roerden, Chris. *Don't Murder Your Mystery.* 2006.

_____. *Don't Sabotage Your Submission.* 2008.

FICTION WRITING

Bickham, Jack M. *Setting.* 1994.

Block, Lawrence. *Telling Lies for Fun and Profit: A Manual for Fiction Writers.* 1981.

Buckham, Mary, & Dianna Love. *Break Into Fiction: Power Plot Your Novel.* 2009.

Card, Orson Scott. *How to Write Science Fiction & Fantasy.* 2001.

Emerson, Kathy Lynn, *How to Write Killer Historical Mysteries.* 2008.

Ephron, Hallie. *Writing and Selling Your Mystery Novel.* 2005.

Gardner, John. *The Art of Fiction.* 1983.

Hayden, G. Miki. *Writing the Mystery.* 2001.

Highsmith, Patricia. *Plotting and Writing Suspense Fiction.* 1990.

Horror Writers Ass'n.*On Writing Horror.* Castle, Mort, ed. 2006.

Johnson, Sarah L. *Historical Fiction: A Guide to the Genre.* 2005.

Lamb, Nancy. *Writer's Guide to Crafting Stories for Children.* 2001.

Lukeman, Noah. *The Plot Thickens.* 2002.

McKee, Robert. *Story: Substance, Structure, Style, and the Principles of Screenwriting.* 1997.

Morrell, David. *Lessons from a Lifetime of Writing.* 2003.

Mystery Writers of America. *Writing Mysteries.* Sue Grafton, ed. 2001.

Orr, Alice. *No More Rejections.* 2004.

Parv, Valerie. *The Art of Romance Writing.* 2005.

Pianca, Phyllis Taylor. *How to Write Romances.* 1998.

Provost, Gary. *Make Your Words Work.* Reissued 2001.

Stein, Sol. *How to Grow a Novel.* 1999.

Tapply, William G. *The Elements of Mystery Fiction.* 2005.

Wainger, Leslie J. *Writing a Romance Novel for Dummies.* 2004.

Walsh, Pat. *78 Reasons Why Your Book May Never Be Published and 14 Reasons Why It Just Might.* 2005.

Wheat, Carolyn. *How to Write Killer Fiction.* 2003.

Yoneda, Kathie Fong. *The Script-Selling Game,* Michael Wiese Prod. 2002.

CHARACTER BUILDING & BEHAVIOR

Douglas, John E., and Mark Olshaker. *Anatomy of Motive: The FBI's Key to Understanding & Catching Violent Criminals.* 1999.

Groetsch, Michael; Chris Roerden, ed. *He Promised He'd Stop.* 1997. Profiles of types of men who abuse women.

Kress, Nancy. *Characters, Emotion & Viewpoint.* 2005.

Samenow, Stanton E. *Inside the Criminal Mind.* 2004.

Tannen, Deborah. *You Just Don't Understand: Women and Men in Conversation.* 1991.

CRIMINAL INVESTIGATION

Brown, Steven Kerry. *The Complete Idiot's Guide to Private Investigating.* 2003.

Campbell, Andrea. *Making Crime Pay: The Writer's Guide to Criminal Law, Evidence, and Procedure.* 2002.

Lofland, Lee. *Police Procedure & Investigation: Guide for Writers.* 2007.

COPYRIGHT

Kozak, Ellen. *Every Writer's Guide to Copyright and Publishing Law,* 3rd ed. 2004.

MARKETING THE MANUSCRIPT

Herman, Jeff. *Guide to Book Publishers, Editors, Literary Agents.* (Annual)

Maass, Donald. *The Career Novelist: A Literary Agent Offers Strategies for Success.* 1996.

Sambuchino, Chuck. *Guide to Literary Agents.* 2008.

Sands, Katharine. *Making the Perfect Pitch: How to Catch a Literary Agent's Eye.* 2004.

MARKETING POST-PUBLICATION

Horowitz, Shel. *Grassroots Marketing for Authors & Publishers.* 2007.

Howard-Johnson, Carolyn. *The Frugal Book Promoter: How To Do What Your Publisher Won't.* 2004.

Kremer, John. *1001 Ways to Market Your Books,* 6th ed. 2006.

Levinson, Frishman, Larsen. *Guerrilla Marketing for Writers.* 2000.

Marks, Jeffrey. *Intent To Sell: Marketing the Genre Novel.* 2005.

OTHER

King, Stephen. *On Writing: A Memoir of the Craft.* 2000.

Lamott, Anne. *Bird by Bird.* 1995.

Prose, Francine. *Reading Like a Writer.* 2006.

Zinsser, William. *On Writing Well.* (new editions every few years)

EXHIBIT C: INTERNET SITES FOR WRITERS

American Crime Writers League, *www.acwl.org/index.html*
American Society of Journalists and Authors, *www.asja.org*
Authors Guild, *www.authorsguild.org*
Canadian Authors Ass'n., *www.canauthors.org* conferences, awards
Crime Writers of Canada, *www.crimewriterscanada.com/index.htm*
Historical Novel Society, *www.historicalnovelsociety.org*
Horror Writers Ass'n., *www.horror.org* articles plus links, Bram Stoker award
International Association of Crime Writers, *www.crimewritersna.org*
International Thriller Writers, *www.thrillerwriters.org* conferences, awards
International Women's Writing Guild, *www.iwwg.com/*
Mystery Writers of America, *www.mysterywriters.org* 11 regional chapters,
  conferences, Edgar® awards
National Writers Union, *www.nwu.org*
Private Eye Writers of America, *www.thrillingdetective.com* Shamus awards
Romance Writers of America, *www.rwanational.org,* local chapters, regional &
  national conferences, awards, online critique groups
Science Fiction and Fantasy Writers of America, Inc., *http://sfwa.org*
Sisters in Crime, *www.sistersincrime.org* listserves, local chapters; Guppies for
  beginners, online critique groups, extensive archives, *www.sinc-guppies.org/*
Society for Children's Writers & Illustrators, *www.scbwi.org*
Western Writers of America, *www.westernwriters.org* conference, awards

BLOGS AND OTHER SITES TO GET ANY WRITER STARTED

www.annemini.com/ Author! Author! from Anne Mini
www.absolutewrite.com/ Absolute Write forums, discussion, archives, Q&A
www.fictionaddiction.net Fiction Addiction networking, articles, Ask the Expert
www.childrenswriter.com/ marketing newsletter
www.underdown.org/ Purple Crayon: writing for children
www.LawandFiction.com articles on using the law in fiction
www.leelofland.com/wordpress crime investigation articles, facts, Q&A
www.megchittenden.com/ writing tips, links, resources
www.charlottedillon.com/ extensive links for research, other resources
www.crimethrutime.com historical mystery discussion group
www.easyreadingwriting.com/ craft from Peter Abresch
www.lorillake.com/articles.html articles, links, from Lori L. Lake
www.sff.net/people/Vonda/pitfalls.htp tips about writing science fiction, craft
www.missssnark.blogspot.com agent's archives still available
www.agentquery.com genre descriptions, agents actively seeking clients
www.authorlink.com networking, information, links
www.anotherealm.com/prededitors/ lists of good and bad agents, editing
  services, and publishers; contacts, links, writers organizations

Additions and corrections are always welcome: please send to chrisroerden@aol.com
and put ADD TO DSYS in the subject line. Also email me if you'd like to learn when my
own blog begins, where I will answer your questions about writing and publishing.

EXHIBIT D: BIBLIOGRAPHY OF EXCERPTS

Abramo, J. L. *Catching Water in a Net.* New York: St. Martin's Press, 2002.

Abresch, Peter. *Bloody Bonsai.* Aurora, CO: Write Way Publishing, 1999.

Adair, Suzanne. *The Blacksmith's Daughter.* Wilmington, NC: Whittler's Bench Press, 2007.

Adams, Deborah. *All the Great Pretenders.* New York: Ballantine, 1992.

Adams, Georgia. *A Well-Manicured Murder.* Novel-in-progress.

Ainslie, Jeanne. *A Country Girl.* New York: Blue Moon Books, 2005.

Allin, Lou. *Memories Are Murder.* Toronto: Rendezvous Press, 2007.

Anderson, Beth. *Murder Online.* Denver: Amber Quill Press, 2003.

Andrews, Donna. *Murder with Peacocks.* New York: St. Martin's Press, 1999.

Antenen, Chris. "Brown." Short-story-in-progress.

Avery, Morgan. *Act of Betrayal.* New York: Pinnacle Books, 2000.

Avocato, Lori. *Deep Sea Dead.* New York: Avon/HarperCollins, 2006.

Baker, Deb. *Dolled Up for Murder.* New York: Berkley Prime Crime, 2006.

_____. *Murder Passes the Buck.* St. Paul, MN: Midnight Ink, 2006.

Balzo, Sandra. *Uncommon Grounds.* Waterville, ME: Five Star, 2004.

Barnes, Linda. *A Trouble of Fools.* New York: Hyperion, 1987.

Barr, Nevada. *Blood Lure.* New York: Putnam, 2001.

Barrett, Kathleen Anne. *Milwaukee Winters Can Be Murder,* in *Homicide for the Holidays.* Aurora, CO: Write Way Publishing, 2000.

Bartholomew, Nancy. *Drag Strip.* New York: St. Martin's Press Minotaur, 1999.

Beamguard, Betty. "One Too Many," in *MoonShine Review,* June 2007, pp. 61-66.

_____. *Rescuing Maria.* Novel-in-progress.

Berry, Linda. *Death and the Hubcap.* Aurora, CO: Write Way Publishing, 2000.

Birmingham, Ruth. *Atlanta Graves.* New York: Berkley Prime Crime, 1998.

Bissell, Sallie. *A Darker Justice.* New York: Bantam Books, 2002.

Bland, Eleanor Taylor. *Done Wrong.* New York: St. Martin's Press, 1995.

Boatwright, Dottie. "By Gawd, We Ain't Like That," in *Catfish Stew, v. 4,* Columbia, SC: South Carolina Writers Workshop, 2006.

Brennan, Allison. *Speak No Evil.* New York: Ballantine, 2007.

Bristol, Barbara. "Eve's Holiday," in *Tales of Travelrotica for Lesbians, v. 2.* Boston: Alyson Press, 2007.

Brookins, Carl. *The Case of the Greedy Lawyers.* Waterville, ME: Five Star, 2008.

Brown, Dan. *The DaVinci Code.* New York: Doubleday, 2003.

Brown, Sandra. *The Alibi.* New York: Warner Books, 1999.

Brown, Steve. *Hurricane Party.* Taylors, SC: Chick Springs Publishing, 2002.

Browning, Pat. *Full Circle.* iUniverse, 2001.

Buchanan, Edna. *Miami, It's Murder.* New York: HarperCollins, 1994.

Burke, James Lee. *A Morning for Flamingos.* New York: Avon Books, 1991.

Burke, Jan. *Flight.* New York: Simon & Schuster, 2001; Pocket Books, 2002.

_____. *Goodnight, Irene.* New York: S&S, 1993; Pocket Books, 2002.

Chittenden, Meg. *More Than You Know.* New York: Berkley Sensation, 2003.

Christie, Agatha. *The Murder of Roger Ackroyd.* New York: S&S, 2001.

Clarey, Joanne. *Skinned.* Kernersville, NC: Alabaster Books, 2007.

Clarke, Arthur C. *2001: A Space Odyssey.* New York: Penguin, 1993.

Cleland, Jane K. *Deadly Appraisal.* New York: St. Martin's Minotaur, 2007.

Coben, Harlan. *Tell No One.* New York: Dell, 2001; Delacorte Press, 2002.

Cole, Meredith. *Posed for Murder.* New York: St. Martin's Press, 2009.

Coleman, Evelyn. *What a Woman's Gotta Do.* New York: S&S, 1998.

Coleman, Reed Farrel. *Soul Patch.* Madison, WI: Bleak House, 2006.

Connelly, Michael. *The Black Echo.* New York: Warner, 2002.

Cook, Dawn. *First Truth.* New York: Berkley, 2002.

Cornwell, Patricia. *Black Notice.* New York: Putnam, 1999.

Coulter, Catherine. *The Edge.* New York: Putnam, 1999; Jove, 2000.

Creekmore, Judy Bartlett. *The Violet-Crowned Corpse.* Novel-in-progress.

Cruse, Lonnie. *Marriage in Metropolis.* Metropolis, IL: NaDaC Pub., 2006.

_____. *Murder in Metropolis.* Martinsburg, WV: Quiet Storm, 2003.

D'Alessandro, Jacquie. *Confessions at Midnight.* New York: Avon, 2008.

D'Amato, Barbara. *Authorized Personnel Only.* New York: Tom Doherty, 2000.

_____. *Killer.app.* New York: Tom Doherty, 1996.

Daniel, Cindy. *Death Warmed Over.* Martinsburg, WV: Quiet Storm, 2003.

Davidson, Mary Janice. *Undead and Unwed.* New York: Berkley, 2004.

Davis, Maya. *Wild Mountain Roses.* Novel-in-progress.

Deaver, Jeffery. *The Coffin Dancer.* New York: Simon & Schuster, 1998.

Delinsky, Barbara. *The Carpenter's Lady.* New York: Harper Torch, 2005.

DePoy, Phillip. *Easy.* New York: Dell Publishing, 1997.

Dietz, Denise. *Footprints in the Butter.* Lee's Summit, MO: Delphi Books, 1999.

du Maurier, Daphne. *Rebecca.* New York: Doubleday, 1938; Avon, 1971.

Dunlap, Susan. *Death and Taxes.* New York: Dell Publishing, 1992.

_____. *Pious Deception.* New York: Dell Publishing, 1989.

Dymmoch, Michael Allen. *The Man Who Understood Cats.* New York: Avon, 1993.

Ehrhart, Peggy. *Sweet Man Is Gone.* Waterville, ME: Five Star, 2008.

Elliott, Myrna. *In Her Blood.* Work-in-progress.

Ellison, J.T. *All The Pretty Girls.* Ontario: MIRA Books, 2007.

Estleman, Loren D. *Sinister Heights.* New York: Mysterious Press, 2002.

Evanovich, Janet. *One for the Money.* New York: HarperPaperbacks, 1995.

Fairstein, Linda. *Final Jeopardy.* New York: Pocket Books, 1997.

Fannin, Teresa. *Mrdr Mystri.* Novel-in-progress.

Farmer, Jerrilyn. *Perfect Sax.* New York: Avon Books, 2004.

Flora, Kate Clark. *Death in Paradise.* New York: Tom Doherty, 1998.

_____. *Playing God.* Waterville, ME: Five Star, 2006.

Ford-Williamson, Estelle. *Abbeville Farewell: A Novel of Early Atlanta and North Georgia.* Decatur, GA. Other Voices Press, 2001.

Foti, Silvia. *The Diva's Fool.* Laurel, MD: Echelon Press, 2007.

French, Christy Tillery. *The Bodyguard and the Show Dog.* Lake Forest, CA: Behler Publications, 2006.

Frommer, Sara Hoskinson. *The Vanishing Violinist.* New York: St. Martin's, 1999.

Garwood, Julie. *Slow Burn.* New York: Ballantine, 2006.

_____. *The Gift.* New York: Pocket Books, 1991.

Gates, Nancy Gotter. *When Push Comes to Death.* Kernersville, NC: Alabaster, 2007.

Geary, Judith. *Getorix: The Eagle and the Bull.* Boone, NC: Claystone Books/Ingalls Publishing Group, 2006.

George, Elizabeth. *For the Sake of Elena.* New York: Bantam, 1992.

Gerber, Daryl Wood. *Cut! Cut! Print.* Novel-in-progress.

Glatzer, Hal. *A Fugue in Hell's Kitchen.* McKinleyville, CA: Perseverance, 2004.

Godden, Anne Segard. "The Garden Lodger," in *Off Center.* Off Center Press, 2007.

Gordon, Betty. "Dead by Breakfast," in *Dead and Breakfast.* Lisa René Smith, Linda Houle, eds. Spring, TX: L&L Dreamspell, 2007.

Grafton, Sue. *"P" is for Peril.* New York: Ballantine Books, 2002.

Grant, Anne Underwood. *Multiple Listing.* New York: Dell, 1998.

Grant, Linda. *A Woman's Place.* New York: Ivy Books, 1994.

_____. *Lethal Genes.* New York: Ivy Books, 1996.

Grimes, Martha. *Foul Matter.* New York: Viking, 2003.

Groundwater, Beth. *A Real Basket Case.* Waterville, ME: Five Star, 2007.

Hall, Parnell. *Murder.* New York: New American Library/Onyx ed, 1989.

Ham, Lorie. *Murder in Four Part Harmony.* America House, 2000.

Harper, Karen. *Below the Surface.* Ontario: MIRA Books, 2008.

Harris, Charlaine. *Dead Over Heels.* New York: Worldwide/Scribner, 1998.

Hart, Erin. *Lake of Sorrows.* New York: Scribner, 2004; Simon & Schuster, 2007.

Hart, John. *The King of Lies.* New York: Thomas Dunne Books, 2006.

Hayden, L.C. *Who's Susan?* Plano, TX: Top Publications, 1995, 1998.

Heilbrun, Robert. *Offer of Proof.* New York: Harper Torch, 2004.

Hellmann, Libby Fischer. *An Eye for Murder.* New York: Berkley, 2002.

Helms, Rick. *Voodoo That You Do.* Weddington, NC: Back Alley Books, 2001.

Highsmith, Patricia. *The Blunderer.* London: Heinemann Ltd., 1956; Penguin, 1988.

Hinze, Vicki. *Duplicity.* New York: St. Martin's Press, 1999.

Hogan, Chuck. "One Good One," in *Ellery Queen,* March/April, 2007.

Holbrook, Teri. *Sad Water.* New York: Bantam Books, 1999.

Holm, Janis. "Shopping with Winona," in *Venuszine.com,* Winter 2006.

Hoover, Terry. *Double Dead.* Waterville, ME: Five Star, 2007.

Hudgins, Maria. *Death of an Obnoxious Tourist.* Waterville, ME: Five Star, 2007.

Hull, Gene. *Hooked on a Horn.* Victoria, BC: Trafford Publishing, 2005.

Hunter, Ellen Elizabeth. *Murder on the Candlelight Tour.* Greensboro: WGOT, 2003.

_____. *Murder on the I.C.W.* Greensboro: Magnolia Mysteries, 2006.

Hunter, Gwen. *Delayed Diagnosis.* Ontario: MIRA Books, 2001.

Huskins, James. *Silent Scream.* Novel-in-progress.

Jaffarian, Sue Ann. *The Curse of the Holy Pail.* St. Paul: Midnight Ink, 2007.

Jance, J. A. *Desert Heat.* New York: Avon Books, 1993.

Johansen, Iris. *Long After Midnight.* New York: Bantam Books, 1997.

Johnson, Heide Anne. *Flash Memory.* Novel-in-progress.

Jones, Pauline Baird. "Do Wah Diddy Die Already," in *Dead and Breakfast.* Lisa René
    Smith, Linda Houle, eds. Spring, TX: L&L Dreamspell, 2007.

_____. *The Key.* Spring, TX: L&L Dreamspell, 2007.

Kenny, Carol. *Closing Time.* Short story-in-progress.

Konrath, J. A. *Whiskey Sour.* New York: Hyperion, 2004.

Krevat, Kathy. *PTA Meetings Are Murder.* Novel-in-progress.

Krich, Rochelle. *Blues in the Night.* New York: Fawcett, 2002; Ballantine, 2003.

Land, Dixie. *Grave Secrets.* Kernersville, NC: Alabaster Books, 2007.

Lanchester, John. *Mr Phillips.* New York: Putnam, 2000.

Lane, Vicki. *Signs in the Blood.* New York: Bantam Dell, 2005.

_____. *Old Wounds.* New York: Bantam Dell, 2007.

Lavene, Joyce and Jim. *Swapping Paint.* Woodbury, MN: Midnight Ink, 2007.

Lehane, Dennis. *Gone, Baby, Gone.* New York: Avon Books, 1998.

Leonard, Elmore. *Glitz.* New York: Mysterious Press, 1985; Warner, 1986.

Lilley, Kathryn. *A Killer Workout.* New York: Signet, 2008.

Lippman, Laura. *Baltimore Blues.* New York: Avon Books, 1997.

Lyon, Dana. *Heart of the Druae.* Baker City, OR; Black Lyon, 2008.

MacDonald, John D. *The Deep Blue Good-by.* Greenwich, CT: Fawcett, 1964.

Mallory, Michael and Marilyn Victor. *Death Roll.* Waterville, ME: Five Star , 2007.

Malone, Michael. *Uncivil Seasons.* Naperville, IL: Sourcebooks, 2001.

Malone, Susan Mary. "The Dream Delicious." Amazon Short. 2007.

Maron, Margaret. *Bootlegger's Daughter.* New York: Mysterious Press, 1992.

_____. *Southern Discomfort.* New York: Mysterious Press, 1993.

Martini, Steve. *Prime Witness.* New York: Putnam, 1993; Jove, 1994.

Mathews, Francine. *Blown.* New York: Bantam, 2005.

Matthews, Alex. *Death's Domain.* Philadelphia: Intrigue Press, 2001.

McBain, Ed. *There Was a Little Girl.* New York: Warner Books, 1994.

McCullough, Karen. *A Question of Fire.* Ontario, Ca: LTDBooks, 2000.

McDermid, Val. *A Place of Execution.* New York: St. Martin's Paperbacks, 2001.

McRae, Cricket. *Lye in Wait.* Woodbury MN: Midnight Ink, 2007.

Miller, John Ramsey. *Side by Side.* New York: Bantam Dell, 2005.

Miller, Rebecca. *Personal Velocity.* New York: Grove Press, 2001.

Mills, Wendy Howell. *Callie & the Dealer & a Dog Named Jake.* Taylorville, IL: Oak Tree Press, 2001.

Mucha, Susan P. *Deadly Deception.* Augusta, GA: Harbor House, 2005.

Muller, Marcia. *The Cheshire Cat's Eye.* 1983; New York: Mysterious Press, 1990.

Munger, Katy. *Legwork.* New York: Avon Books, 1997.

Myers, Tamar. *The Dark Side of Heaven.* Rock Hill, SC: Bella Rosa, 2006.

_____. *The Ming and I.* New York: Avon Books, 1991.

Nehring, Radine Trees. *A Wedding to Die For.* Wichita, KS: St. Kitts Press, 2006.

Neri, Kris. *Revenge of the Gypsy Queen.* New York: Worldwide, 2003.

Nicholson, Scott. *The Harvest.* New York: Kensington, 2003.

Orwell, George. *Nineteen Eighty-four.* New York: Harcourt, Brace, 1949.

Paretsky, Sara. *Blood Shot.* New York: Delacorte Press, 1988; Dell, 1989.

Park, Christopher M. *Longer the Night.* Novel-in-progress.

Parrish, P. J. *A Thousand Bones.* New York: Pocket Books, 2007.

Parshall, Sandra. *The Heat of the Moon.* Scottsdale: Poisoned Pen Press, 2006.

Patton, Lois. "The Empty Chair." Short-story-in-progress.

Peters, Elizabeth. *Naked Once More.* New York: Warner Books, 1989.

Phelan, Twist. *Spurred Ambition.* Scottsdale, AZ: Poisoned Pen Press, 2006.

_____. *Family Claims.* Scottsdale, AZ: Poisoned Pen Press, 2004.

Pickard, Nancy. *The Virgin of Small Plains.* New York: Ballantine Books, 2006.

_____. *No Body.* New York: Pocket Books, 1986.

Pickens, Cathy. *Done Gone Wrong.* New York: St. Martin's Press, 2005.

_____. *Hog Wild.* New York: Thomas Dunne Books, 2007.

Picoult, Jodi. *The Tenth Circle.* New York: Washington Square Press, 2006.

Proulx, Suzanne. *Bad Luck.* New York: Ballantine, 2000.

Rawls, Randy. *Jasmine's Fate.* Boonsboro, MD: Hilliard & Harris, 2007.

Read, June Willson. *Frontier Madam.* Guilford, CT: TwoDot, 2008.

Reichs, Kathy. *Death du Jour.* New York: Scribner, 1999; Pocket Books, 2000.

Reuben, Shelly. *Weeping.* Cambridge, MA: Kate's Mystery Books, 2004.

Roberts, Nora. *Irish Rebel.* New York: Silhouette Books, 2007.

Rogers, Stephen D. "Bodyshop Blues," in *Nocturnal Ooze Magazine,* 2004.

Rogow, Roberta. *The Problem of the Evil Editor.* New York: St. Martin's, 2000.

Rozan, S. J. *A Bitter Feast.* New York: St. Martin's Press, 1998.

_____. *Winter and Night.* New York: St. Martin's Press, 2002.

Ryan, Hank Phillippi. *Air Time.* Ontario: MIRA Books, 2008.

Salisbury, Michael. *Thou Shalt Kill Thy Neighbor.* Novel-in-progress.

Sandford, John. *Rules of Prey.* New York: Putnam, 1989; Berkley, 1990.

Saums, Mary. *Midnight Hour.* Johnson City, TN: Silver Dagger, 2000.

_____. *Thistle and Twigg.* New York: St. Martin's Press, 2007.

Schneider, Ilene. *Chanukah Guilt.* Arlington, TX: Swimming Kangaroo, 2007.

Schumacher, Aileen. *Framework for Death.* Aurora, CO: Write Way, 1998.

Scottoline, Lisa. *Final Appeal.* New York: HarperCollins, 1994.

_____. *Dead Ringer.* New York: HarperCollins, 2004.

Shaber, Sarah R. *Snipe Hunt.* New York: St. Martin's Press, 2000.

Shaw, June. *Relative Danger.* Waterville, ME: Five Star, 2006.

Shelton, Connie. *Memories Can Be Murder.* Philadelphia: Intrigue Press, 1999.

Shlian, Deborah and Joel. *Rabbit in the Moon.* Ipswich, MA: Oceanview, 2008.

_____. *Wednesday's Child.* New York: Pocket Books, 1986.

Singer, Gammy L. *A Landlord's Tale.* New York: Kensington Publishers, 2005.

Sokoloff, Alexandra. *The Harrowing.* New York: St. Martin's Press, 2006.

Sorrells, Walter. *Will to Murder.* New York: Avon Books, 1996.

Sprinkle, Patricia. *Murder in the Charleston Manner.* New York: St. Martin's, 1990.

Squire, Elizabeth Daniels. *Memory Can Be Murder.* New York: Berkley, 1995.

_____. *Who Killed What's-Her-Name?* New York: Berkley Prime Crime, 1994.

Swanson, Denise. *Murder of a Small-Town Honey.* New York: Signet, 2000.

_____. *Murder of a Sweet Old Lady.* New York: Signet, 2001.

Sweeney, Leann. *Pick Your Poison.* New York: NAL/Signet, 2004.

Szymanski, Therese. *Another One Bites the Dust,* in *It's All Smoke & Mirrors.* Tallahassee: Bella Books, 2007.

Taichert, Pari Noskin. *The Clovis Incident.* Albuquerque: UNM Press, 2004.

Terrell, Elizabeth. *Too Close to Evil.* Lincoln, NE: iUniverse, 2004.

Terrell, Joseph L.S. *The Other Side of Silence.* Rock Hill, SC: Bella Rosa, 2007.

Thiel, Kristin. "Pilgrim for Hire," in *VoiceCatcher2.* Portland, OR: VoiceCatcher Editorial Collective, Jennifer Lalime, ed. pp. 25-31. 2007.

Thompson, Vicki Lewis. *Over Hexed.* New York: Onyx, 2007.

Tiller, Denise. *Calculated Risk.* Allen, TX: Timberwolf Press, 2000.

Tillery, Debra. *Myth Maker.* Work-in-progress.

Todd, Charles. *A Test of Wills.* New York: St. Martin's, 1996; Bantam, 1998.

Toole, John Kennedy. *A Confederacy of Dunces.* Louisiana State University Press, 1980; New York: Grove Weidenfeld, 1987.

Tooley, S. D. *When the Dead Speak.* Schererville, IN: Full Moon Publishing, 1999.

Toussaint, Maggie. *No Second Chance.* Adams Basin, NY: Wild Rose Press, 2008.

Turner, J.R. *Stark Knight.* Memphis, TN: Echelon Press, 2005.

Viehl, Lynn. *Dark Need.* New York: Signet Eclipse, 2006.

Wait, Lea. *Seaward Born.* New York: Simon & Schuster Children's, 2003.

Wall, Kathryn R. *Resurrection Road.* New York: St. Martin's Press, 2005.

_____. *In for a Penny.* Beaufort, SC: Coastal Villages Press, 2001.

Wallace, Brenda. *Mind Trip.* Novel-in-progress.

Wareham, Evonn. *Out of Sight, Out of Mind.* Novel-in-progress.

Webb, Betty. *Desert Noir.* Scottsdale, AZ: Poisoned Pen, 2001; Worldwide, 2003.

West, Chassie. *Sunrise.* New York: HarperPaperbacks, 1994.

West, Nancy Glass. *Nine Days to Evil.* Bangor, ME: Booklocker, 2004.

Westerson, Jeri. "The Tin Box," in *St. Anthony Messenger,* Sept. 2003.

Wheat, Carolyn. *Fresh Kills.* New York: Berkley Prime Crime, 1995.

Whelan, Kathleen. *Cocktail Cove.* Novel-in-progress.

Whitney, Phyllis A. *Woman Without a Past.* New York: Doubleday, 1991.

Wigglesworth, Gayle. "I Love a Parade!" in *Dead and Breakfast.* Lisa René Smith, Linda Houle, eds. Spring, TX: L&L Dreamspell, 2007.

Williams, N.L. *A Matter of Destiny.* Diggory Press, 2006; Chattanooga TN: Springflower Publishing, 2008.

Wright, Nancy Means. *Mad Cow Nightmare.* New York: Thomas Dunne, 2005.

Wyle, Dirk. *Pharmacology Is Murder.* Highland City, FL: Rainbow Books, 1998.

Zelvin, Elizabeth. *Death Will Get You Sober.* New York: St. Martin's, 2008.

_____. "Death Will Clean Your Closet," in *Murder New York Style.* Spring, TX: L&L Dreamspell, 2007.

CROSS-EXAMINATION: INDEX

THE WITNESS BOX
ACKNOWLEDGMENTS

I solemnly swear that many thousands of readers and writers made this book happen. Your overwhelming support for its predecessor, *Don't Murder Your Mystery,* showed that a version for all genres would be welcomed.

"Solemnly" does not accurately reflect my feelings, though, because I get goosebumps whenever I realize how many of you made winning the Agatha Award possible. Words could not express then or now how profound my gratitude is to the members of Sisters in Crime, the Guppies, and Mystery Writers of America for your support, and the many writers who continue to make the workshops and conferences where I meet you exciting and fun.

To Joye Barnes, Chris Antenen, and Therese Szymanski, thank you so much for your kind and generous feedback on my manuscript.

To Shannon Bodie and David Tipton, I'm extremely grateful for your outstanding professional talents.

My sincere appreciation to Joe Gallehugh and Rod Hunter for your generous support and special expertise.

Love and appreciation to Peter and Morris Gandelman for the good ideas you came up with, and to Phyllis Rosoff and Mary McKeown for being with me at an especially joyous time.

As for special people being there for me, never-ending hugs and gratitude to Susan Schreyer, Kim Mattox, and Shawn Pace for your exceptional care and concern. How fortunate I am to have you three as very special friends.

Above all, my deepest gratitude to Pat Meller, my astute first reader, hard-working business partner, and dearest friend. Your unflagging help and support, and your warm sense of humor, are priceless. I'm truly privileged to have you in my life.

Chris

THE PERPETRATOR

ABOUT THE AUTHOR

Editor, writer, and workshop leader, Chris Roerden enjoys sharing what she's learned from 45-plus years in niche publishing—a career that began when she graduated from New York City's H. S. of Music & Art at age 16. Twelve years and two children later, her first book was published, motivating her to enroll at the University of Maine. There she earned a BA in English *summa cum laude,* was invited to stay on as an instructor of writing, became the first president of the graduate student body, and received the first MA in English awarded from the Portland campus.

With a family transfer to Syracuse, NY, she mentored independent study students for Empire State College of SUNY. Another transfer, and she was elected president of a 3,000-member Wisconsin women's organization, and in the mid-nineties became president of a trade association of 250 Midwest publishers and university presses.

After twenty years in publishing she left a busy managing editor's job to become an even busier independent book editor. Authors she's edited are published by St. Martin's, Berkley Prime Crime, Midnight Ink, Viking, Intrigue, Oceanview, Rodale, Walker & Co., and many more. For eight years she taught nights for the University of Wisconsin-Milwaukee, and one summer taught schoolteachers in South Korea for UNESCO.

Chris served on the southeast regional board of Mystery Writers of America six years, and in 2007 received its highest honor, the Magnolia Award. She is also a member of Sisters in Crime, Romance Writers of America, Publishers Marketing Association, and Mensa.

She is the proud grandmother of Eli, Zach, and Ben, who live near Boston with her son Doug and daughter-in-law, Laura, also an editor. Two granddogs share a hillside home with her son Ken in Southern California.

Now settled in Greensboro, NC, Chris celebrates pansies blooming in February and not having worn snow boots since the 20th century.

P. M.

LaVergne, TN USA
15 April 2010
179420LV00001B/116/P